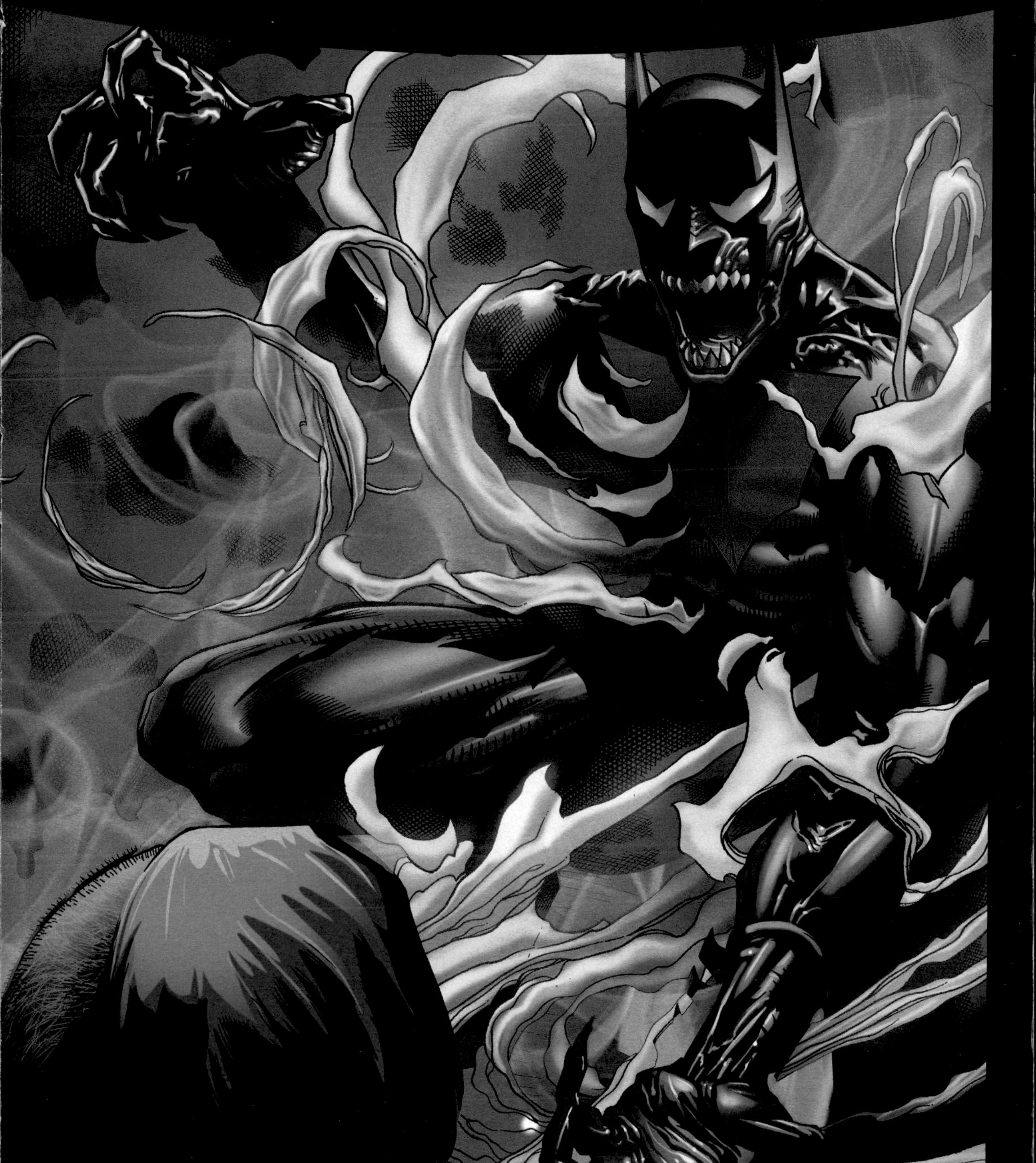

BATMAN BEYOND

VOL.4 TARGET: BATMAN

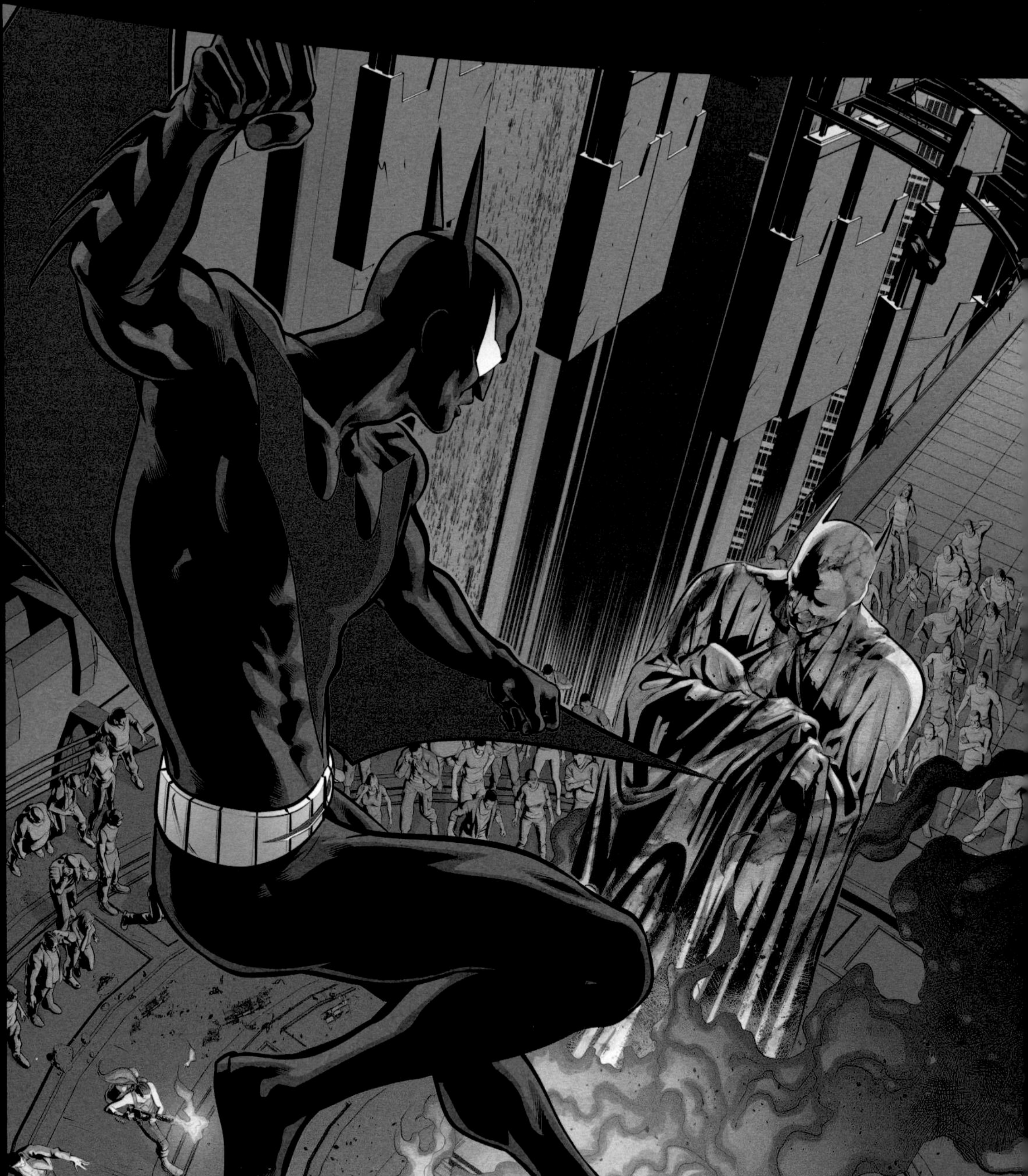

BATMAN BEYOND
VOL.4 TARGET: BATMAN

DAN JURGENS
writer

WILL CONRAD
MARCO CASTIELLO * MARK MORALES
artists

DAVID BARON
WIL QUINTANA
colorists

TRAVIS LANHAM
letterer

VIKTOR KALVACHEV
collection cover artist

BATMAN created by BOB KANE with BILL FINGER

ROB LEVIN Editor - Original Series
JEB WOODARD Group Editor - Collected Editions · **ERIKA ROTHBERG** Editor - Collected Edition
STEVE COOK Design Director - Books · **SHANNON STEWART** Publication Design

BOB HARRAS Senior VP - Editor-in-Chief, DC Comics · **PAT McCALLUM** Executive Editor, DC Comics

DAN DiDIO Publisher · **JIM LEE** Publisher & Chief Creative Officer
AMIT DESAI Executive VP - Business & Marketing Strategy, Direct to Consumer & Global Franchise Management
BOBBIE CHASE VP & Executive Editor, Young Reader & Talent Development · **MARK CHIARELLO** Senior VP - Art, Design & Collected Editions
JOHN CUNNINGHAM Senior VP - Sales & Trade Marketing · **BRIAR DARDEN** VP - Business Affairs
ANNE DePIES Senior VP - Business Strategy, Finance & Administration · **DON FALLETTI** VP - Manufacturing Operations
LAWRENCE GANEM VP - Editorial Administration & Talent Relations · **ALISON GILL** Senior VP - Manufacturing & Operations
JASON GREENBERG VP - Business Strategy & Finance · **HANK KANALZ** Senior VP - Editorial Strategy & Administration
JAY KOGAN Senior VP - Legal Affairs · **NICK J. NAPOLITANO** VP - Manufacturing Administration
LISETTE OSTERLOH VP - Digital Marketing & Events · **EDDIE SCANNELL** VP - Consumer Marketing
COURTNEY SIMMONS Senior VP - Publicity & Communications · **JIM (SKI) SOKOLOWSKI** VP - Comic Book Specialty Sales & Trade Marketing
NANCY SPEARS VP - Mass, Book, Digital Sales & Trade Marketing · **MICHELE R. WELLS** VP - Content Strategy

BATMAN BEYOND VOL. 4: TARGET: BATMAN

DC Comics, 2900 West Alameda Ave., Burbank, CA 91505
Printed by LSC Communications, Kendallville, IN, USA. 11/23/18. First Printing.
ISBN: 978-1-4012-8563-0

Library of Congress Cataloging-in-Publication Data is available.

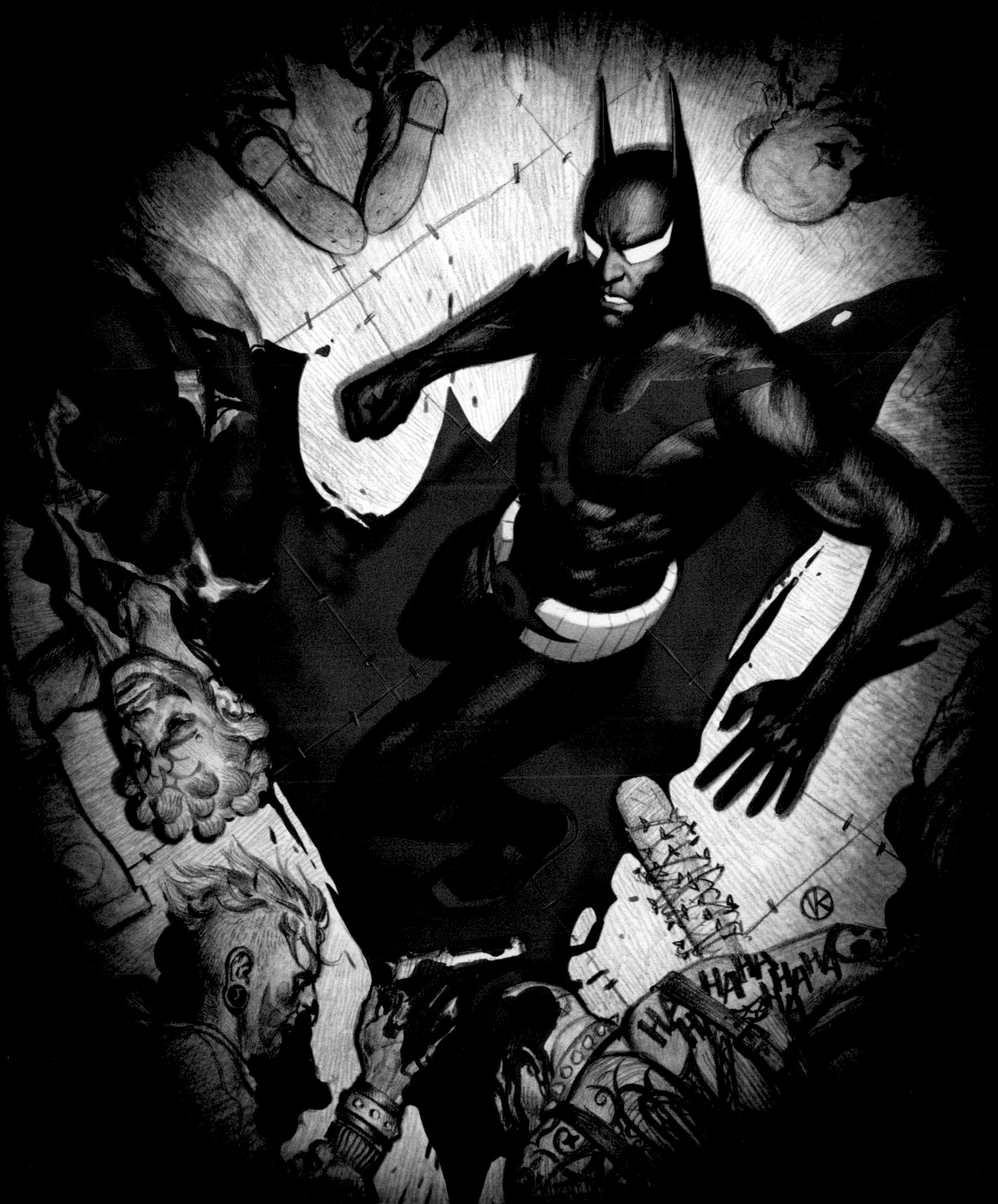

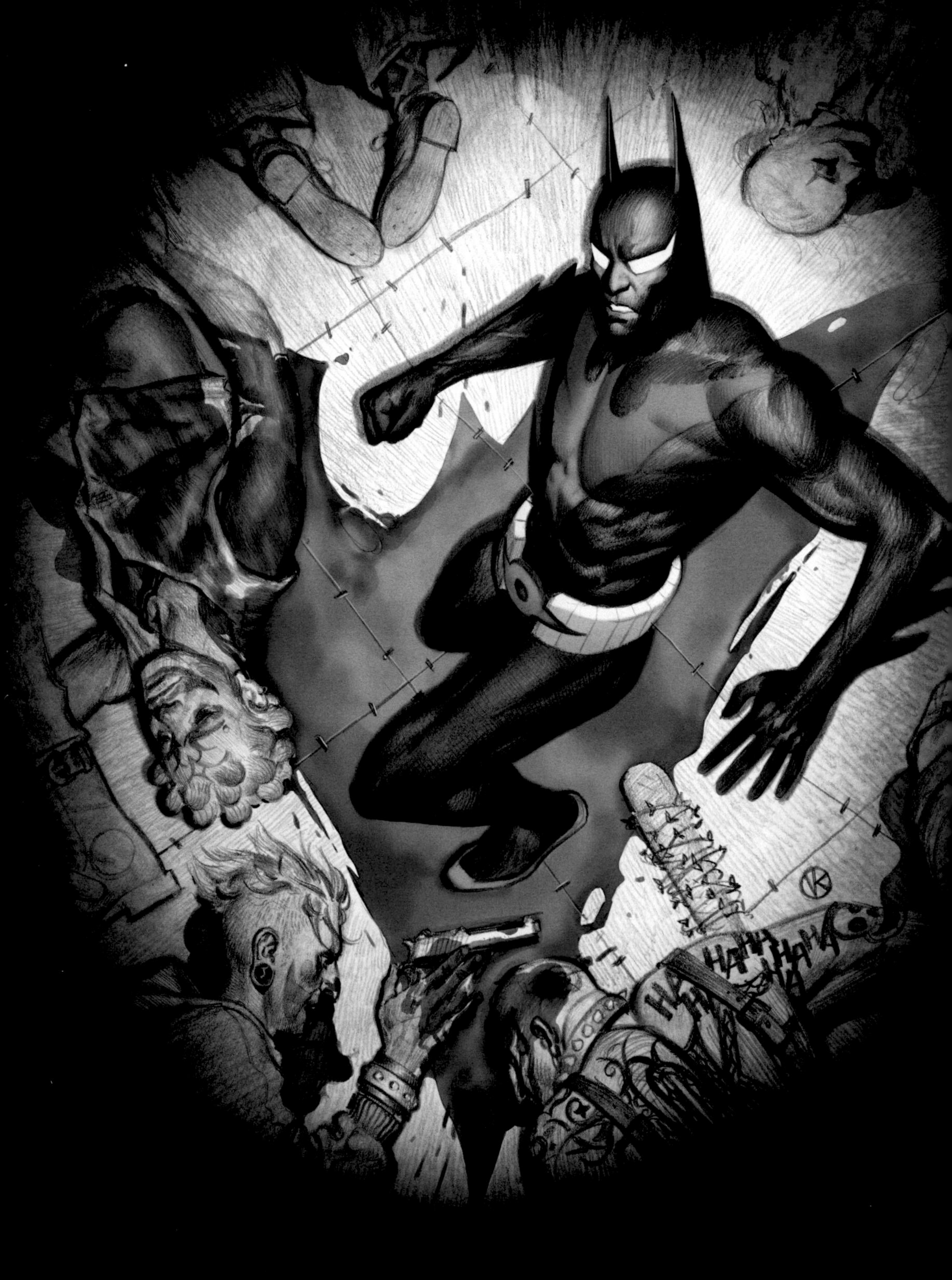
HAHA HAHA HA

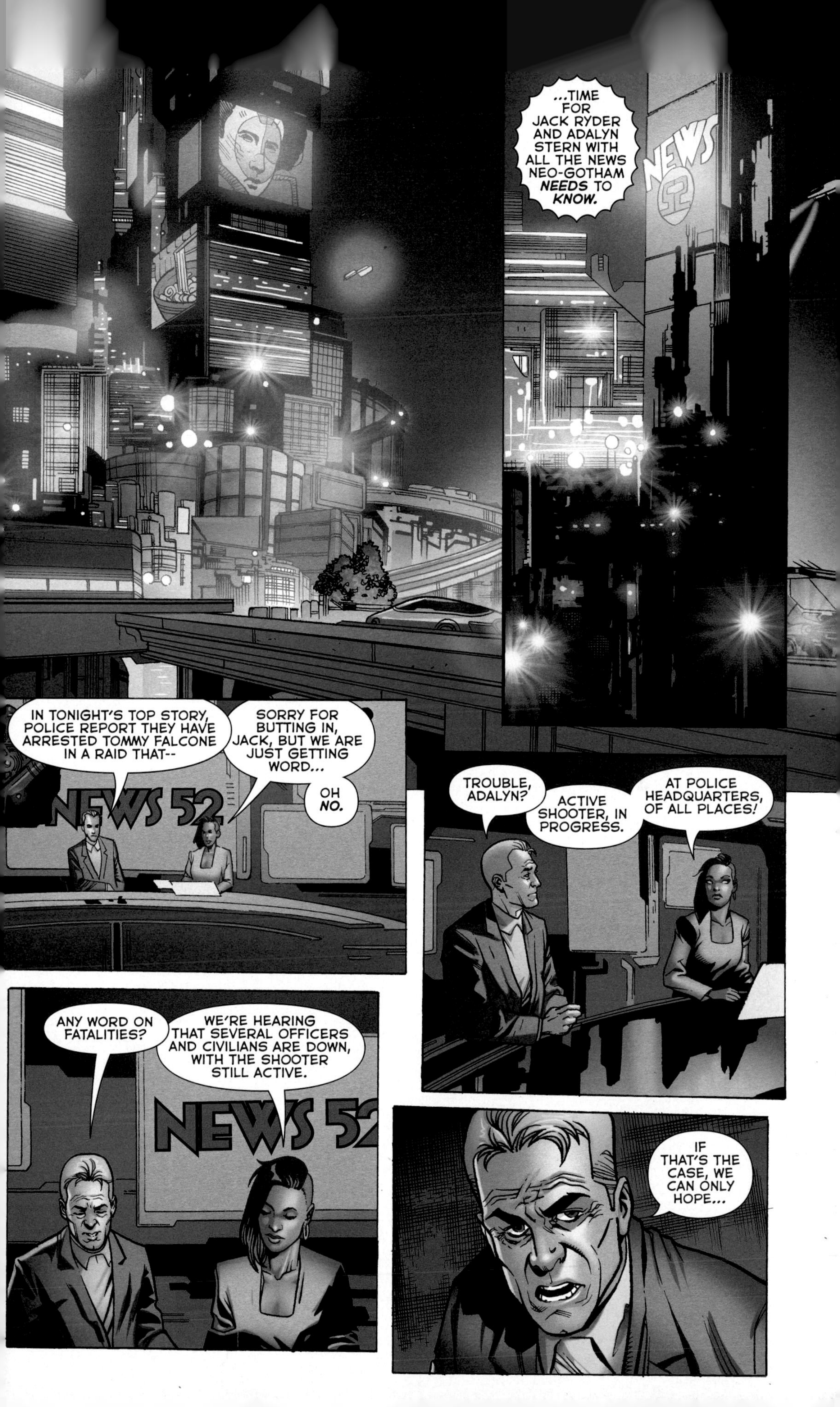

...TIME FOR JACK RYDER AND ADALYN STERN WITH ALL THE NEWS NEO-GOTHAM *NEEDS* TO *KNOW.*
NEWS 52
IN TONIGHT'S TOP STORY, POLICE REPORT THEY HAVE ARRESTED TOMMY FALCONE IN A RAID THAT--
SORRY FOR BUTTING IN, JACK, BUT WE ARE JUST GETTING WORD...
OH *NO.*
NEWS 52
TROUBLE, ADALYN?
ACTIVE SHOOTER, IN PROGRESS.
AT POLICE HEADQUARTERS, OF ALL PLACES!
ANY WORD ON FATALITIES?
WE'RE HEARING THAT SEVERAL OFFICERS AND CIVILIANS ARE DOWN, WITH THE SHOOTER STILL ACTIVE.
NEWS 52
IF THAT'S THE CASE, WE CAN ONLY HOPE...

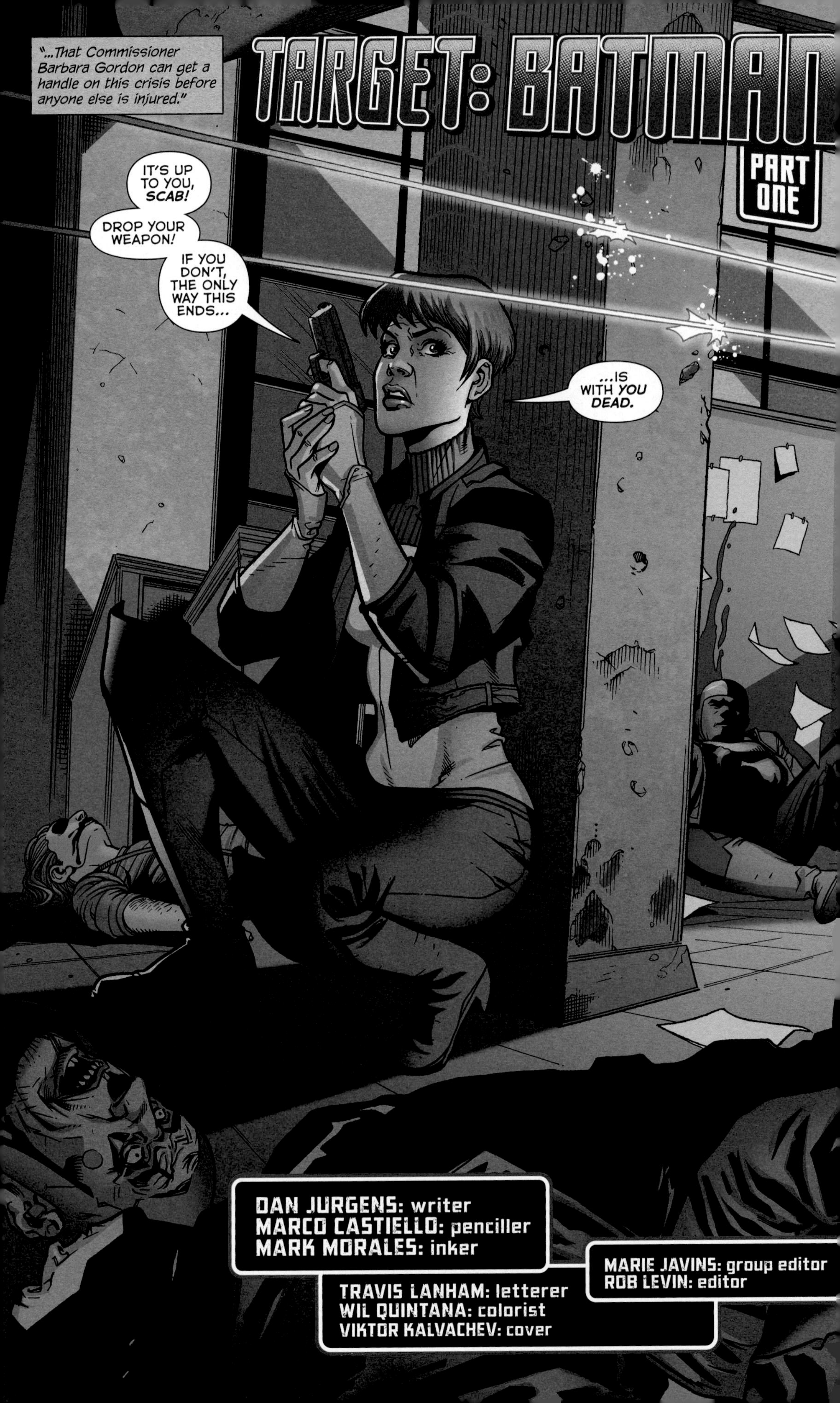

"...That Commissioner Barbara Gordon can get a handle on this crisis before anyone else is injured."
TARGET: BATMAN
PART ONE
IT'S UP TO YOU, SCAB!
DROP YOUR WEAPON!
IF YOU DON'T, THE ONLY WAY THIS ENDS...
...IS WITH YOU DEAD.
DAN JURGENS: writer
MARCO CASTIELLO: penciller
MARK MORALES: inker
TRAVIS LANHAM: letterer
WIL QUINTANA: colorist
VIKTOR KALVACHEV: cover
MARIE JAVINS: group editor
ROB LEVIN: editor

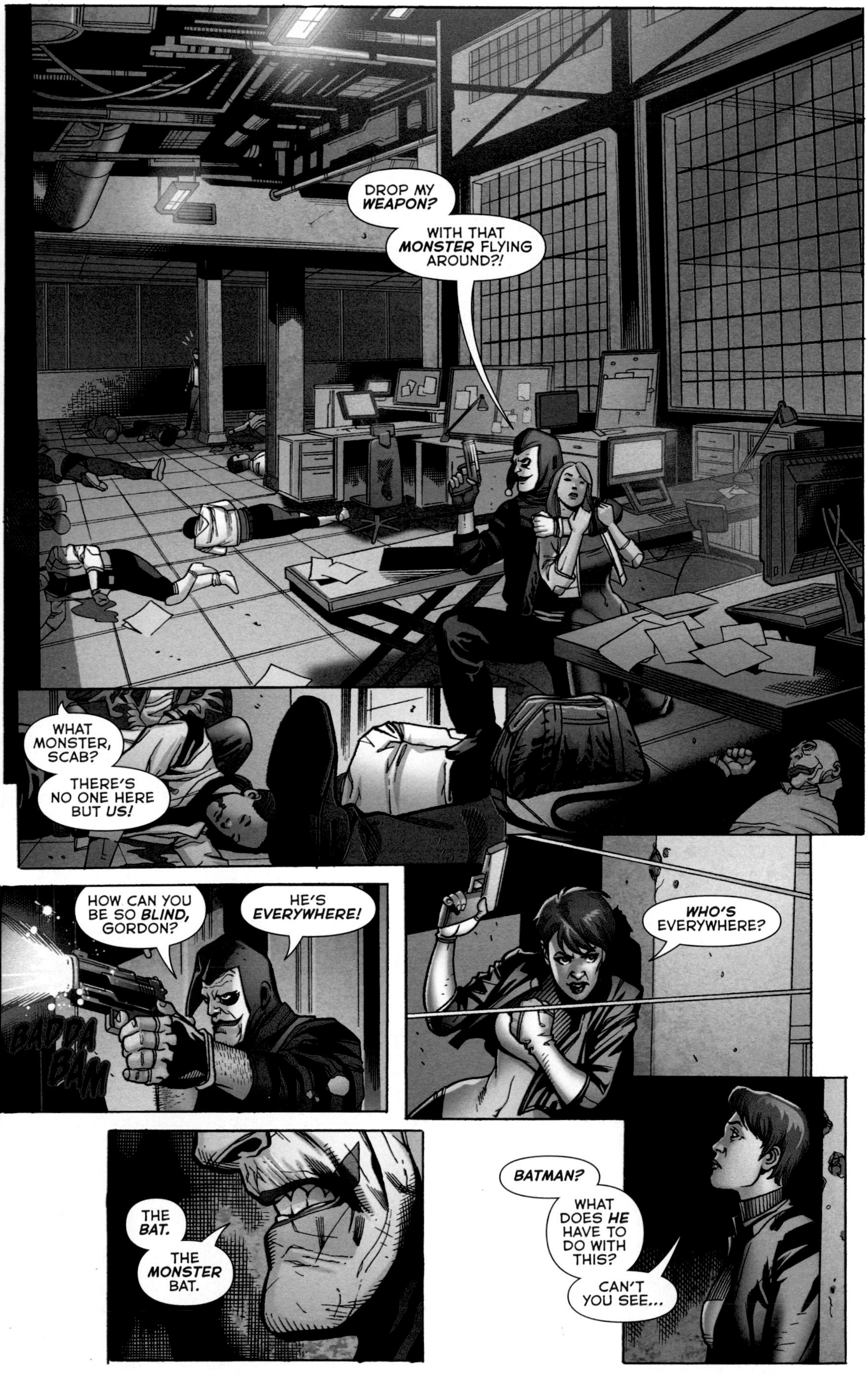
DROP MY WEAPON?
WITH THAT MONSTER FLYING AROUND?!
WHAT MONSTER, SCAB?
THERE'S NO ONE HERE BUT US!
HOW CAN YOU BE SO BLIND, GORDON?
HE'S EVERYWHERE!
BADDA BAM
WHO'S EVERYWHERE?
THE BAT.
THE MONSTER BAT.
BATMAN?
WHAT DOES HE HAVE TO DO WITH THIS?
CAN'T YOU SEE...

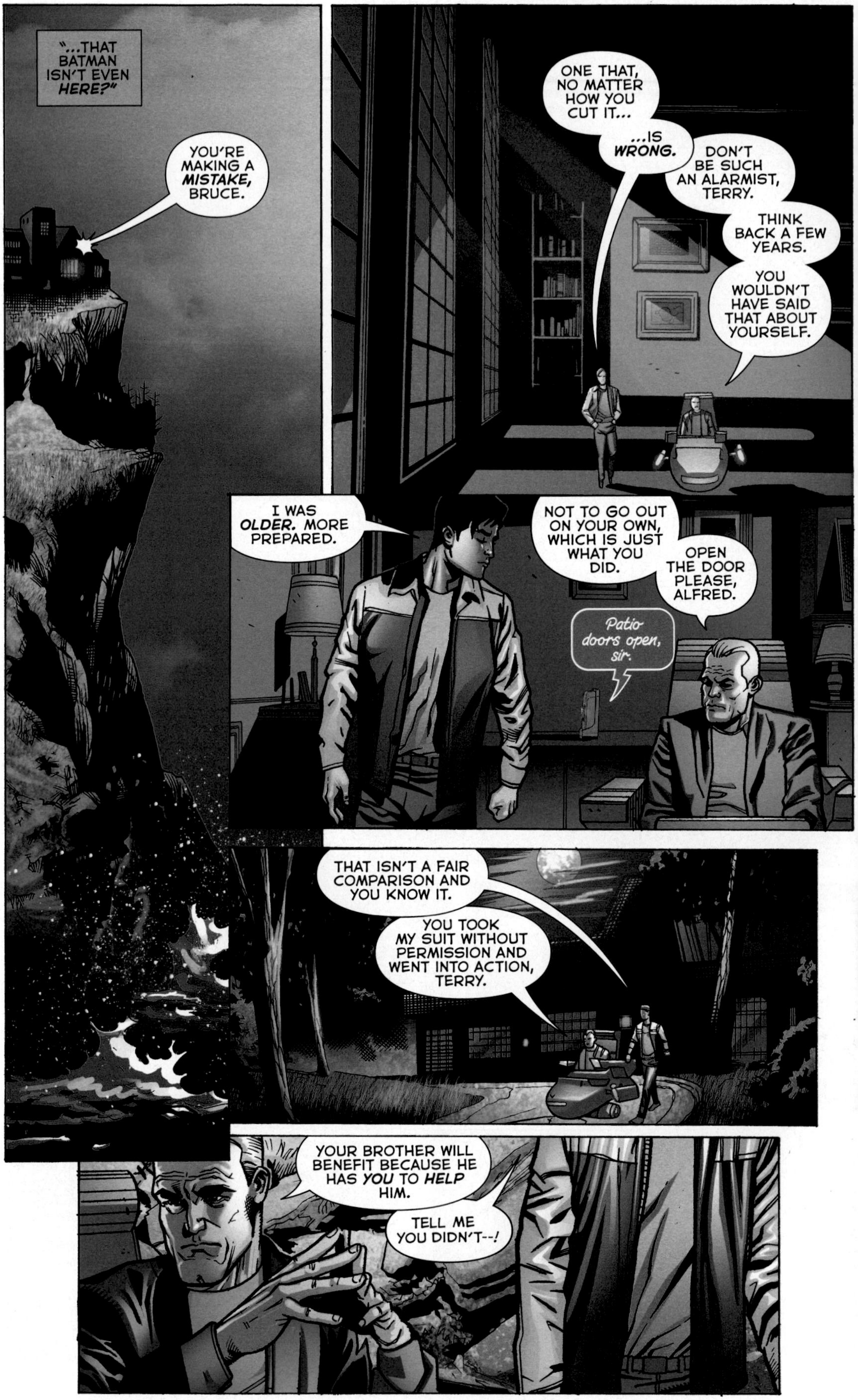

"...THAT BATMAN ISN'T EVEN HERE?"
YOU'RE MAKING A MISTAKE, BRUCE.
ONE THAT, NO MATTER HOW YOU CUT IT...
...IS WRONG.
DON'T BE SUCH AN ALARMIST, TERRY.
THINK BACK A FEW YEARS.
YOU WOULDN'T HAVE SAID THAT ABOUT YOURSELF.
I WAS OLDER. MORE PREPARED.
NOT TO GO OUT ON YOUR OWN, WHICH IS JUST WHAT YOU DID.
OPEN THE DOOR PLEASE, ALFRED.
Patio doors open, sir.
THAT ISN'T A FAIR COMPARISON AND YOU KNOW IT.
YOU TOOK MY SUIT WITHOUT PERMISSION AND WENT INTO ACTION, TERRY.
YOUR BROTHER WILL BENEFIT BECAUSE HE HAS YOU TO HELP HIM.
TELL ME YOU DIDN'T--!

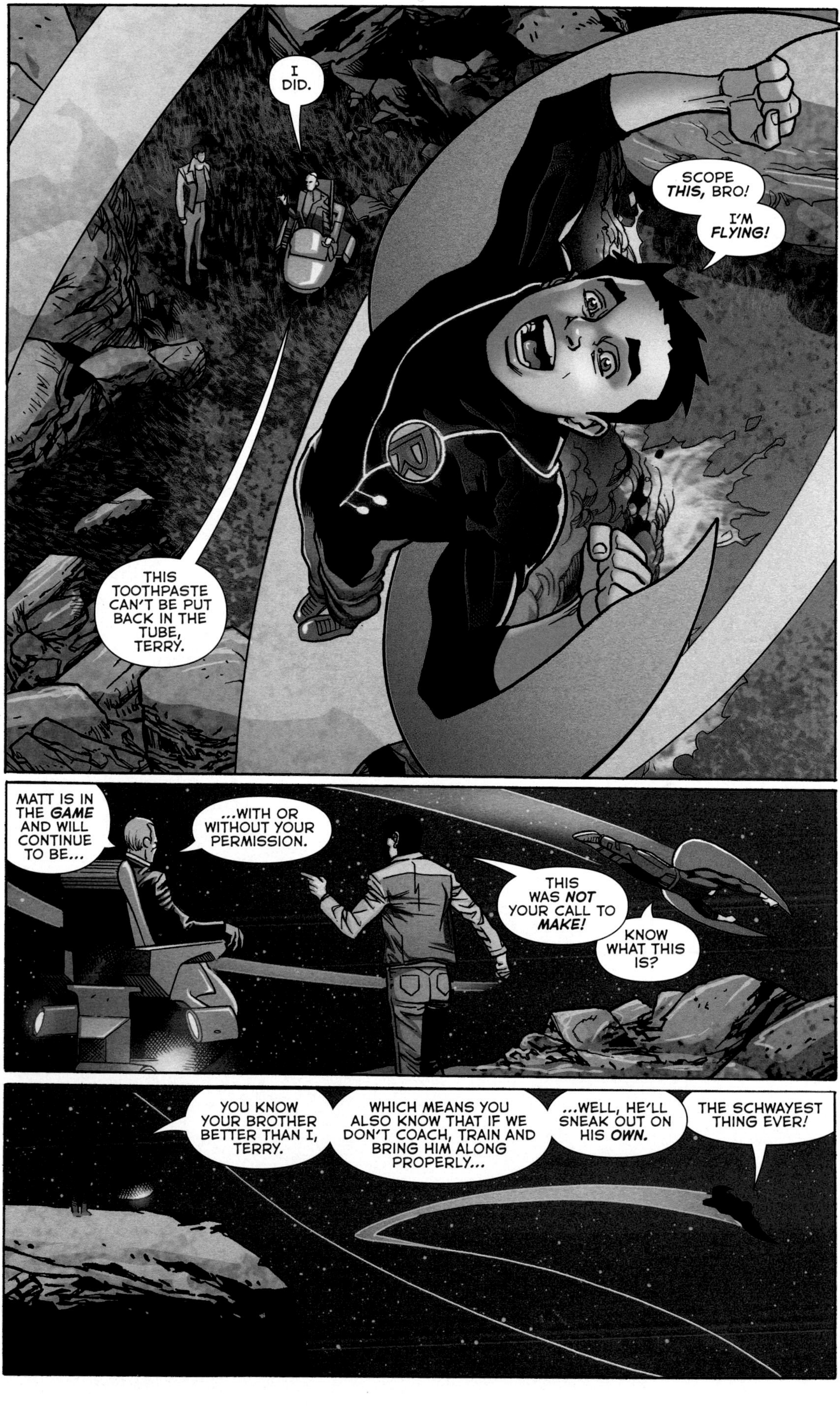
I DID.
SCOPE THIS, BRO!
I'M FLYING!
THIS TOOTHPASTE CAN'T BE PUT BACK IN THE TUBE, TERRY.
MATT IS IN THE GAME AND WILL CONTINUE TO BE...
...WITH OR WITHOUT YOUR PERMISSION.
THIS WAS NOT YOUR CALL TO MAKE!
KNOW WHAT THIS IS?
YOU KNOW YOUR BROTHER BETTER THAN I, TERRY.
WHICH MEANS YOU ALSO KNOW THAT IF WE DON'T COACH, TRAIN AND BRING HIM ALONG PROPERLY...
...WELL, HE'LL SNEAK OUT ON HIS OWN.
THE SCHWAYEST THING EVER!

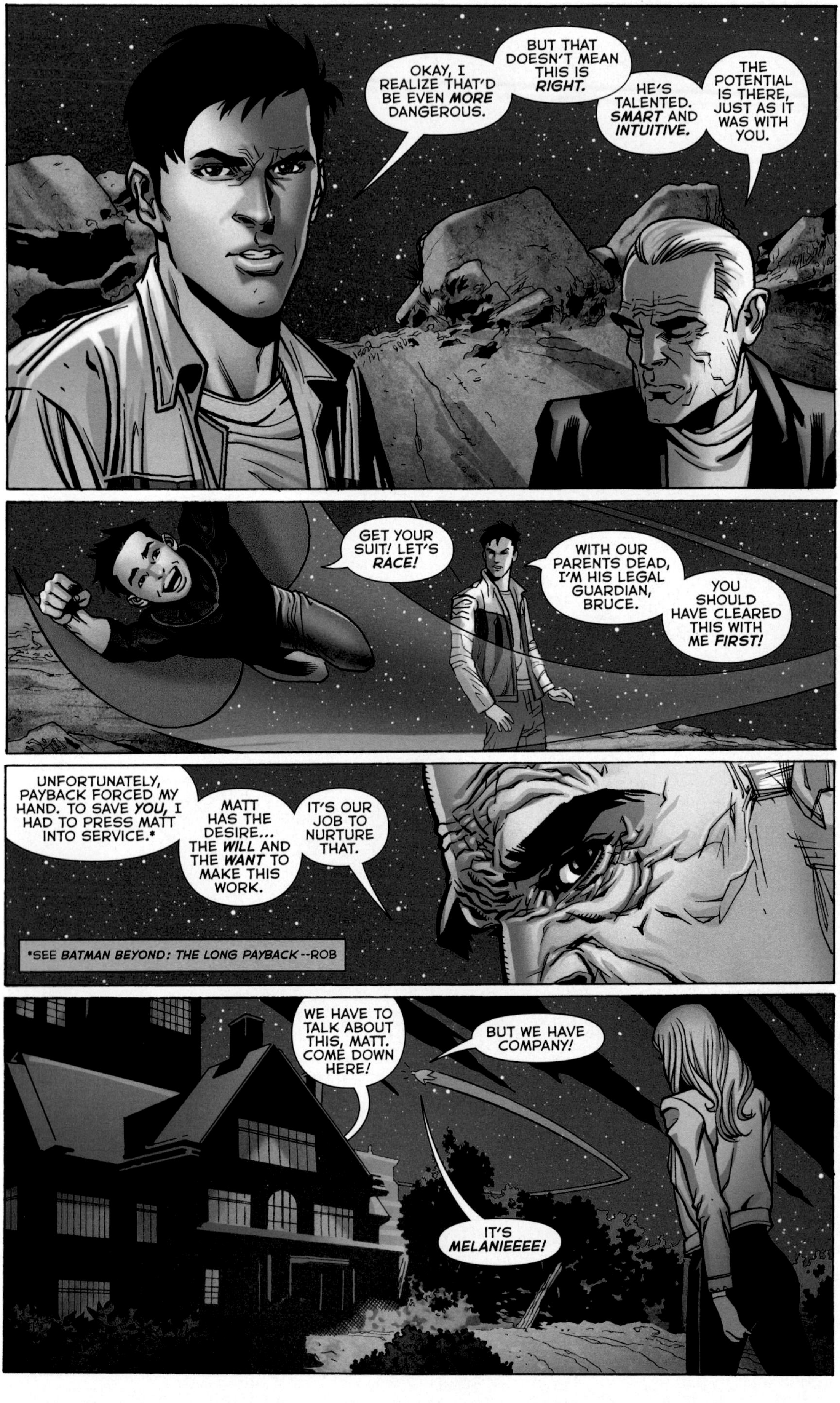
OKAY, I REALIZE THAT'D BE EVEN MORE DANGEROUS.
BUT THAT DOESN'T MEAN THIS IS RIGHT.
HE'S TALENTED. SMART AND INTUITIVE.
THE POTENTIAL IS THERE, JUST AS IT WAS WITH YOU.
GET YOUR SUIT! LET'S RACE!
WITH OUR PARENTS DEAD, I'M HIS LEGAL GUARDIAN, BRUCE.
YOU SHOULD HAVE CLEARED THIS WITH ME FIRST!
UNFORTUNATELY, PAYBACK FORCED MY HAND. TO SAVE YOU, I HAD TO PRESS MATT INTO SERVICE.*
MATT HAS THE DESIRE... THE WILL AND THE WANT TO MAKE THIS WORK.
IT'S OUR JOB TO NURTURE THAT.
*SEE BATMAN BEYOND: THE LONG PAYBACK --ROB
WE HAVE TO TALK ABOUT THIS, MATT. COME DOWN HERE!
BUT WE HAVE COMPANY!
IT'S MELANIEEEE!

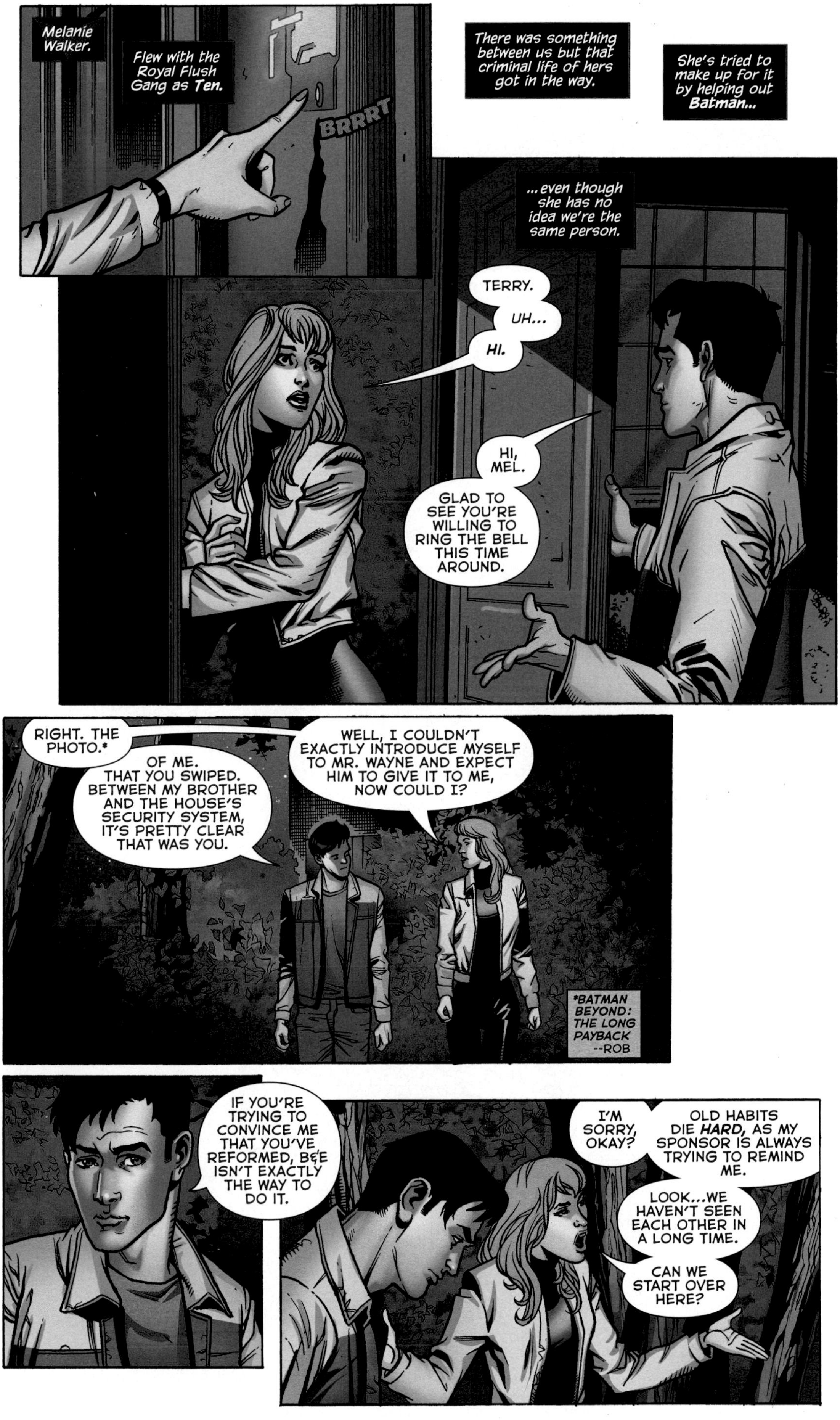
Melanie Walker.
Flew with the Royal Flush Gang as Ten.
BRRRT
There was something between us but that criminal life of hers got in the way.
She's tried to make up for it by helping out Batman...
...even though she has no idea we're the same person.
TERRY.
UH...
HI.
HI, MEL.
GLAD TO SEE YOU'RE WILLING TO RING THE BELL THIS TIME AROUND.
RIGHT. THE PHOTO.*
OF ME. THAT YOU SWIPED. BETWEEN MY BROTHER AND THE HOUSE'S SECURITY SYSTEM, IT'S PRETTY CLEAR THAT WAS YOU.
WELL, I COULDN'T EXACTLY INTRODUCE MYSELF TO MR. WAYNE AND EXPECT HIM TO GIVE IT TO ME, NOW COULD I?
*BATMAN BEYOND: THE LONG PAYBACK --ROB
IF YOU'RE TRYING TO CONVINCE ME THAT YOU'VE REFORMED, B&E ISN'T EXACTLY THE WAY TO DO IT.
I'M SORRY, OKAY?
OLD HABITS DIE HARD, AS MY SPONSOR IS ALWAYS TRYING TO REMIND ME.
LOOK...WE HAVEN'T SEEN EACH OTHER IN A LONG TIME.
CAN WE START OVER HERE?

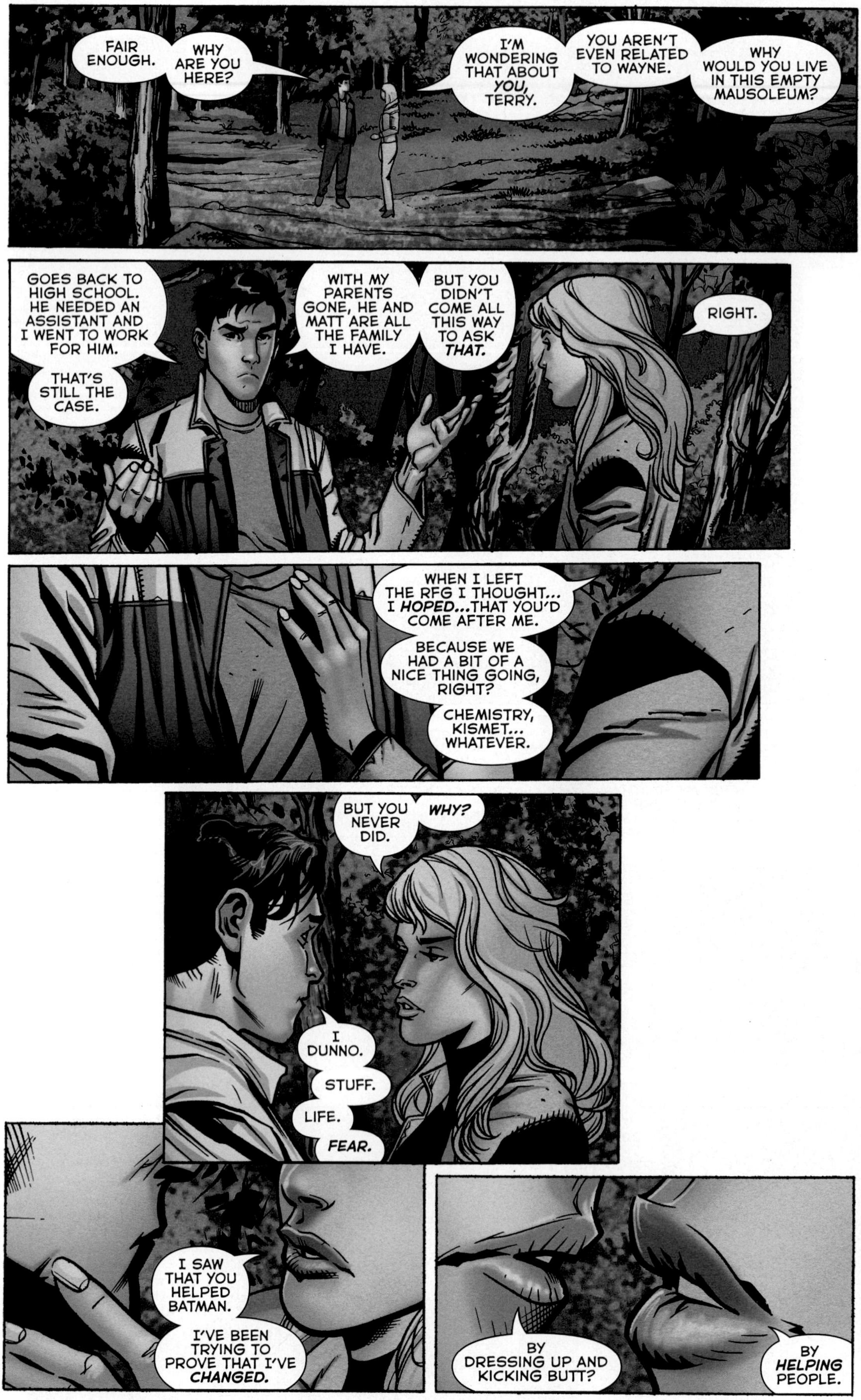

FAIR ENOUGH.
WHY ARE YOU HERE?
I'M WONDERING THAT ABOUT *YOU,* TERRY.
YOU AREN'T EVEN RELATED TO WAYNE.
WHY WOULD YOU LIVE IN THIS EMPTY MAUSOLEUM?
GOES BACK TO HIGH SCHOOL. HE NEEDED AN ASSISTANT AND I WENT TO WORK FOR HIM.
THAT'S STILL THE CASE.
WITH MY PARENTS GONE, HE AND MATT ARE ALL THE FAMILY I HAVE.
BUT YOU DIDN'T COME ALL THIS WAY TO ASK *THAT.*
RIGHT.
WHEN I LEFT THE RFG I THOUGHT... I *HOPED*...THAT YOU'D COME AFTER ME.
BECAUSE WE HAD A BIT OF A NICE THING GOING, RIGHT?
CHEMISTRY, KISMET... WHATEVER.
BUT YOU NEVER DID.
WHY?
I DUNNO.
STUFF.
LIFE.
FEAR.
I SAW THAT YOU HELPED BATMAN.
I'VE BEEN TRYING TO PROVE THAT I'VE *CHANGED.*
BY DRESSING UP AND KICKING BUTT?
BY *HELPING* PEOPLE.

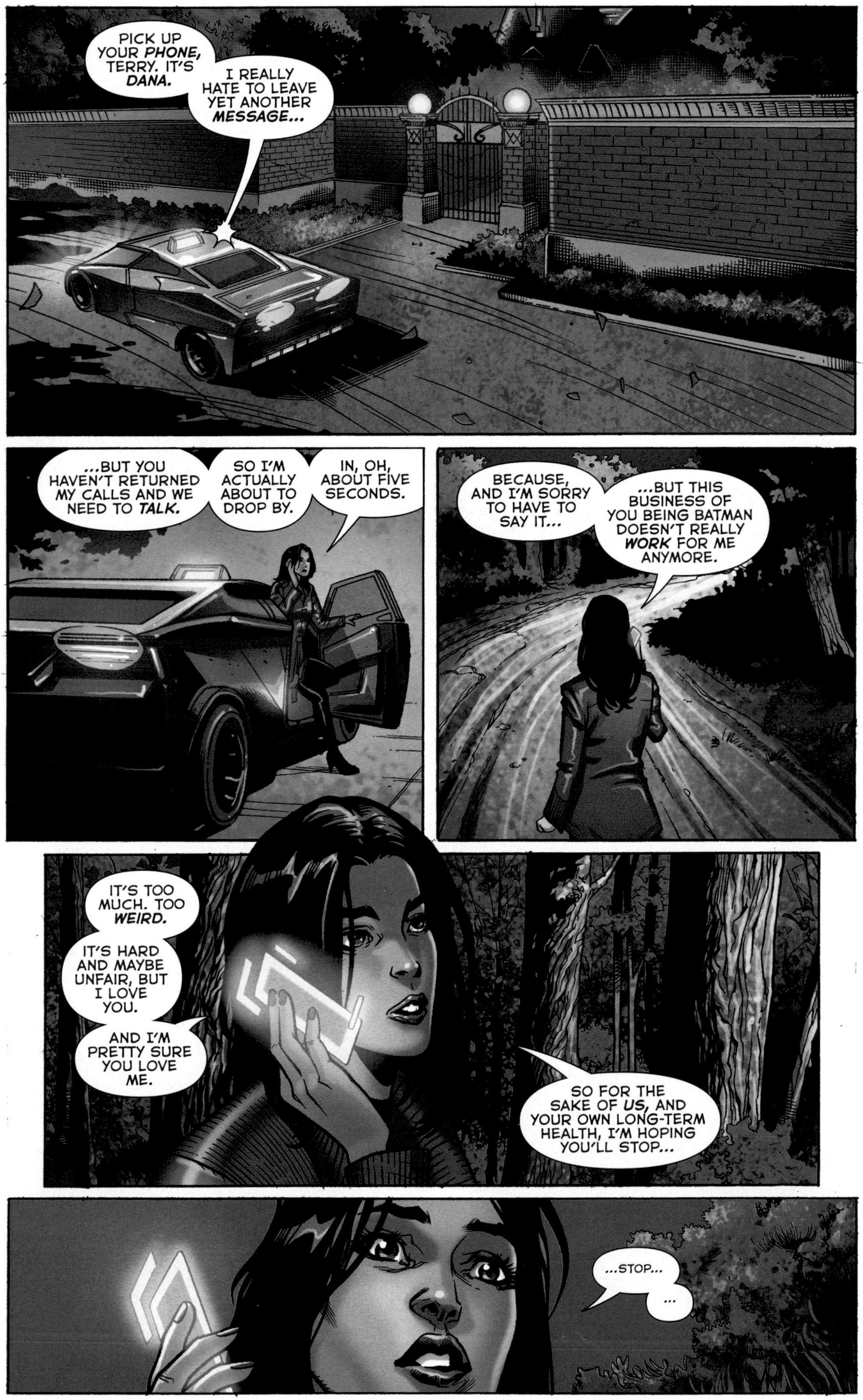
PICK UP YOUR PHONE, TERRY. IT'S DANA.
I REALLY HATE TO LEAVE YET ANOTHER MESSAGE...
...BUT YOU HAVEN'T RETURNED MY CALLS AND WE NEED TO TALK.
SO I'M ACTUALLY ABOUT TO DROP BY.
IN, OH, ABOUT FIVE SECONDS.
BECAUSE, AND I'M SORRY TO HAVE TO SAY IT...
...BUT THIS BUSINESS OF YOU BEING BATMAN DOESN'T REALLY WORK FOR ME ANYMORE.
IT'S TOO MUCH. TOO WEIRD.
IT'S HARD AND MAYBE UNFAIR, BUT I LOVE YOU.
AND I'M PRETTY SURE YOU LOVE ME.
SO FOR THE SAKE OF US, AND YOUR OWN LONG-TERM HEALTH, I'M HOPING YOU'LL STOP...
...STOP...
...

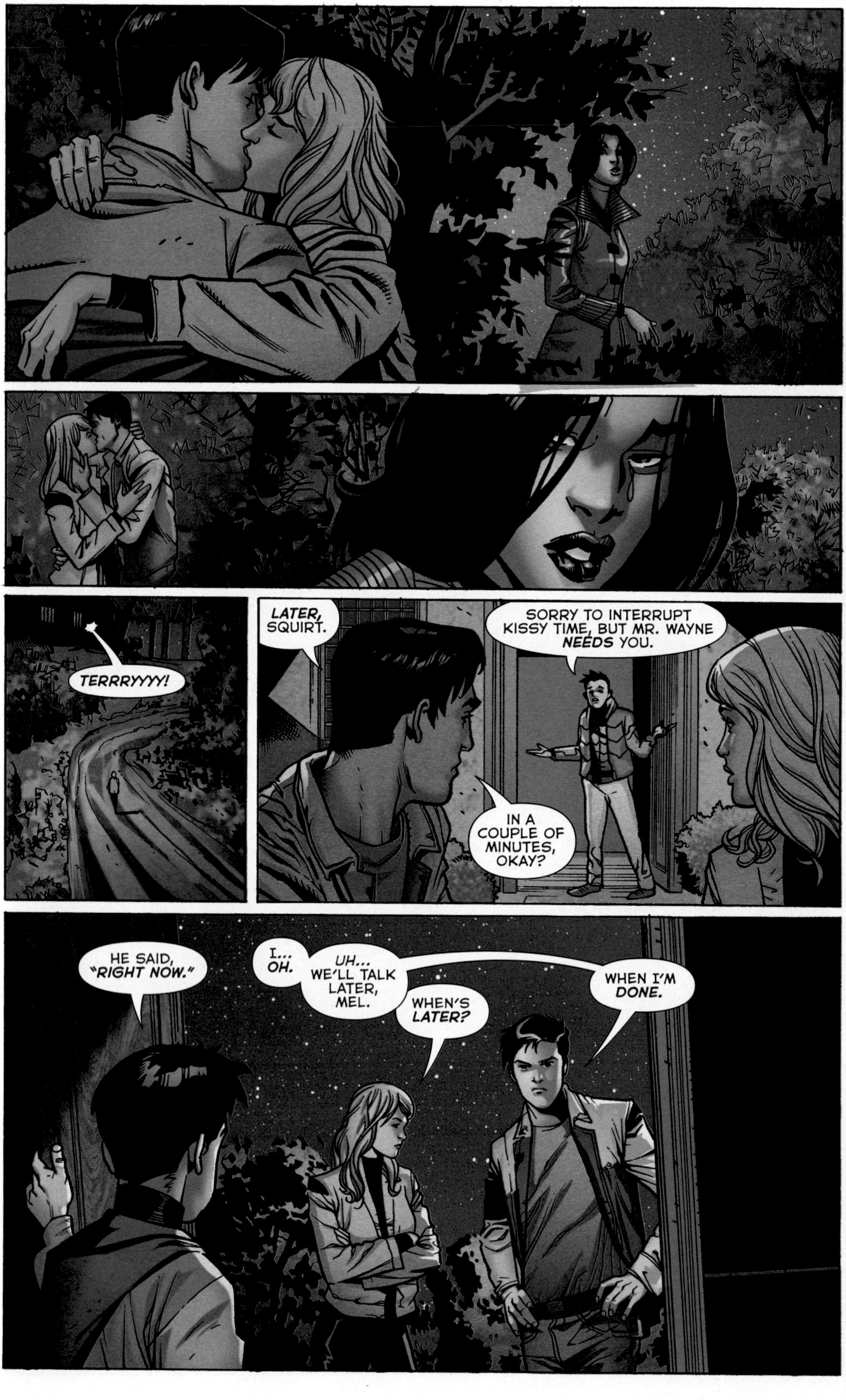
TERRRYYYY!
LATER, SQUIRT.
SORRY TO INTERRUPT KISSY TIME, BUT MR. WAYNE NEEDS YOU.
IN A COUPLE OF MINUTES, OKAY?
HE SAID, "RIGHT NOW."
I... OH.
UH... WE'LL TALK LATER, MEL.
WHEN'S LATER?
WHEN I'M DONE.

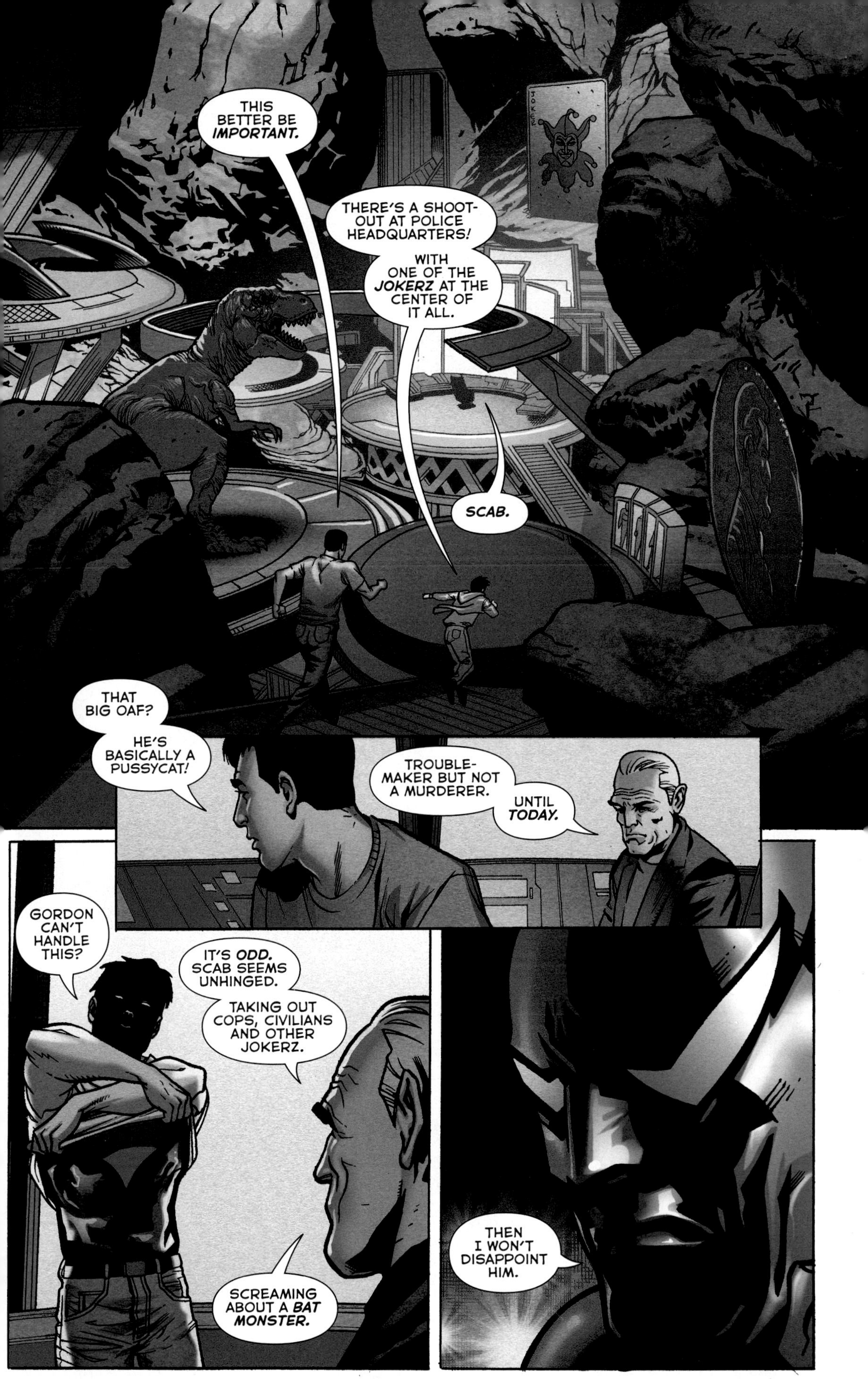
THIS BETTER BE *IMPORTANT.*
THERE'S A SHOOT-OUT AT POLICE HEADQUARTERS!
WITH ONE OF THE *JOKERZ* AT THE CENTER OF IT ALL.
SCAB.
THAT BIG OAF?
HE'S BASICALLY A PUSSYCAT!
TROUBLE-MAKER BUT NOT A MURDERER.
UNTIL *TODAY.*
GORDON CAN'T HANDLE THIS?
IT'S *ODD.* SCAB SEEMS UNHINGED.
TAKING OUT COPS, CIVILIANS AND OTHER JOKERZ.
SCREAMING ABOUT A *BAT MONSTER.*
THEN I WON'T DISAPPOINT HIM.

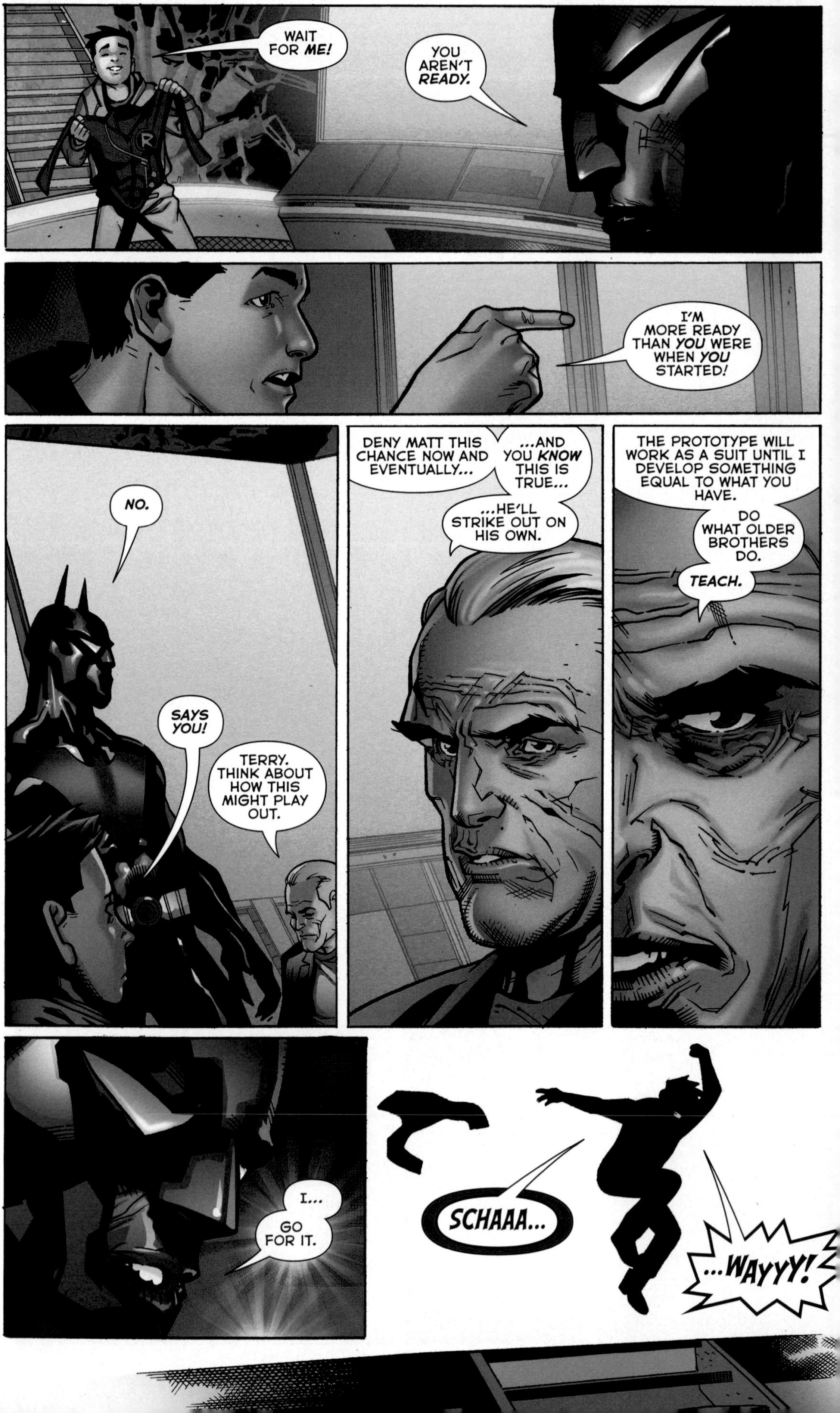
WAIT FOR ME!
YOU AREN'T READY.
I'M MORE READY THAN YOU WERE WHEN YOU STARTED!
NO.
SAYS YOU!
TERRY. THINK ABOUT HOW THIS MIGHT PLAY OUT.
DENY MATT THIS CHANCE NOW AND EVENTUALLY...
...AND YOU KNOW THIS IS TRUE...
...HE'LL STRIKE OUT ON HIS OWN.
THE PROTOTYPE WILL WORK AS A SUIT UNTIL I DEVELOP SOMETHING EQUAL TO WHAT YOU HAVE.
DO WHAT OLDER BROTHERS DO.
TEACH.
I...
GO FOR IT.
SCHAAA...
...WAYYY!

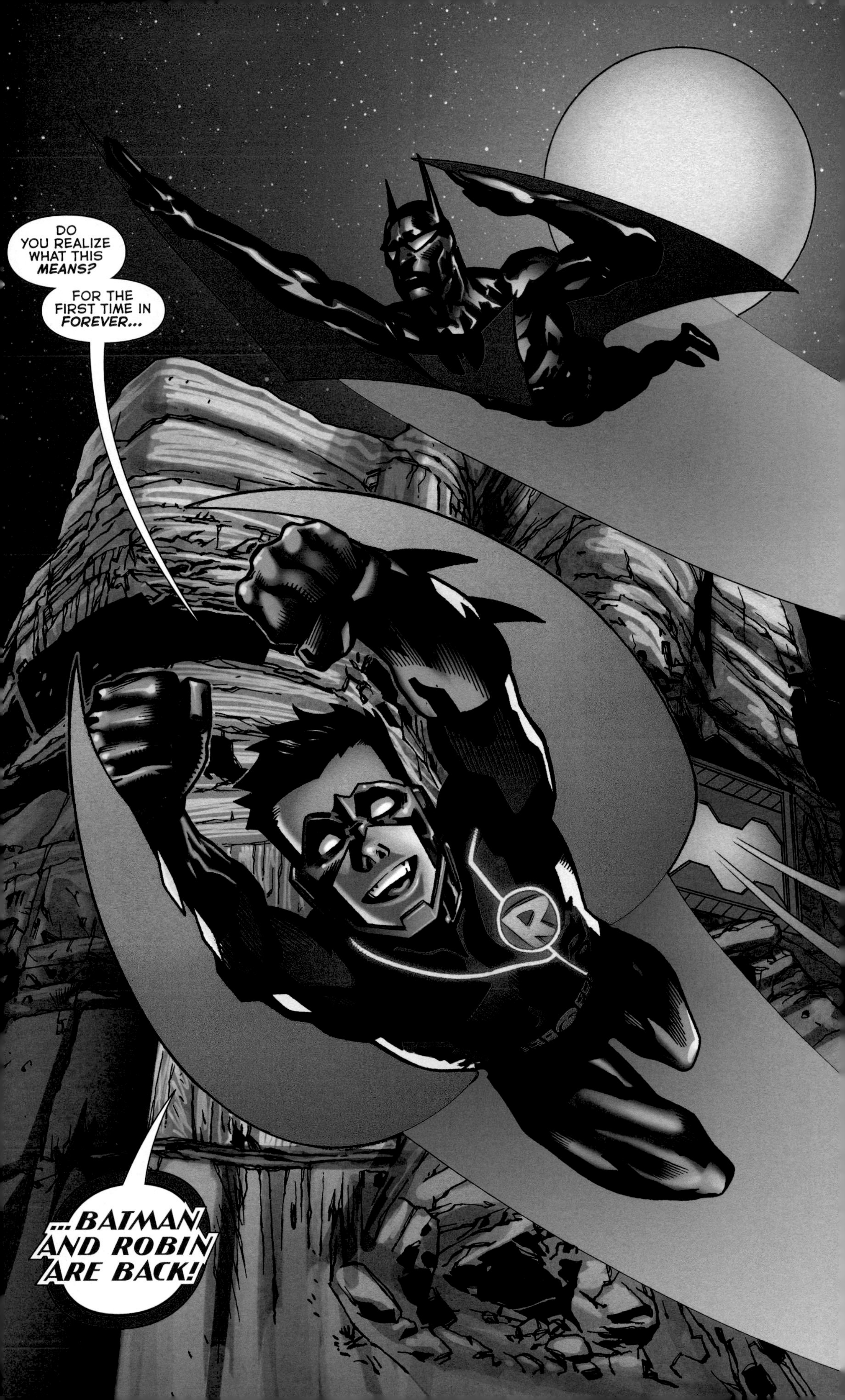
DO YOU REALIZE WHAT THIS MEANS?
FOR THE FIRST TIME IN FOREVER...
...BATMAN AND ROBIN ARE BACK!

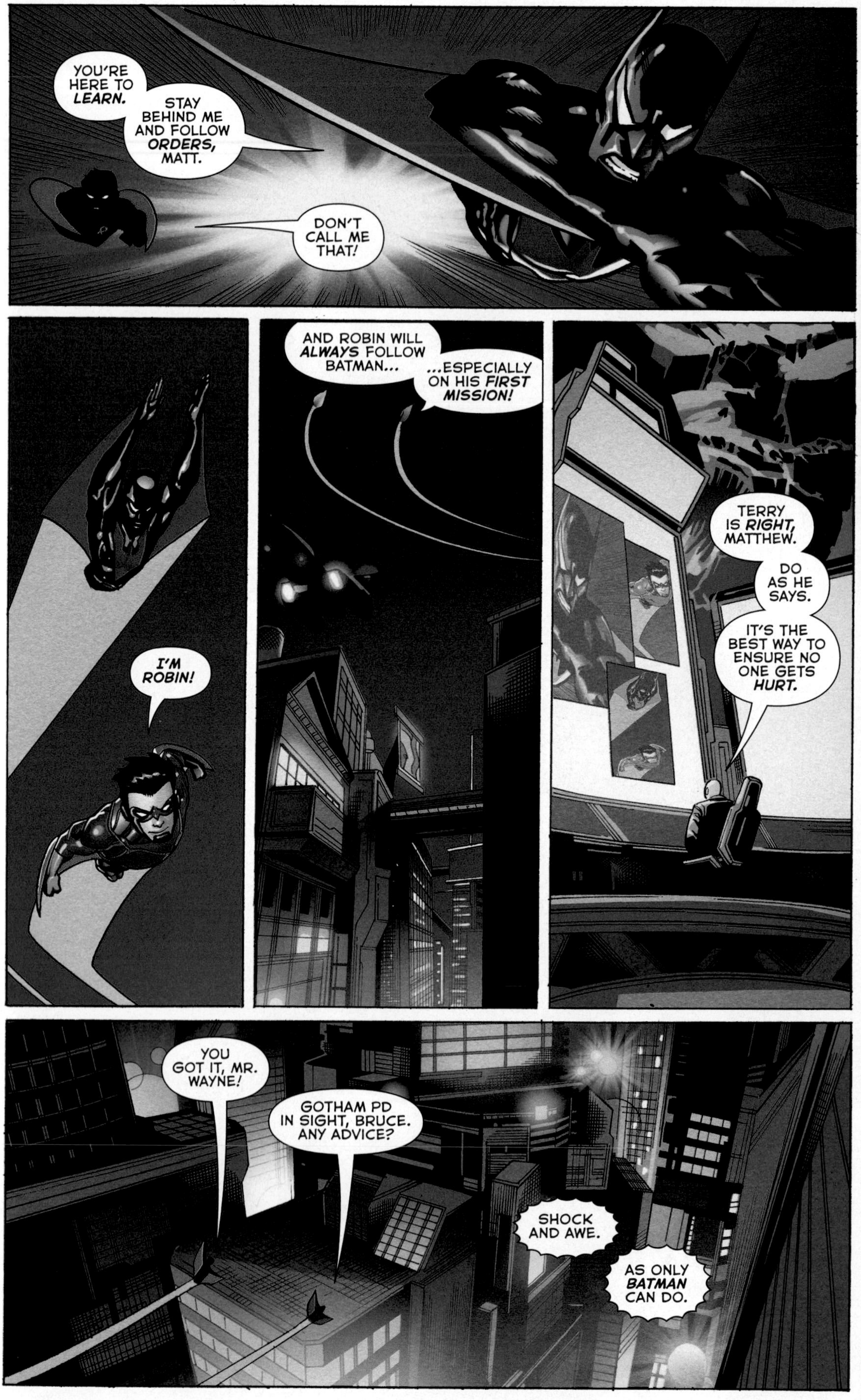

YOU'RE HERE TO LEARN.
STAY BEHIND ME AND FOLLOW ORDERS, MATT.
DON'T CALL ME THAT!
I'M ROBIN!
AND ROBIN WILL ALWAYS FOLLOW BATMAN...
...ESPECIALLY ON HIS FIRST MISSION!
TERRY IS RIGHT, MATTHEW.
DO AS HE SAYS.
IT'S THE BEST WAY TO ENSURE NO ONE GETS HURT.
YOU GOT IT, MR. WAYNE!
GOTHAM PD IN SIGHT, BRUCE. ANY ADVICE?
SHOCK AND AWE.
AS ONLY BATMAN CAN DO.

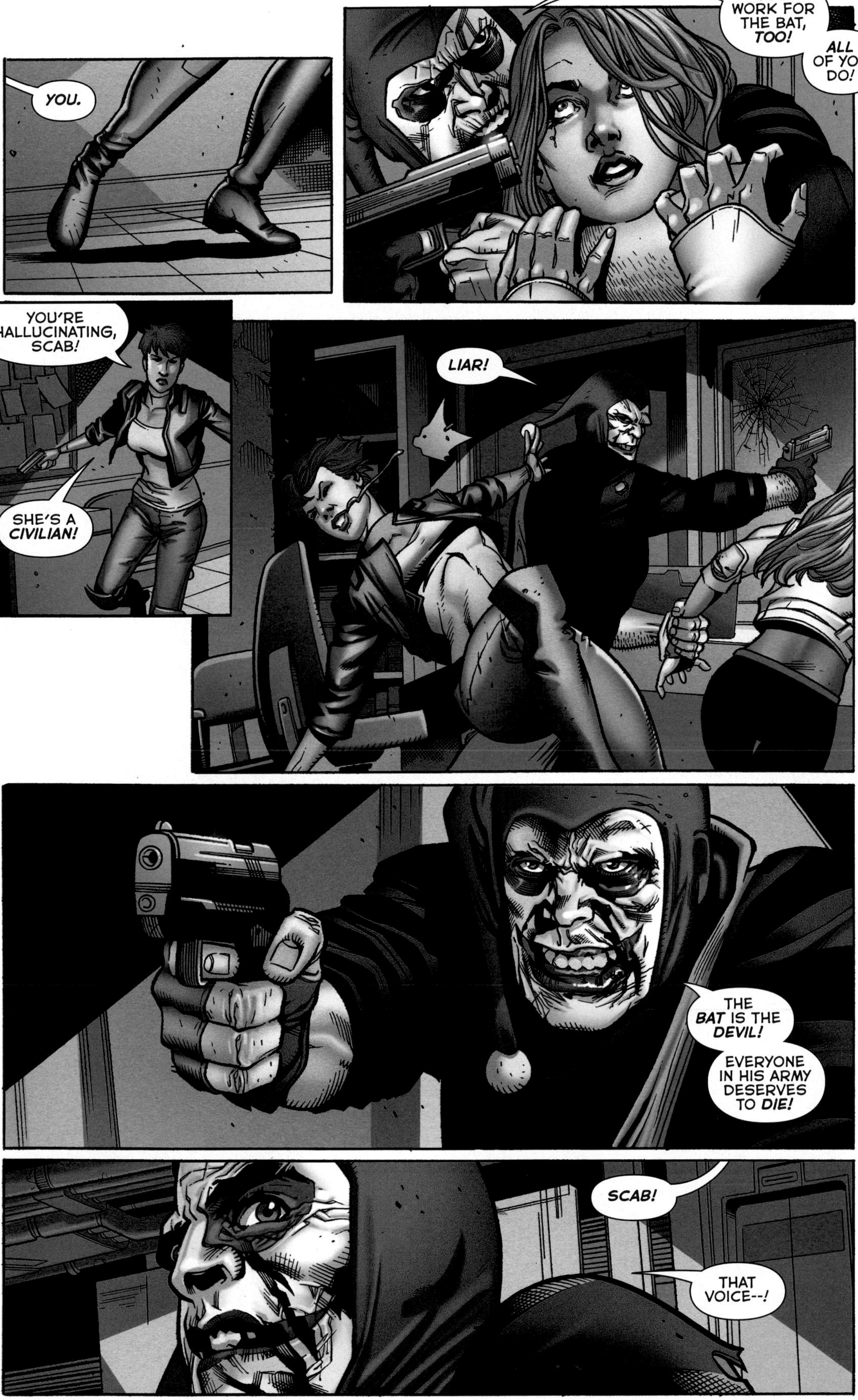
YOU.
YOU WORK FOR THE BAT, TOO!
ALL OF YOU DO!
YOU'RE HALLUCINATING, SCAB!
SHE'S A CIVILIAN!
LIAR!
THE BAT IS THE DEVIL!
EVERYONE IN HIS ARMY DESERVES TO DIE!
SCAB!
THAT VOICE--!

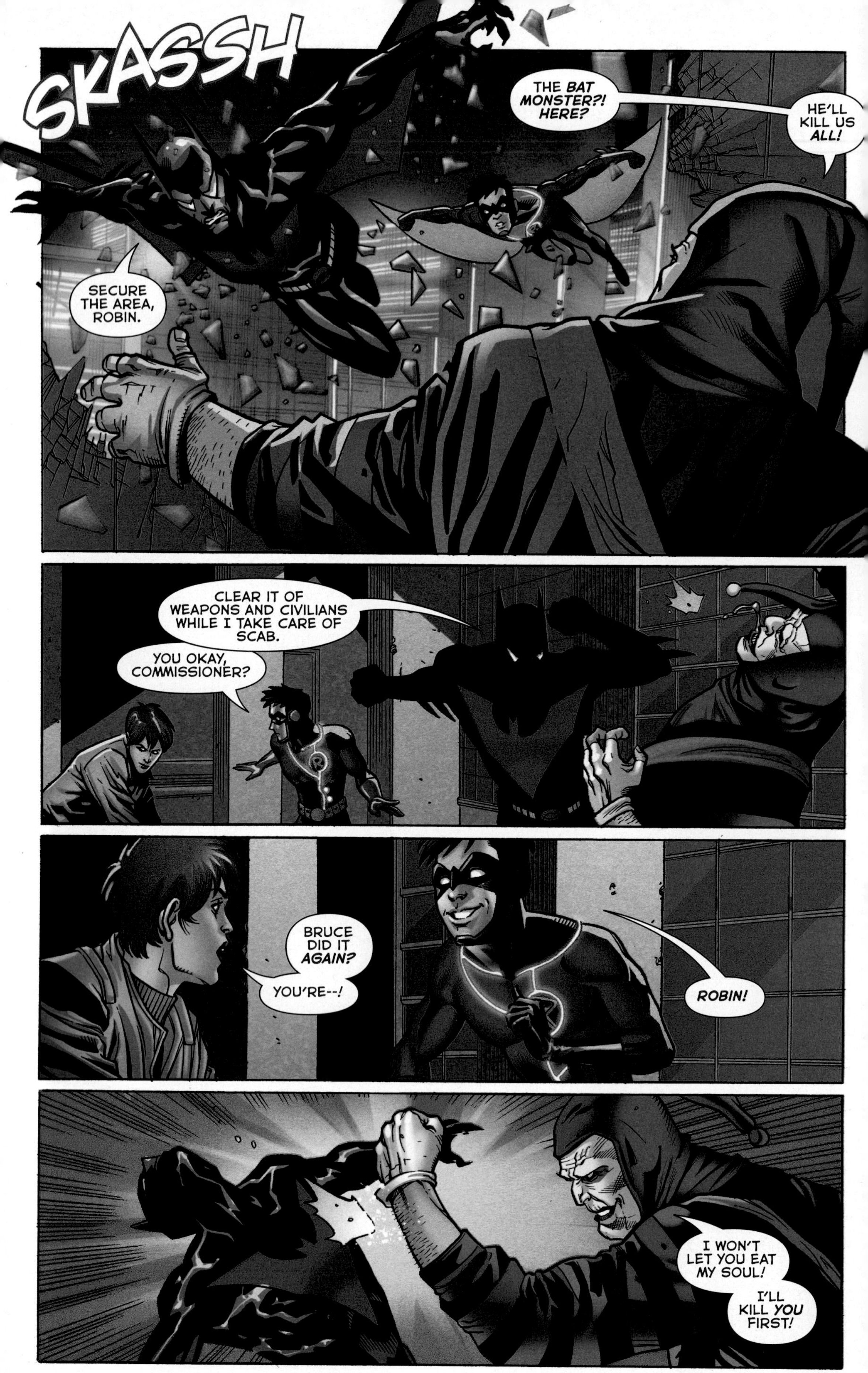
SKASSH
THE BAT MONSTER?! HERE?
HE'LL KILL US ALL!
SECURE THE AREA, ROBIN.
CLEAR IT OF WEAPONS AND CIVILIANS WHILE I TAKE CARE OF SCAB.
YOU OKAY, COMMISSIONER?
BRUCE DID IT AGAIN?
YOU'RE--!
ROBIN!
I WON'T LET YOU EAT MY SOUL!
I'LL KILL YOU FIRST!

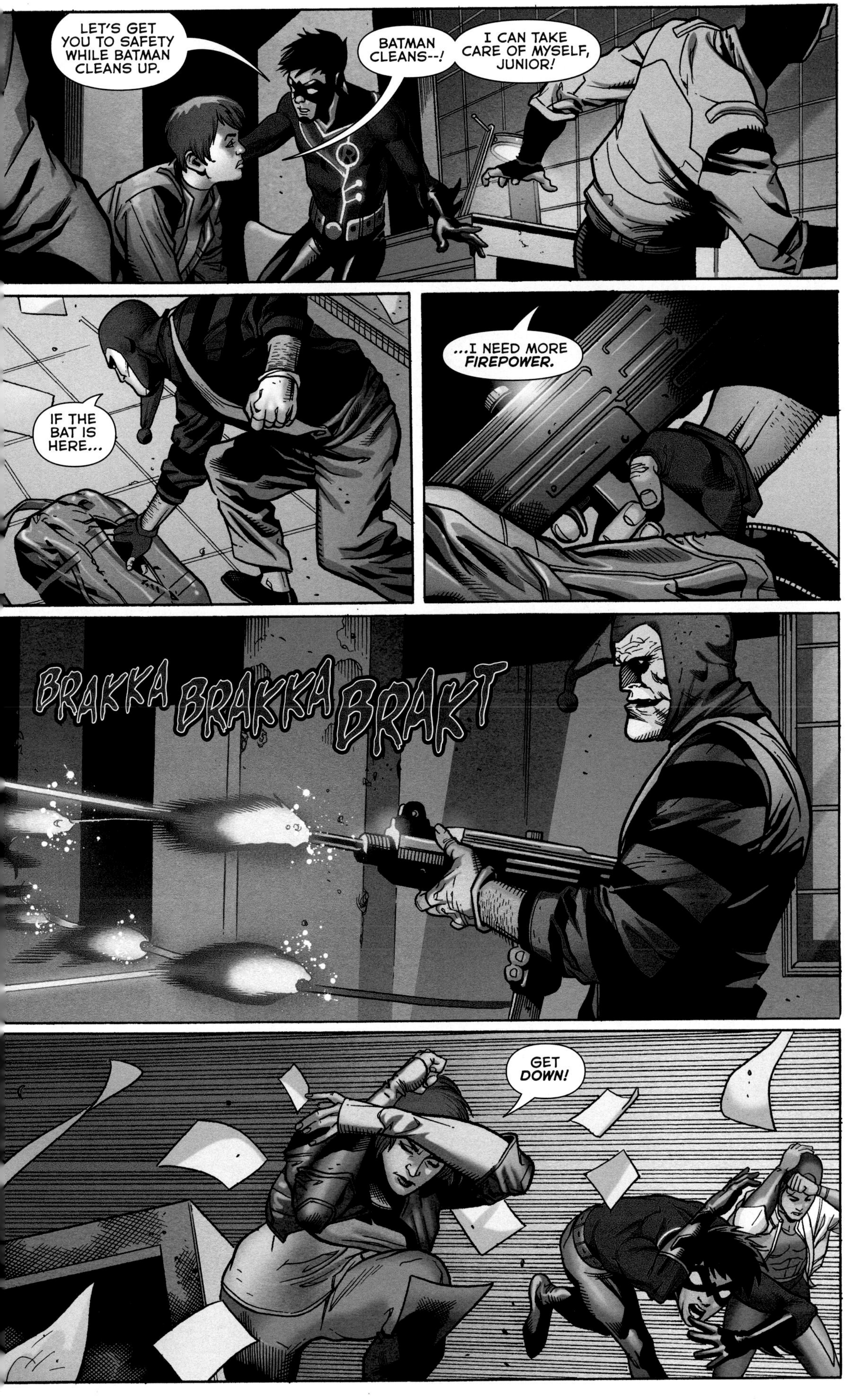
LET'S GET YOU TO SAFETY WHILE BATMAN CLEANS UP.
BATMAN CLEANS--!
I CAN TAKE CARE OF MYSELF, JUNIOR!
IF THE BAT IS HERE...
...I NEED MORE FIREPOWER.
BRAKKA BRAKKA BRAKT
GET DOWN!

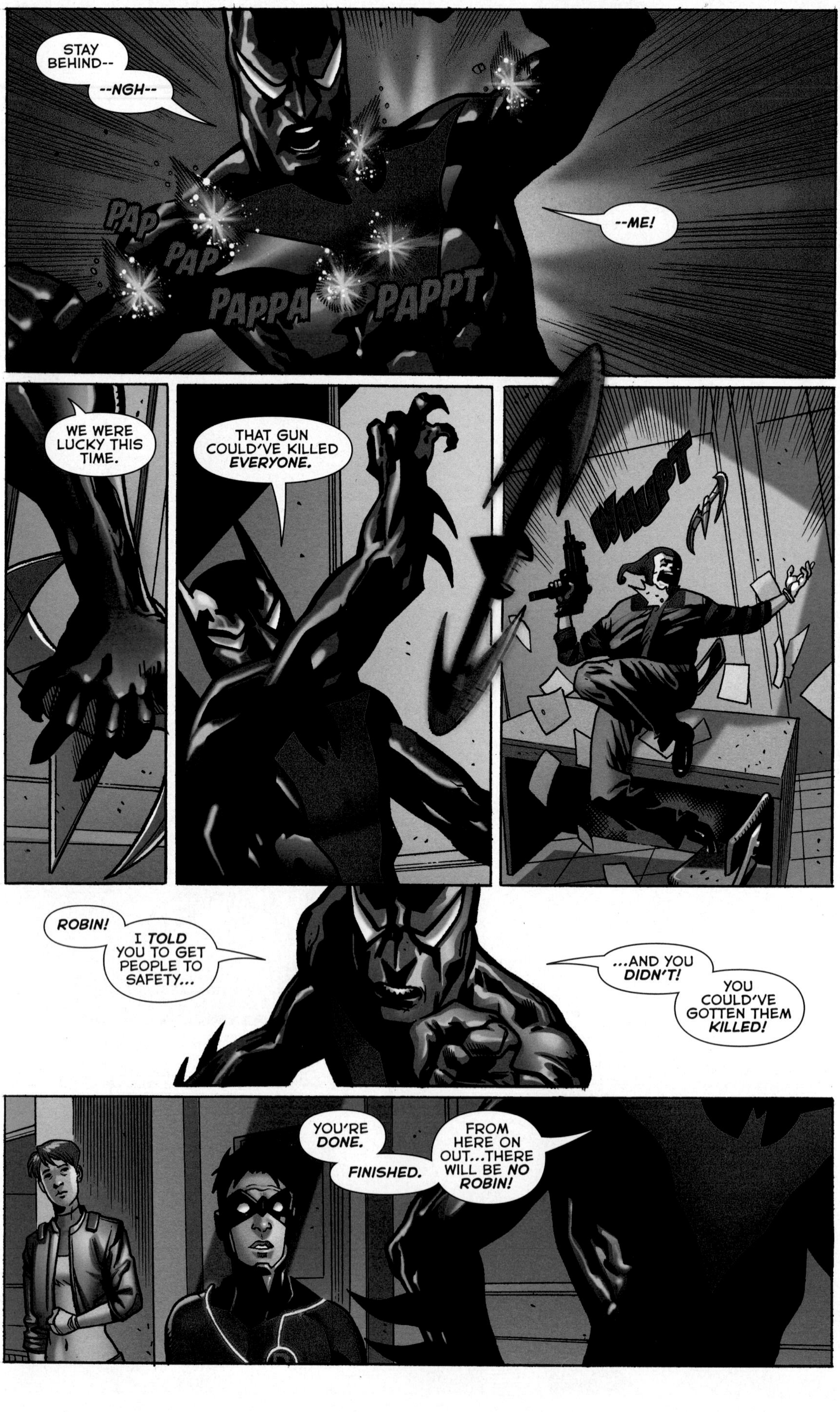
STAY BEHIND--
--NGH--
PAP
PAP
PAPPA
PAPPT
--ME!
WE WERE LUCKY THIS TIME.
THAT GUN COULD'VE KILLED *EVERYONE.*
WHUPT
ROBIN!
I *TOLD* YOU TO GET PEOPLE TO SAFETY...
...AND YOU *DIDN'T!*
YOU COULD'VE GOTTEN THEM *KILLED!*
YOU'RE *DONE.*
FINISHED.
FROM HERE ON OUT...THERE WILL BE *NO ROBIN!*

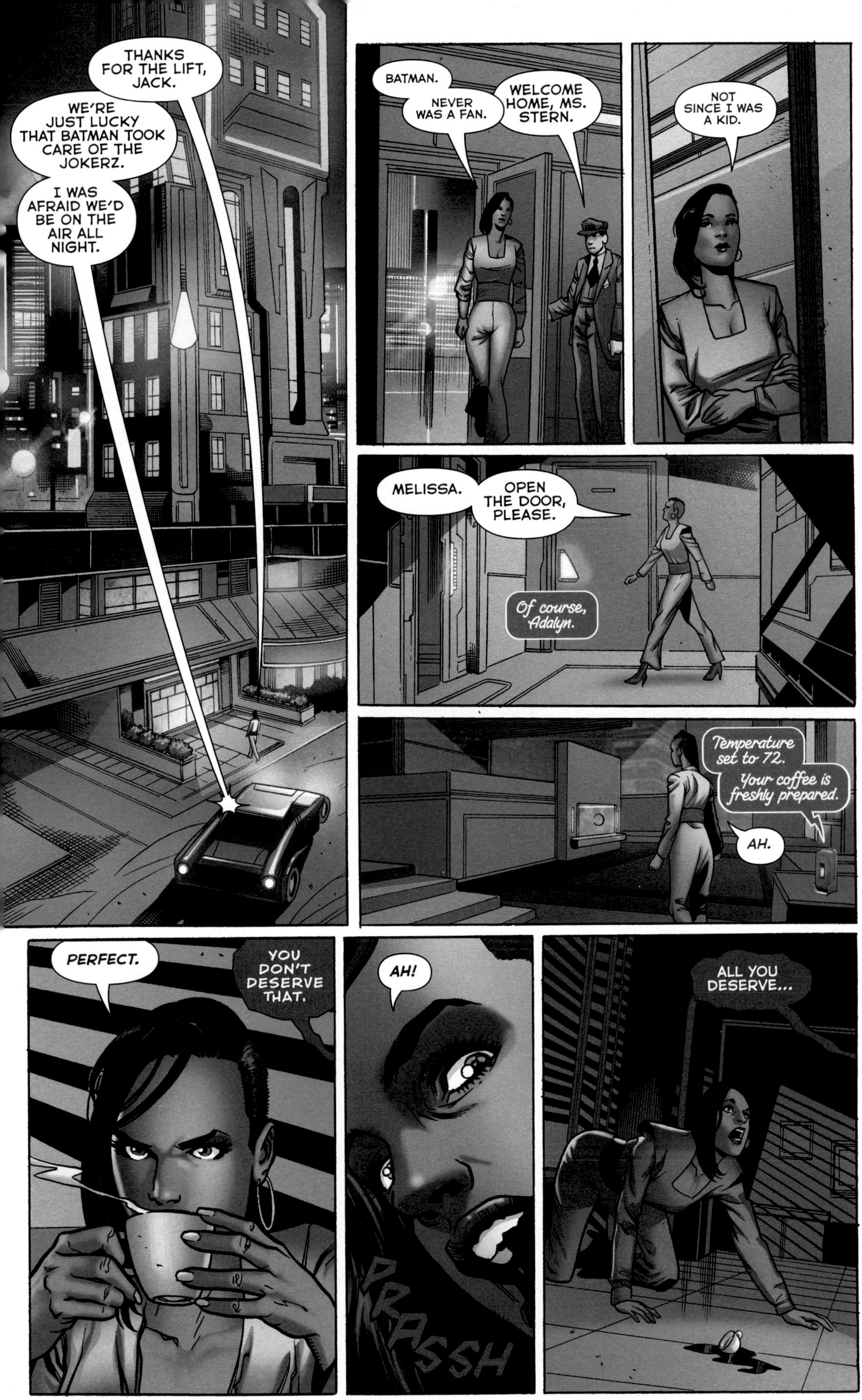
THANKS FOR THE LIFT, JACK.
WE'RE JUST LUCKY THAT BATMAN TOOK CARE OF THE JOKERZ.
I WAS AFRAID WE'D BE ON THE AIR ALL NIGHT.
BATMAN.
NEVER WAS A FAN.
WELCOME HOME, MS. STERN.
NOT SINCE I WAS A KID.
MELISSA.
OPEN THE DOOR, PLEASE.
Of course, Adalyn.
Temperature set to 72.
Your coffee is freshly prepared.
AH.
PERFECT.
YOU DON'T DESERVE THAT.
AH!
DRASSH
ALL YOU DESERVE...

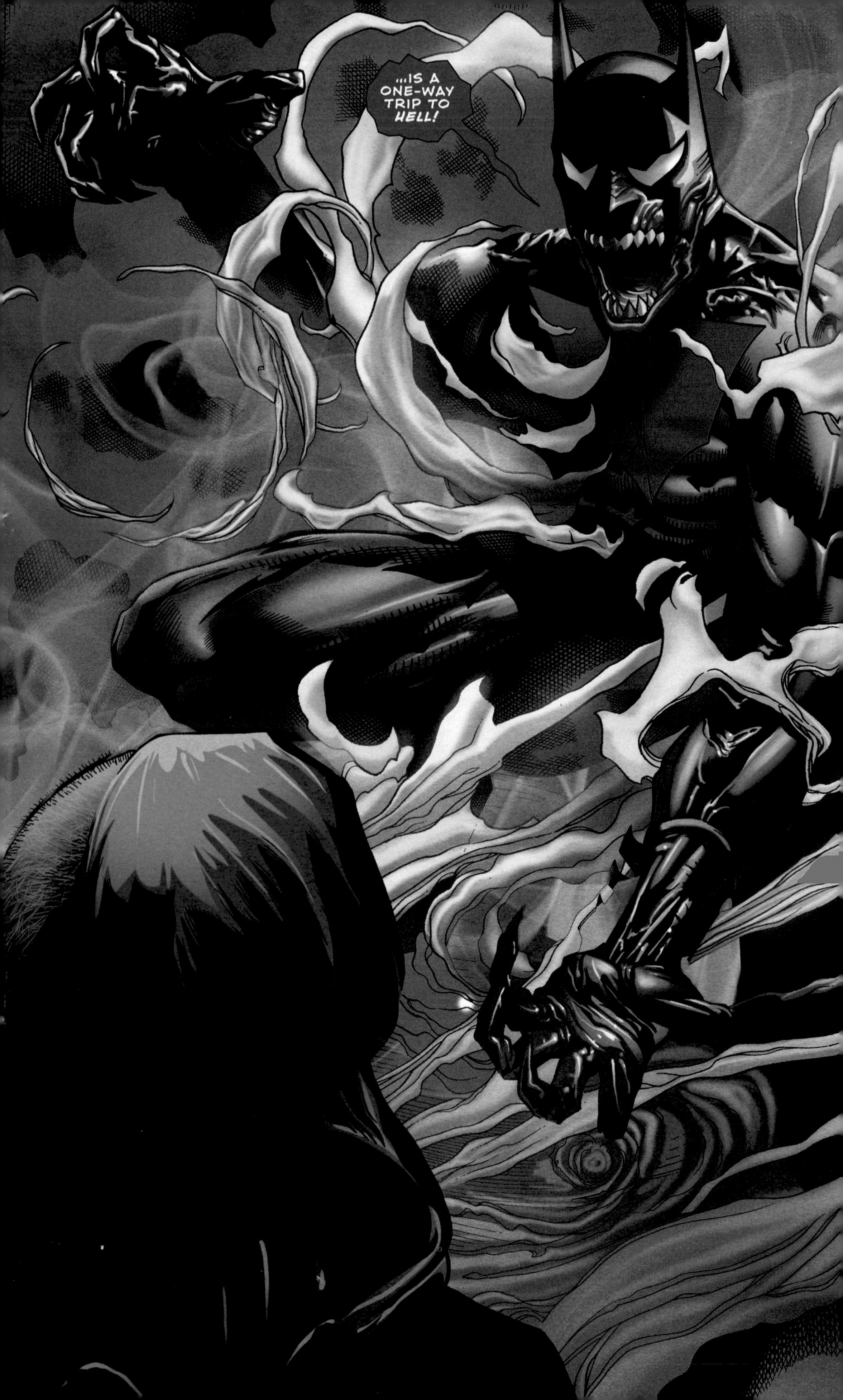
...IS A ONE-WAY TRIP TO HELL!

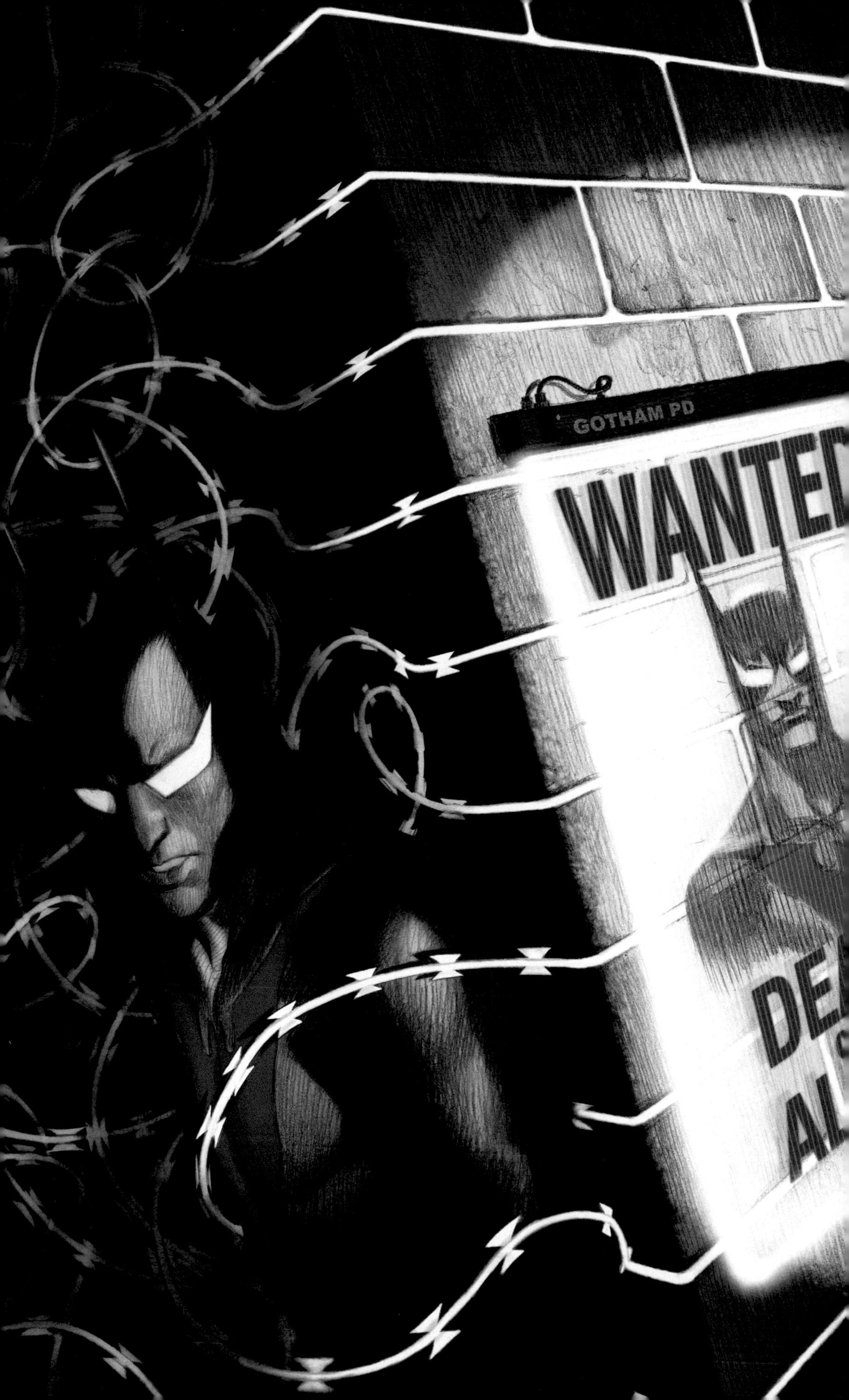
GOTHAM PD
WANTED

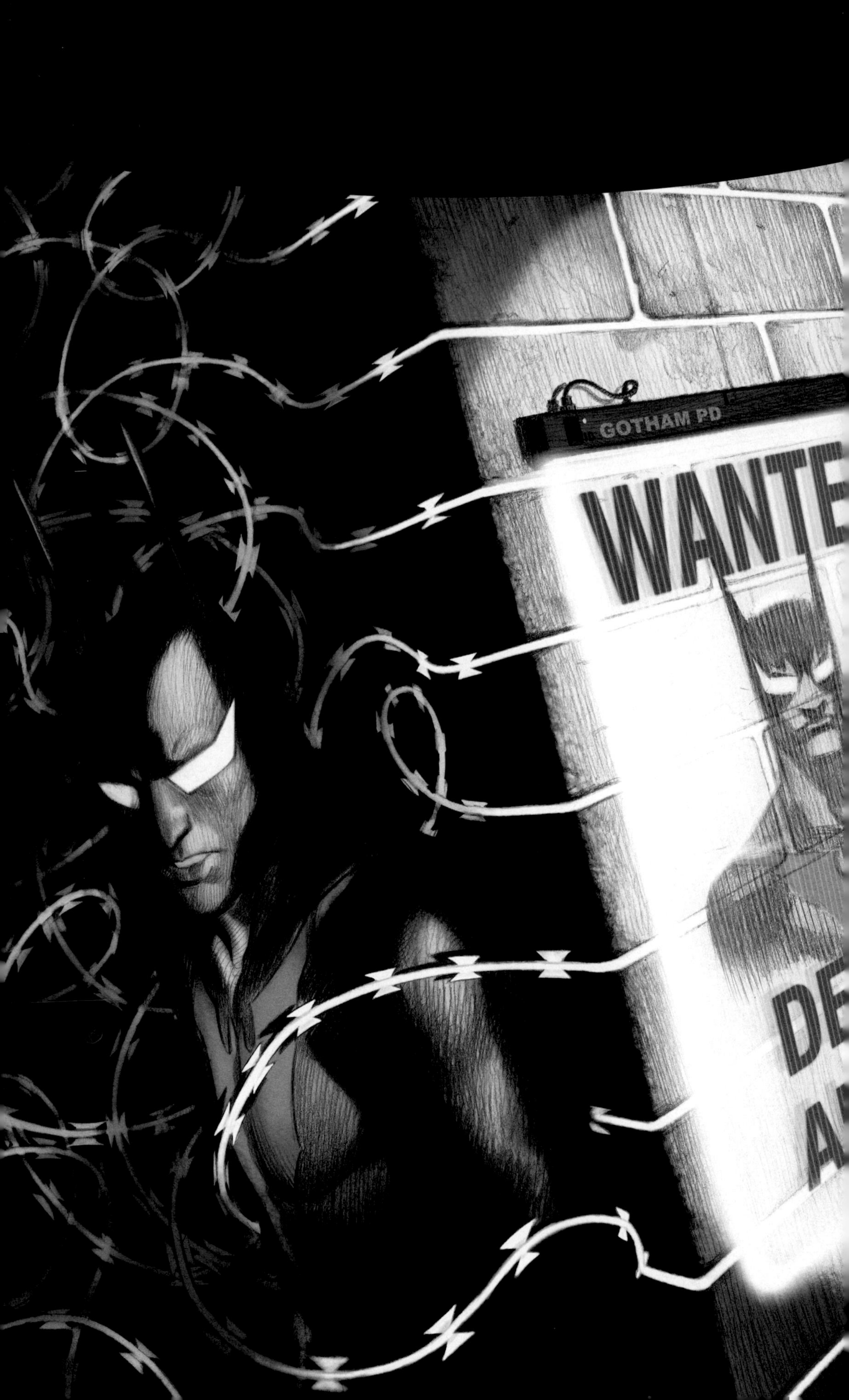
GOTHAM PD
WANTE
DE
A

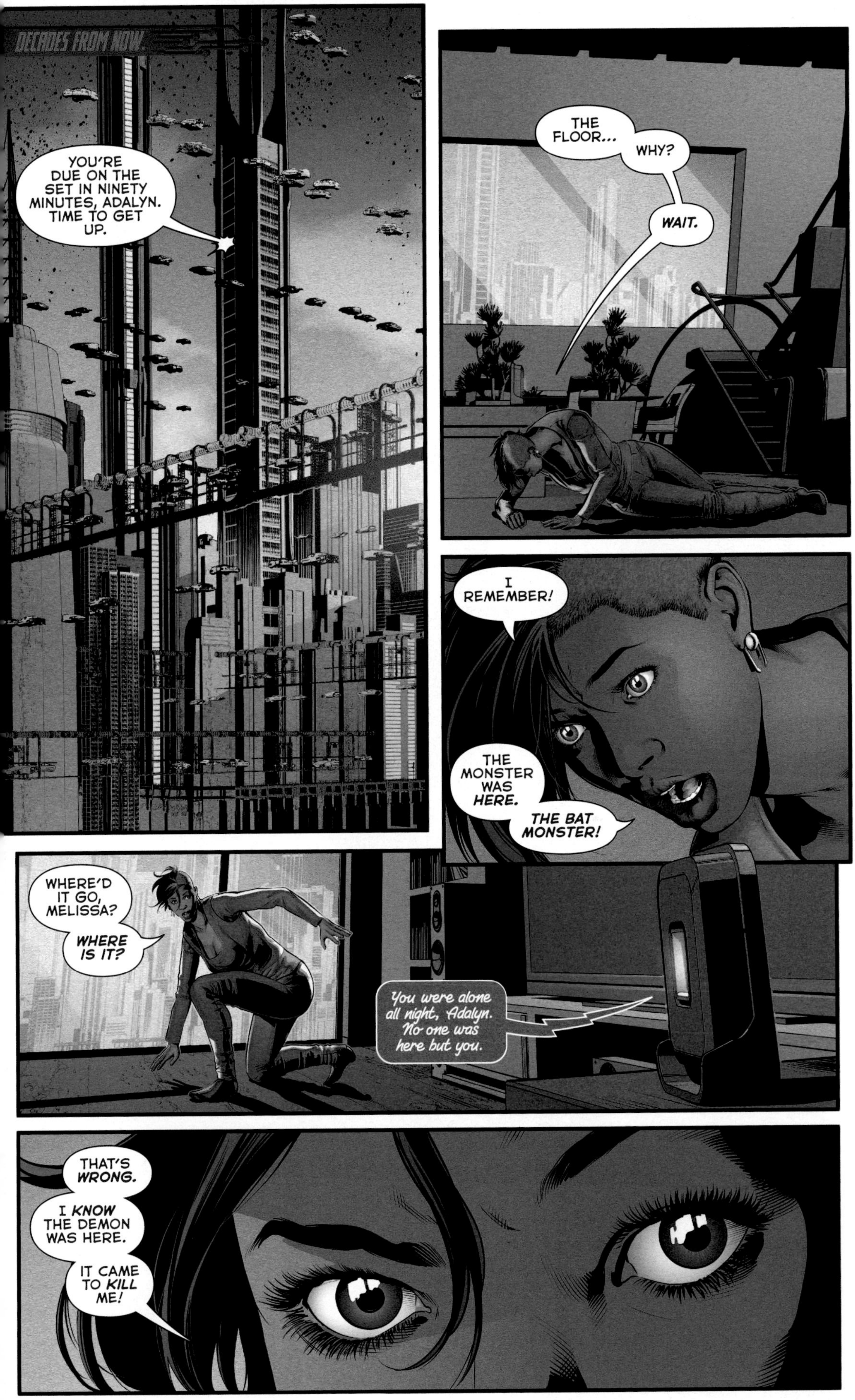
DECADES FROM NOW
YOU'RE DUE ON THE SET IN NINETY MINUTES, ADALYN. TIME TO GET UP.
THE FLOOR...
WHY?
WAIT.
I REMEMBER!
THE MONSTER WAS HERE.
THE BAT MONSTER!
WHERE'D IT GO, MELISSA?
WHERE IS IT?
You were alone all night, Adalyn. No one was here but you.
THAT'S WRONG.
I KNOW THE DEMON WAS HERE.
IT CAME TO KILL ME!

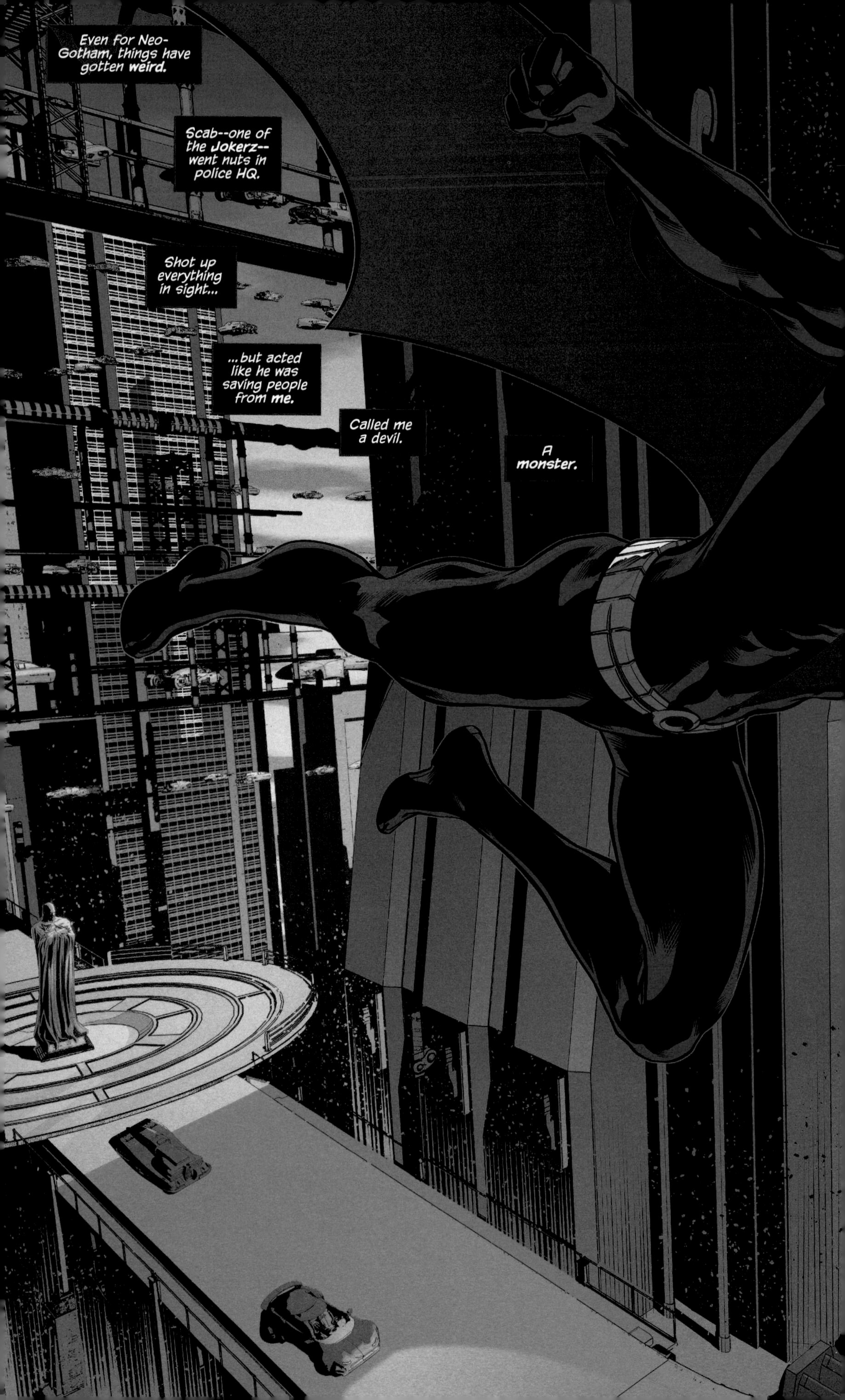
Even for Neo-Gotham, things have gotten **weird.**
Scab--one of the **Jokerz**--went nuts in police HQ.
Shot up everything in sight...
...but acted like he was saving people from **me.**
Called me a devil.
A monster.

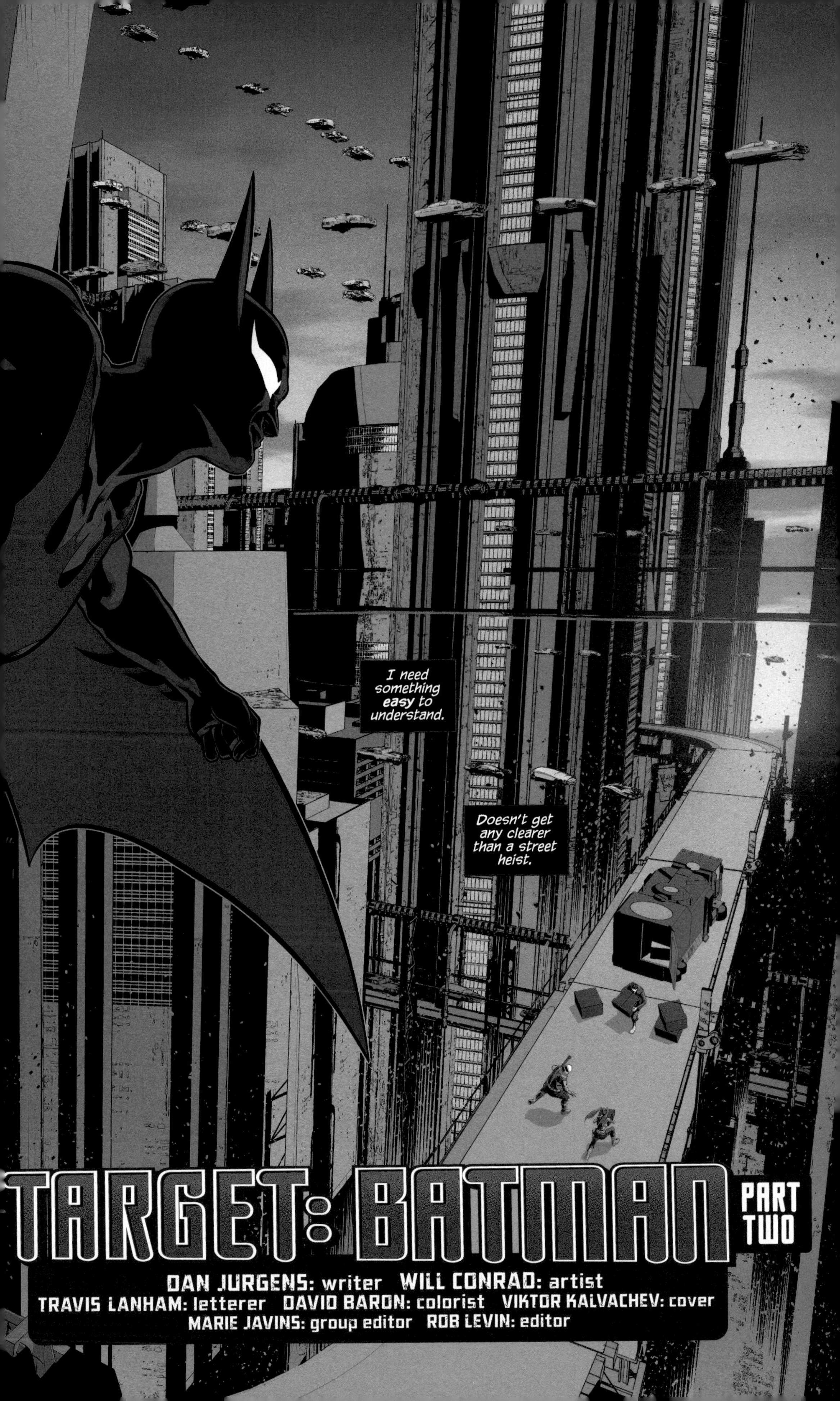
I need something easy to understand.
Doesn't get any clearer than a street heist.
TARGET: BATMAN PART TWO
DAN JURGENS: writer WILL CONRAD: artist
TRAVIS LANHAM: letterer DAVID BARON: colorist VIKTOR KALVACHEV: cover
MARIE JAVINS: group editor ROB LEVIN: editor

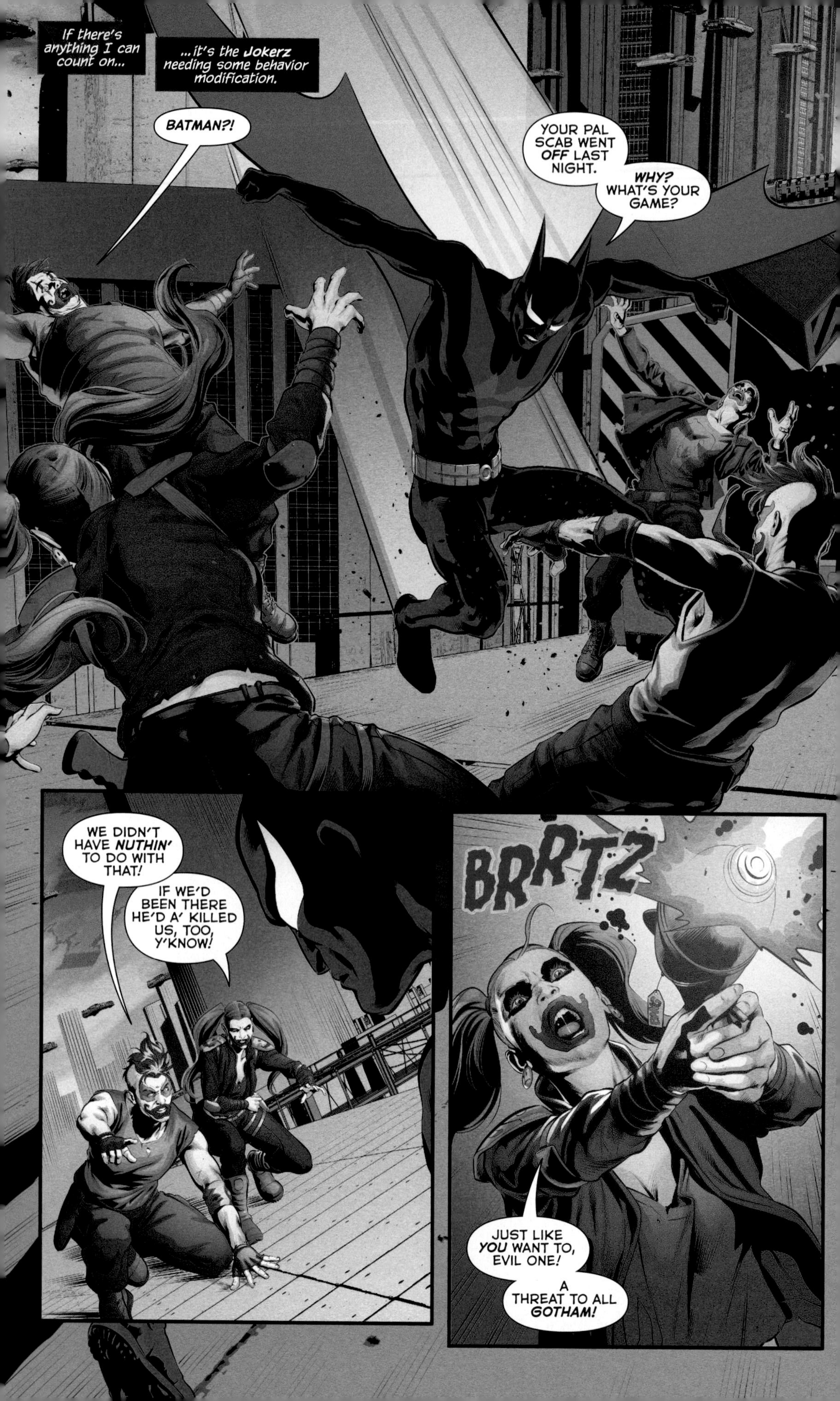
If there's anything I can count on...
...it's the Jokerz needing some behavior modification.
BATMAN?!
YOUR PAL SCAB WENT OFF LAST NIGHT.
WHY? WHAT'S YOUR GAME?
WE DIDN'T HAVE NUTHIN' TO DO WITH THAT!
IF WE'D BEEN THERE HE'D A' KILLED US, TOO, Y'KNOW!
BRRTZ
JUST LIKE YOU WANT TO, EVIL ONE!
A THREAT TO ALL GOTHAM!

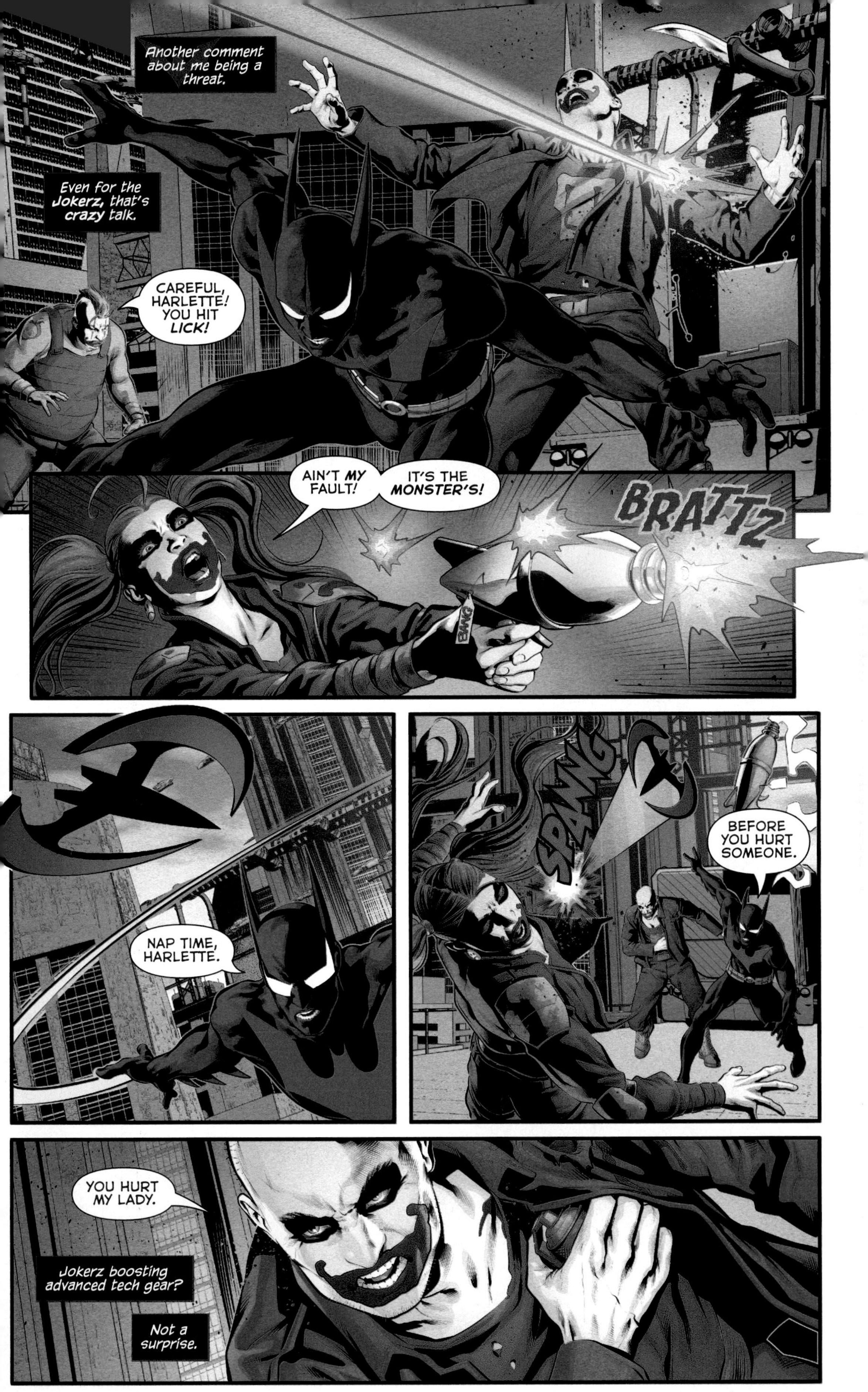
Another comment about me being a threat.
Even for the Jokerz, that's crazy talk.
CAREFUL, HARLETTE! YOU HIT LICK!
AIN'T MY FAULT!
IT'S THE MONSTER'S!
BRATTZ
BANG
NAP TIME, HARLETTE.
SPANNG
BEFORE YOU HURT SOMEONE.
YOU HURT MY LADY.
Jokerz boosting advanced tech gear?
Not a surprise.

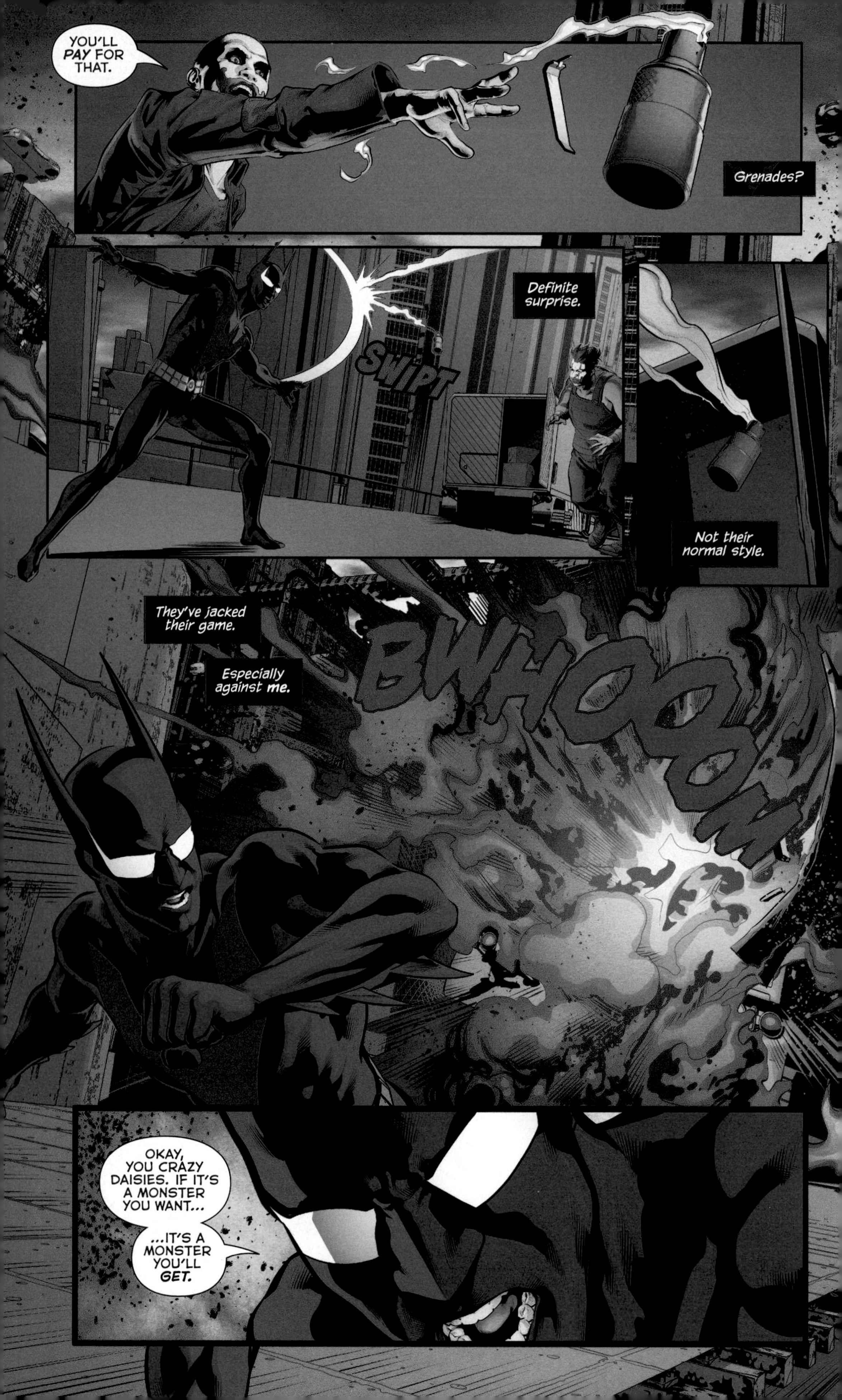

YOU'LL PAY FOR THAT.
Grenades?
Definite surprise.
SWIPT
Not their normal style.
They've jacked their game.
Especially against me.
BWHOOOM
OKAY, YOU CRAZY DAISIES. IF IT'S A MONSTER YOU WANT...
...IT'S A MONSTER YOU'LL GET.

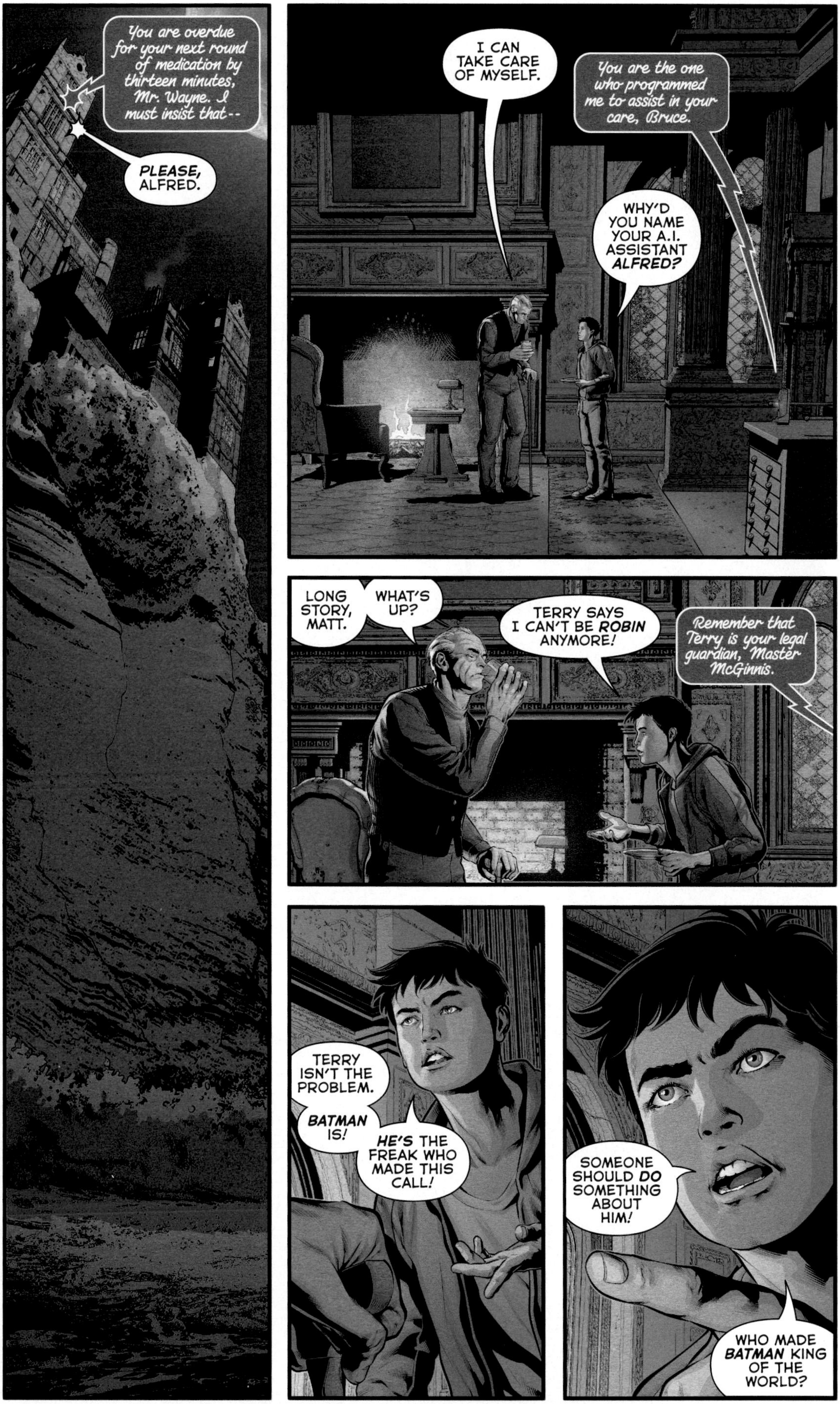

You are overdue for your next round of medication by thirteen minutes, Mr. Wayne. I must insist that--
PLEASE, ALFRED.
I CAN TAKE CARE OF MYSELF.
You are the one who programmed me to assist in your care, Bruce.
WHY'D YOU NAME YOUR A.I. ASSISTANT ALFRED?
LONG STORY, MATT.
WHAT'S UP?
TERRY SAYS I CAN'T BE ROBIN ANYMORE!
Remember that Terry is your legal guardian, Master McGinnis.
TERRY ISN'T THE PROBLEM.
BATMAN IS!
HE'S THE FREAK WHO MADE THIS CALL!
SOMEONE SHOULD DO SOMETHING ABOUT HIM!
WHO MADE BATMAN KING OF THE WORLD?

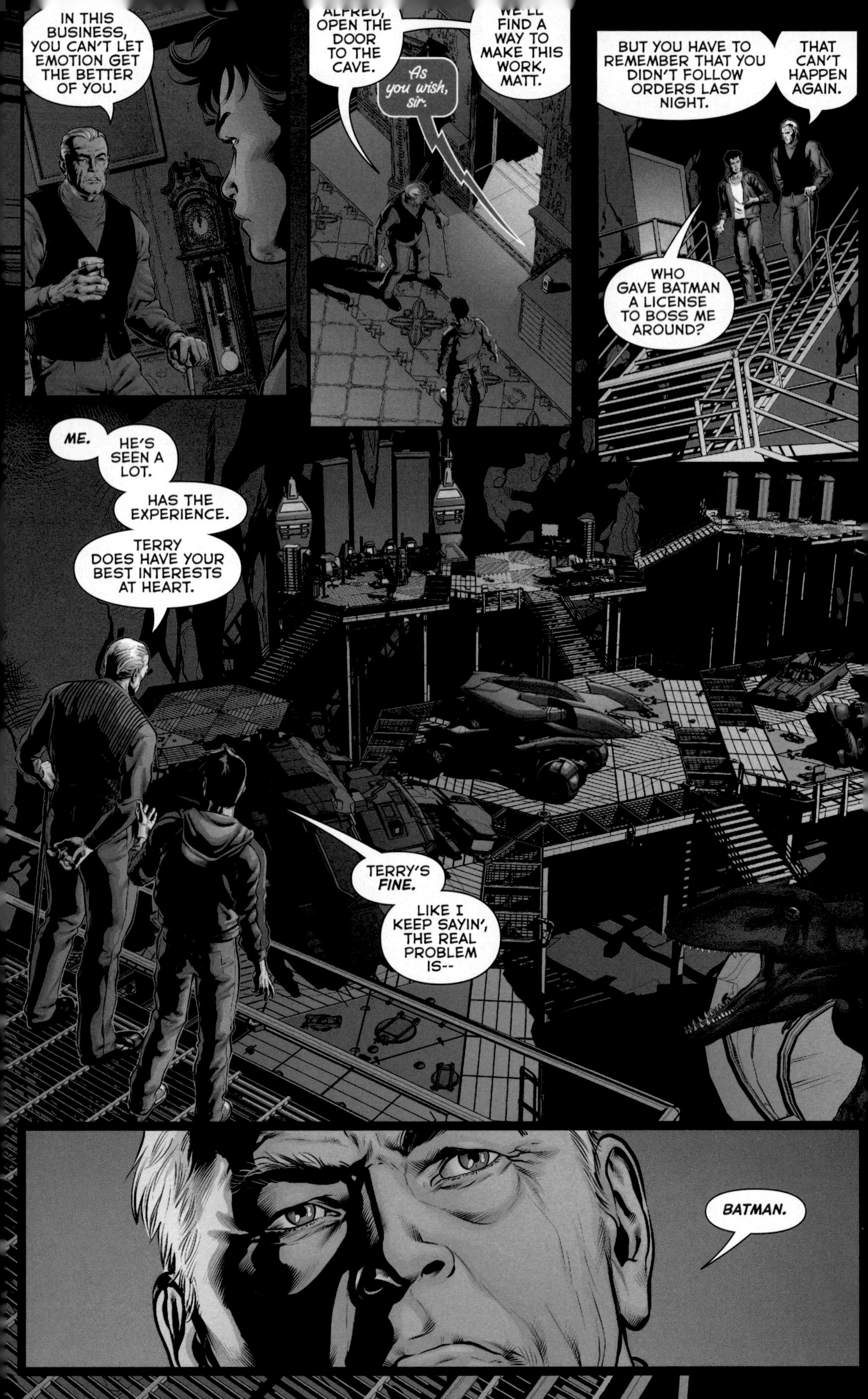
IN THIS BUSINESS, YOU CAN'T LET EMOTION GET THE BETTER OF YOU.
ALFRED, OPEN THE DOOR TO THE CAVE.
As you wish, sir.
WE'LL FIND A WAY TO MAKE THIS WORK, MATT.
BUT YOU HAVE TO REMEMBER THAT YOU DIDN'T FOLLOW ORDERS LAST NIGHT.
THAT CAN'T HAPPEN AGAIN.
WHO GAVE BATMAN A LICENSE TO BOSS ME AROUND?
ME.
HE'S SEEN A LOT.
HAS THE EXPERIENCE.
TERRY DOES HAVE YOUR BEST INTERESTS AT HEART.
TERRY'S FINE.
LIKE I KEEP SAYIN', THE REAL PROBLEM IS--
BATMAN.

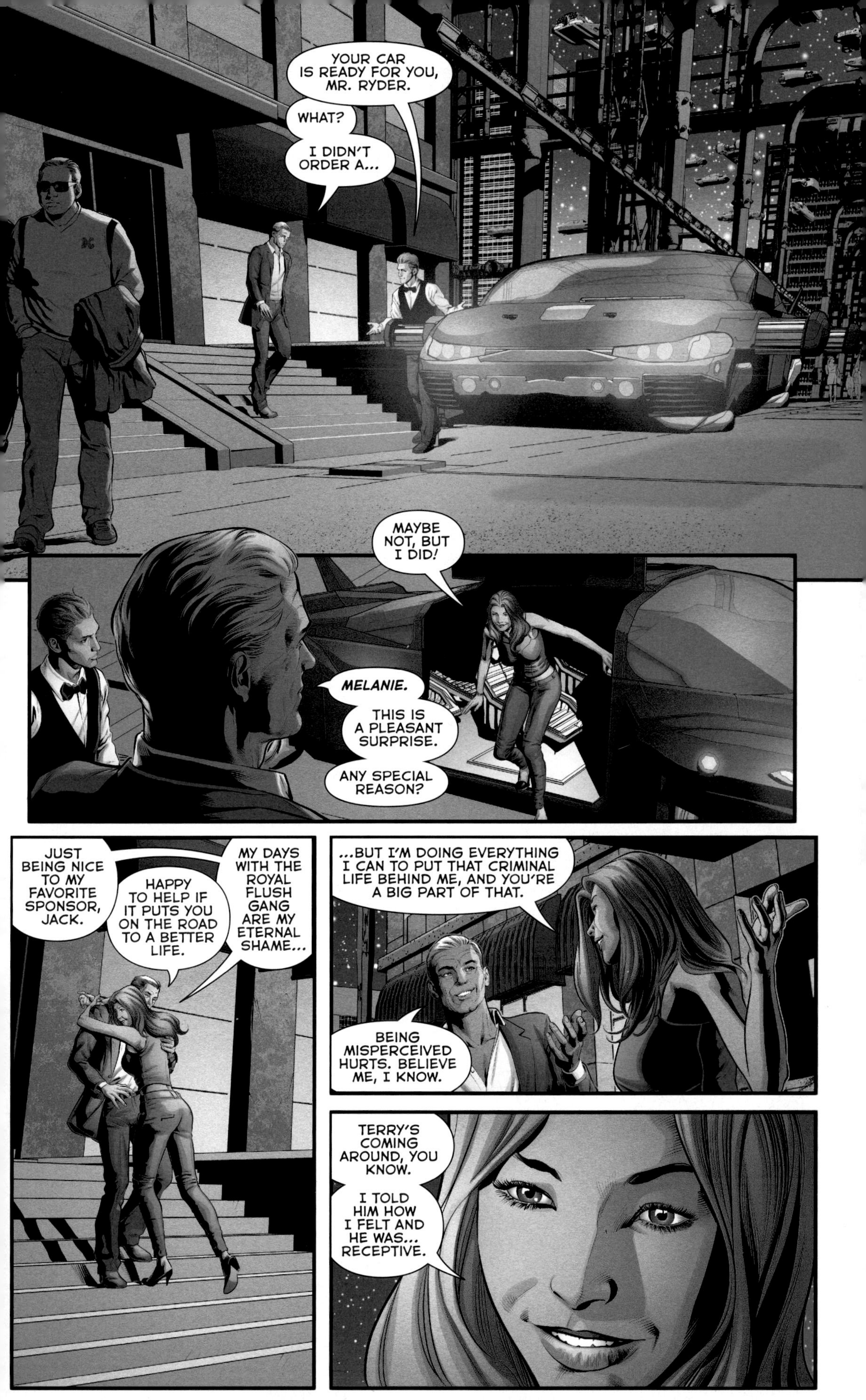
YOUR CAR IS READY FOR YOU, MR. RYDER.
WHAT?
I DIDN'T ORDER A...
MAYBE NOT, BUT I DID!
MELANIE.
THIS IS A PLEASANT SURPRISE.
ANY SPECIAL REASON?
JUST BEING NICE TO MY FAVORITE SPONSOR, JACK.
HAPPY TO HELP IF IT PUTS YOU ON THE ROAD TO A BETTER LIFE.
MY DAYS WITH THE ROYAL FLUSH GANG ARE MY ETERNAL SHAME...
...BUT I'M DOING EVERYTHING I CAN TO PUT THAT CRIMINAL LIFE BEHIND ME, AND YOU'RE A BIG PART OF THAT.
BEING MISPERCEIVED HURTS. BELIEVE ME, I KNOW.
TERRY'S COMING AROUND, YOU KNOW.
I TOLD HIM HOW I FELT AND HE WAS... RECEPTIVE.

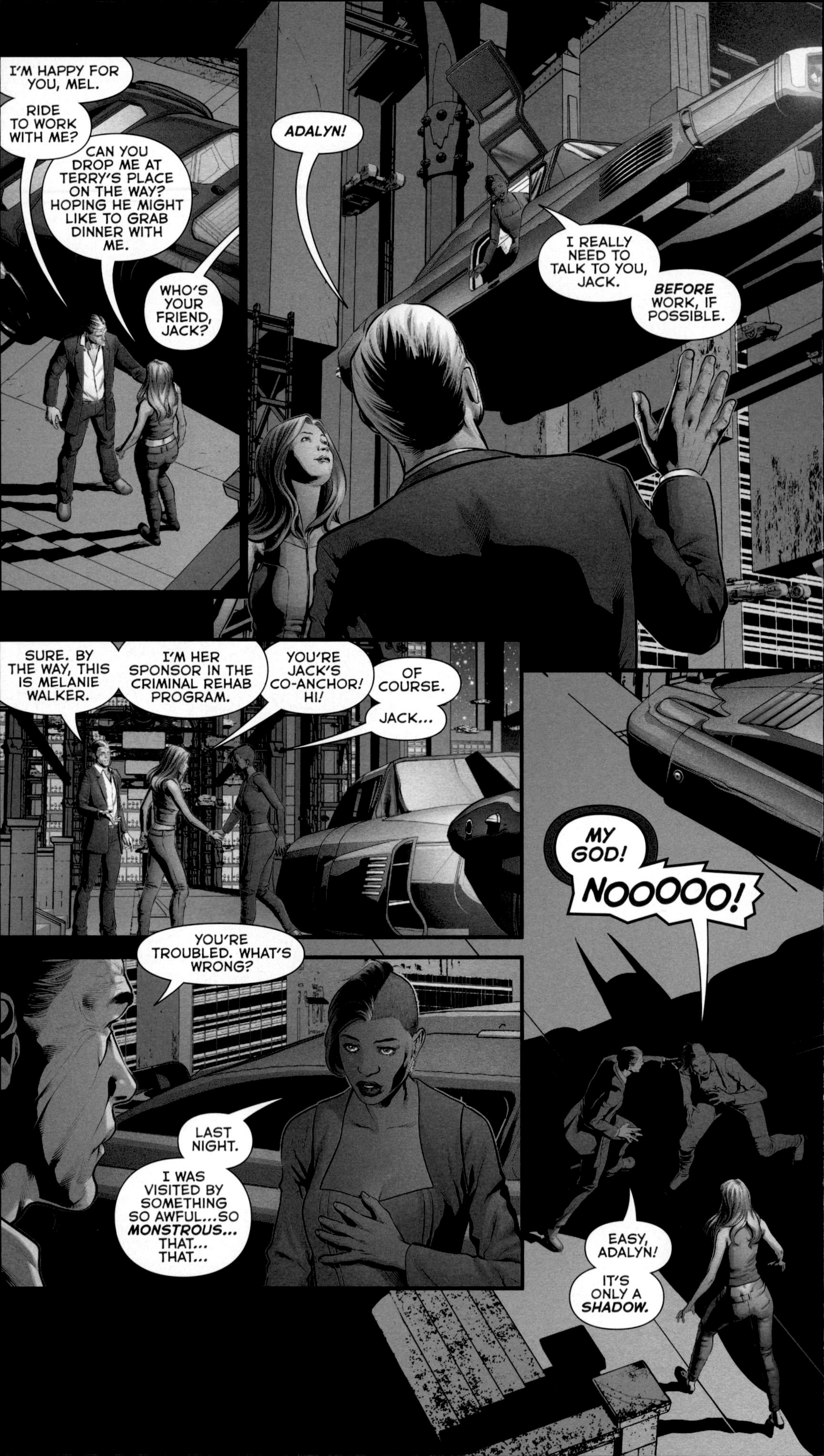

I'M HAPPY FOR YOU, MEL.
RIDE TO WORK WITH ME?
CAN YOU DROP ME AT TERRY'S PLACE ON THE WAY? HOPING HE MIGHT LIKE TO GRAB DINNER WITH ME.
WHO'S YOUR FRIEND, JACK?
ADALYN!
I REALLY NEED TO TALK TO YOU, JACK.
BEFORE WORK, IF POSSIBLE.
SURE. BY THE WAY, THIS IS MELANIE WALKER.
I'M HER SPONSOR IN THE CRIMINAL REHAB PROGRAM.
YOU'RE JACK'S CO-ANCHOR! HI!
OF COURSE.
JACK...
YOU'RE TROUBLED. WHAT'S WRONG?
LAST NIGHT.
I WAS VISITED BY SOMETHING SO AWFUL...SO MONSTROUS... THAT... THAT...
MY GOD!
NOOOOO!
EASY, ADALYN!
IT'S ONLY A SHADOW.

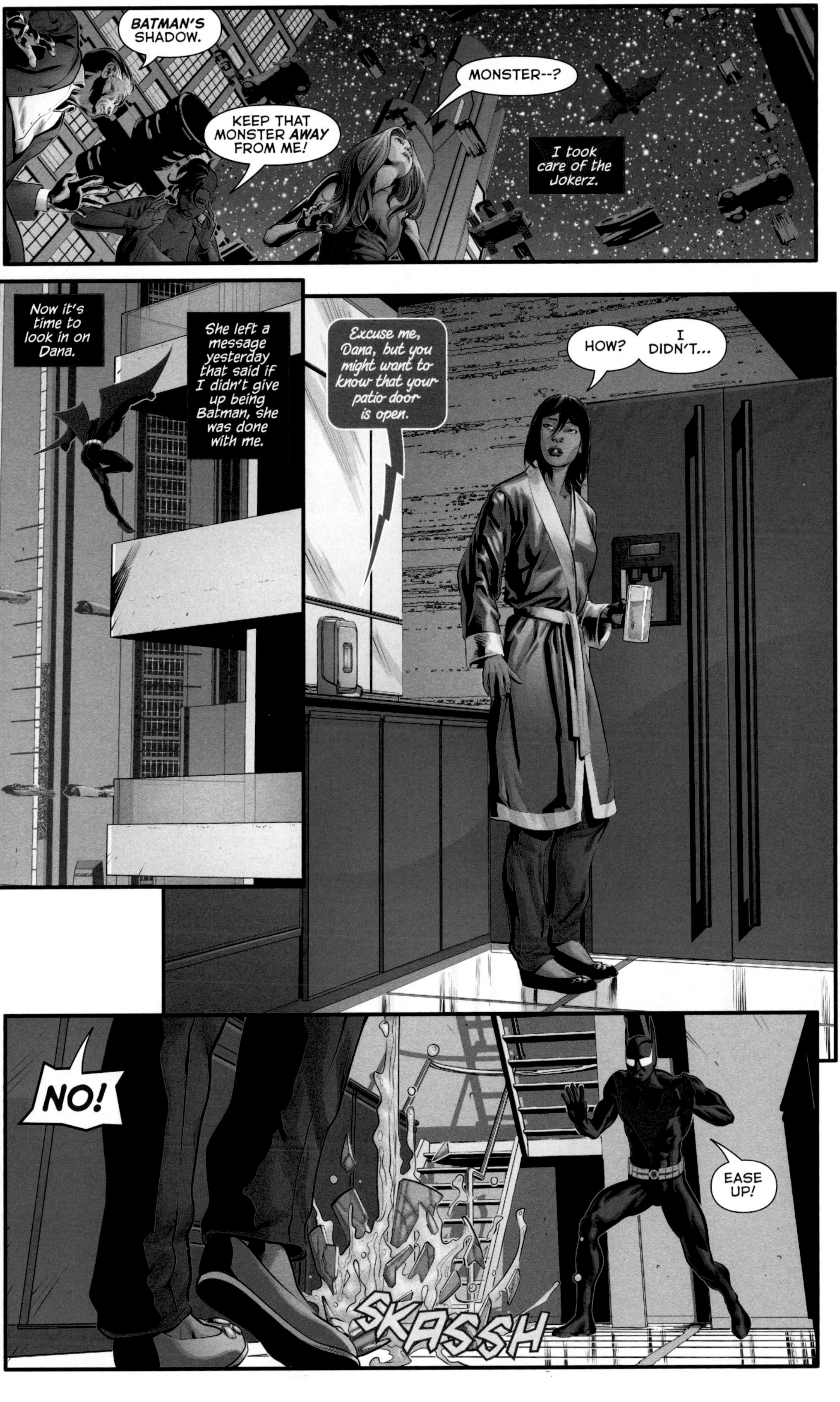
BATMAN'S SHADOW.
KEEP THAT MONSTER AWAY FROM ME!
MONSTER--?
I took care of the Jokerz.
Now it's time to look in on Dana.
She left a message yesterday that said if I didn't give up being Batman, she was done with me.
Excuse me, Dana, but you might want to know that your patio door is open.
HOW?
I DIDN'T...
NO!
SKASSH
EASE UP!

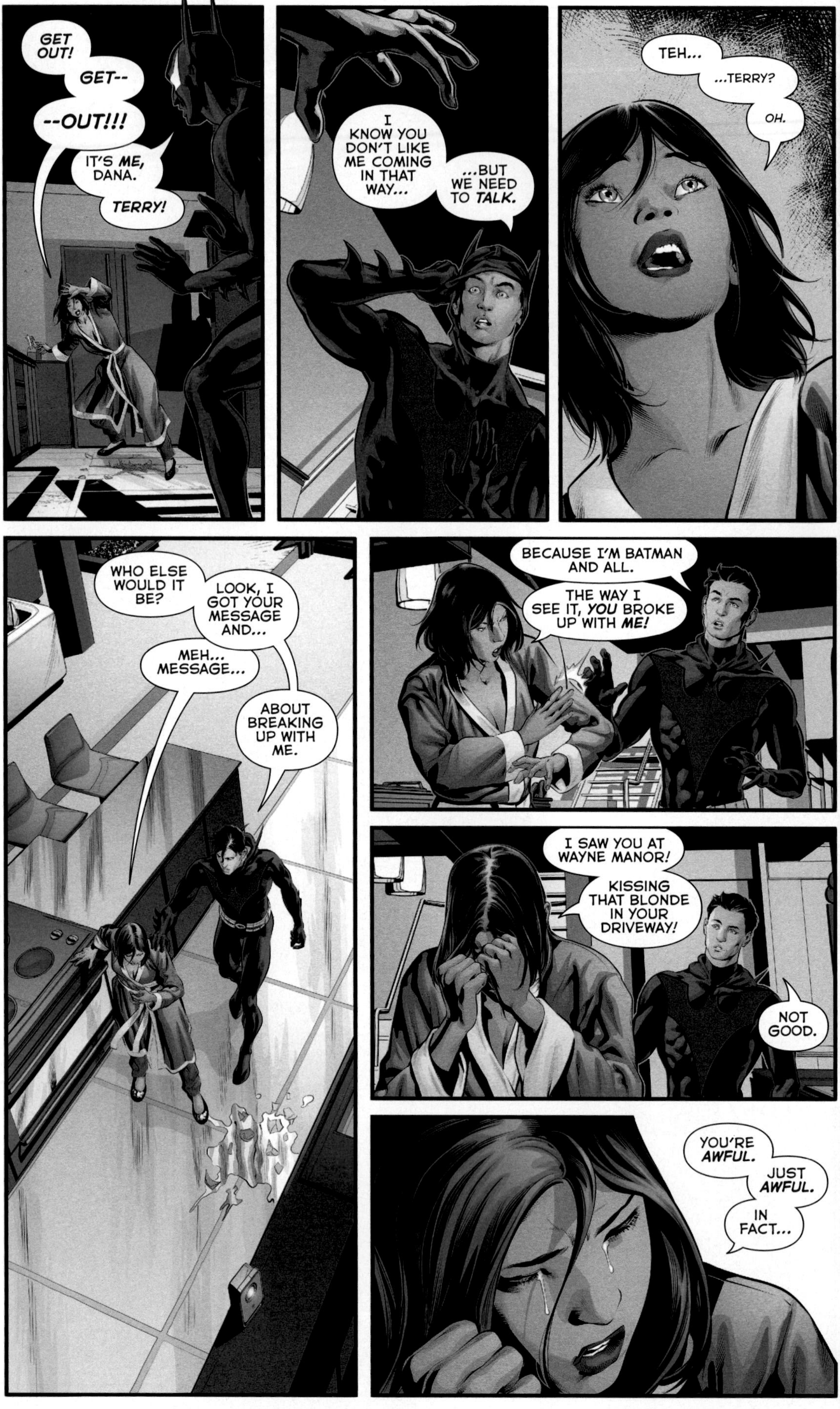

GET OUT!
GET--
--OUT!!!
IT'S ME, DANA.
TERRY!
I KNOW YOU DON'T LIKE ME COMING IN THAT WAY...
...BUT WE NEED TO TALK.
TEH...
...TERRY?
OH.
WHO ELSE WOULD IT BE?
LOOK, I GOT YOUR MESSAGE AND...
MEH... MESSAGE...
ABOUT BREAKING UP WITH ME.
BECAUSE I'M BATMAN AND ALL.
THE WAY I SEE IT, YOU BROKE UP WITH ME!
I SAW YOU AT WAYNE MANOR!
KISSING THAT BLONDE IN YOUR DRIVEWAY!
NOT GOOD.
YOU'RE AWFUL.
JUST AWFUL.
IN FACT...

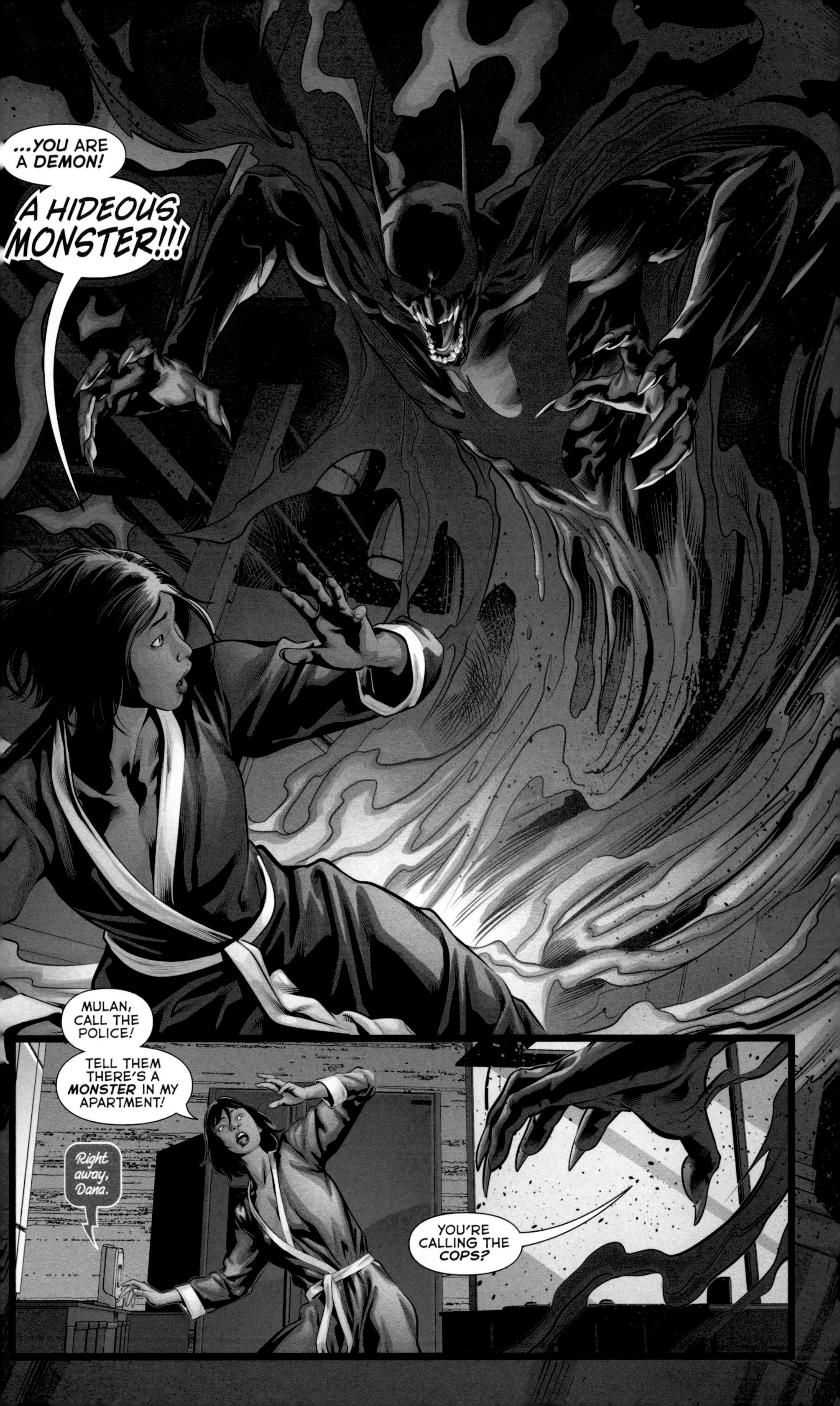

...YOU ARE A DEMON!
A HIDEOUS MONSTER!!!
MULAN, CALL THE POLICE!
TELL THEM THERE'S A MONSTER IN MY APARTMENT!
Right away, Dana.
YOU'RE CALLING THE COPS?

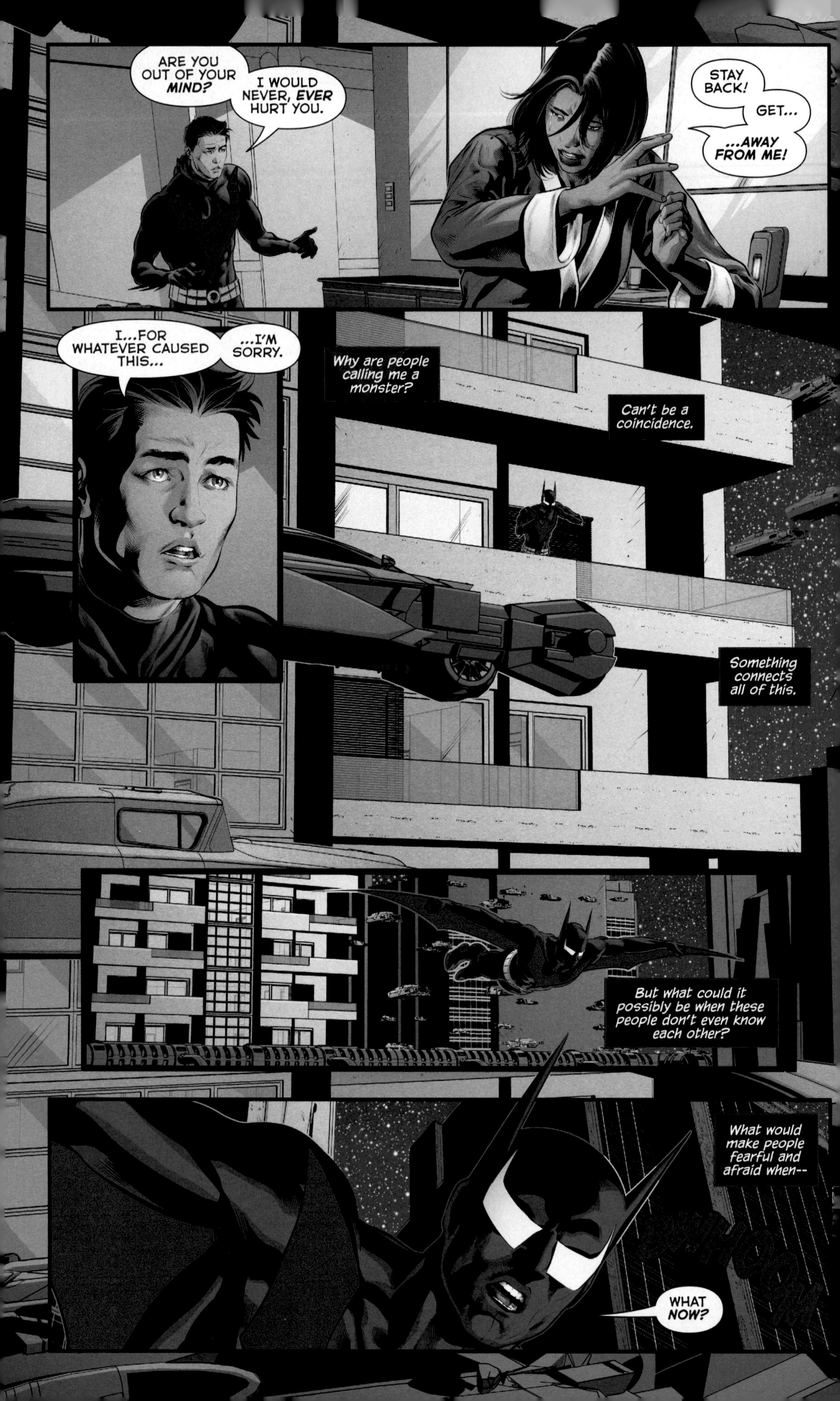
ARE YOU OUT OF YOUR *MIND?*
I WOULD NEVER, *EVER* HURT YOU.
STAY BACK!
GET...
...*AWAY FROM ME!*
I...FOR WHATEVER CAUSED THIS...
...I'M SORRY.
Why are people calling me a monster?
Can't be a coincidence.
Something connects all of this.
But what could it possibly be when these people don't even know each other?
What would make people fearful and afraid when--
WHAT *NOW?*

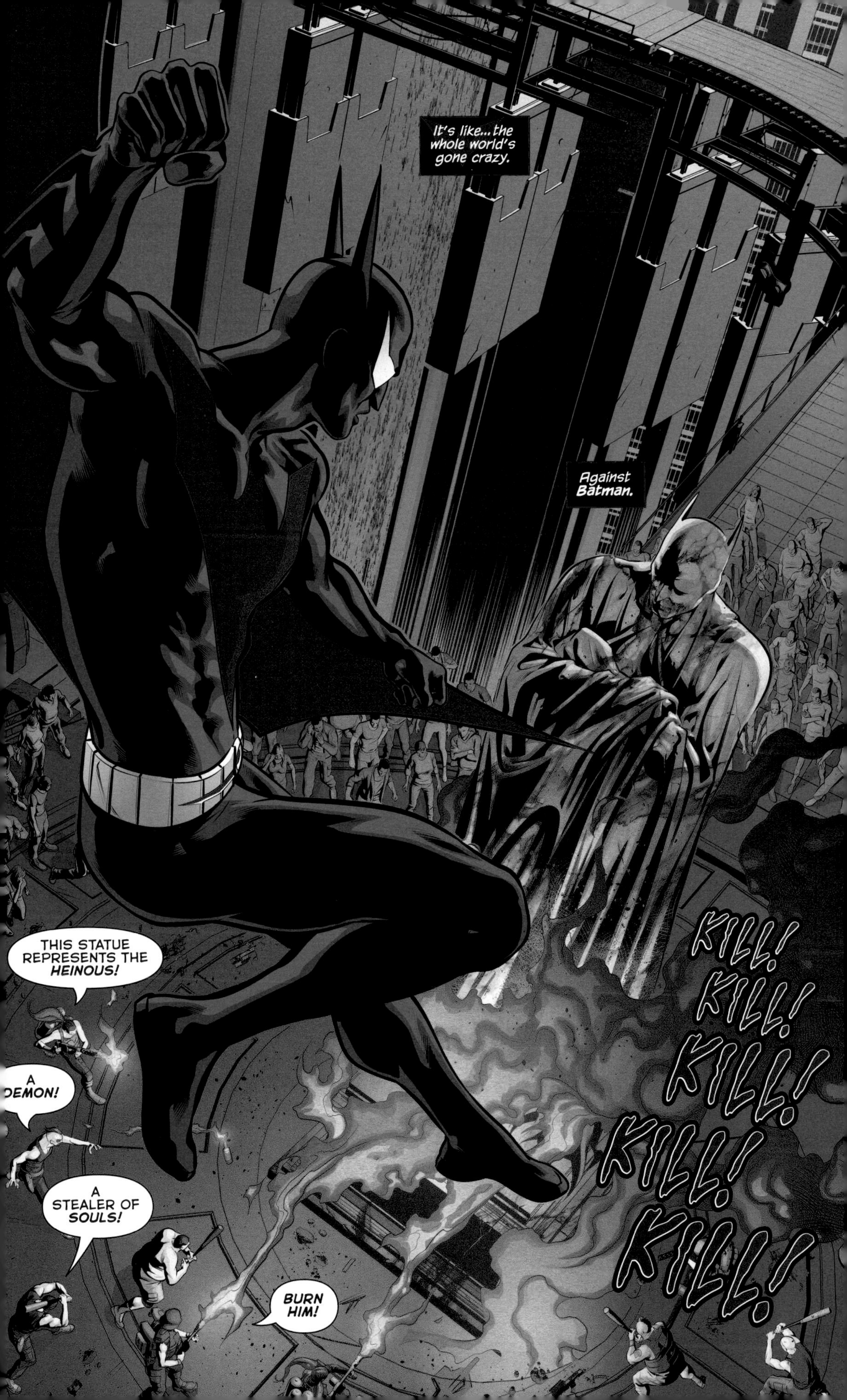
It's like...the whole world's gone crazy.
Against Batman.
THIS STATUE REPRESENTS THE HEINOUS!
A DEMON!
A STEALER OF SOULS!
BURN HIM!
KILL! KILL! KILL! KILL! KILL!

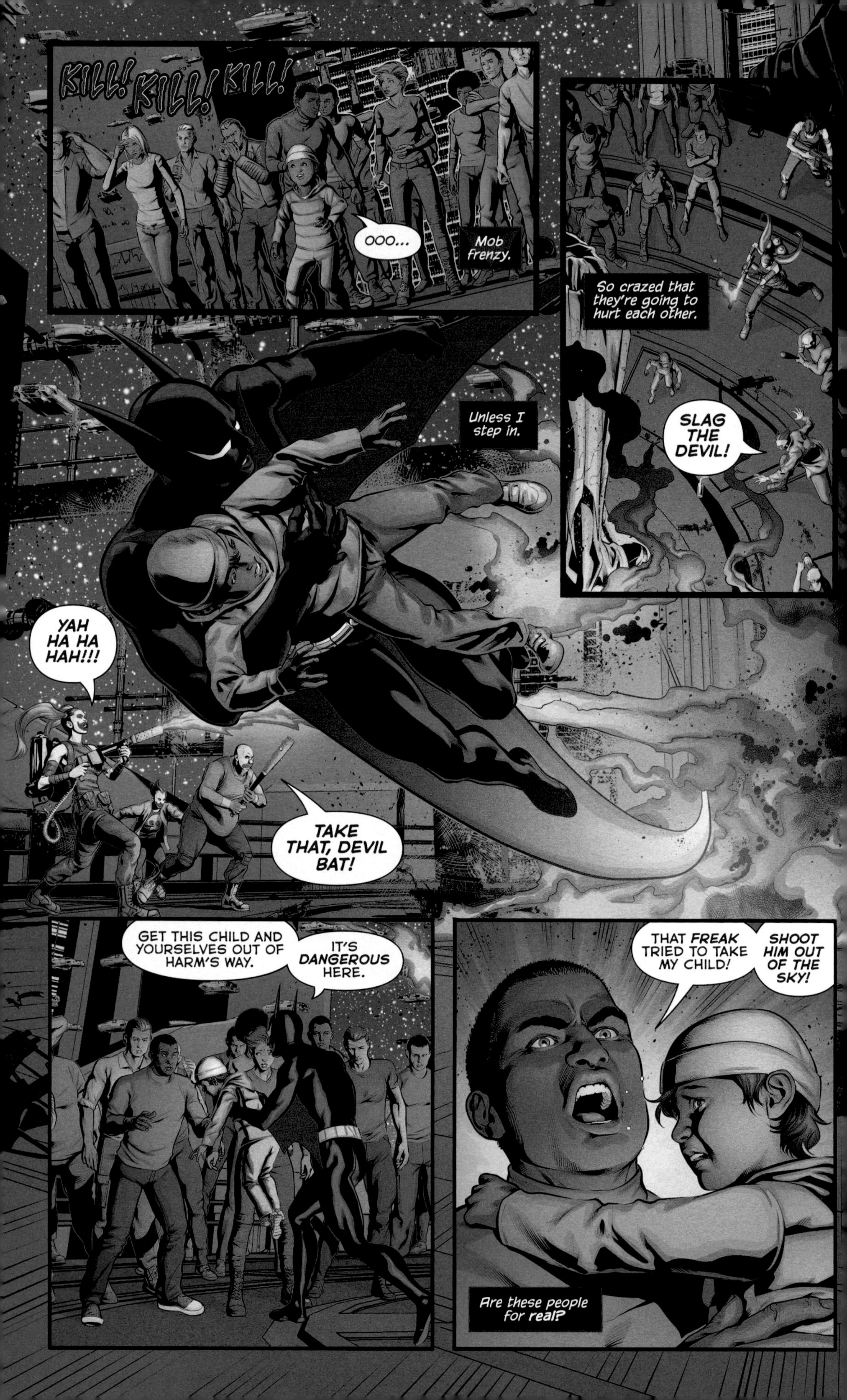
KILL! KILL! KILL!
OOO...
Mob frenzy.
So crazed that they're going to hurt each other.
Unless I step in.
SLAG THE DEVIL!
YAH HA HA HAH!!!
TAKE THAT, DEVIL BAT!
GET THIS CHILD AND YOURSELVES OUT OF HARM'S WAY.
IT'S DANGEROUS HERE.
THAT FREAK TRIED TO TAKE MY CHILD!
SHOOT HIM OUT OF THE SKY!
Are these people for real?

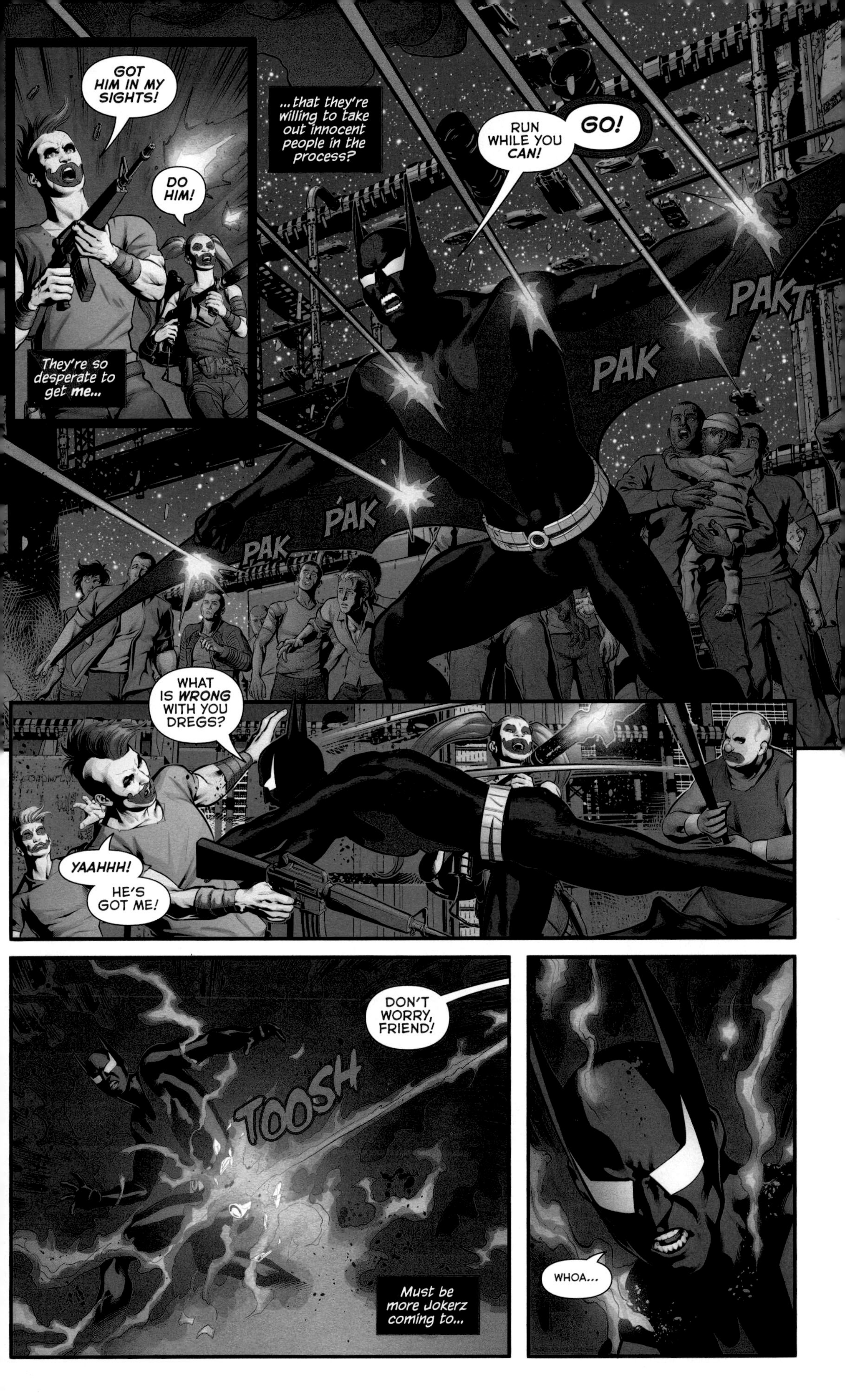
GOT HIM IN MY SIGHTS!
DO HIM!
They're so desperate to get me...
...that they're willing to take out innocent people in the process?
RUN WHILE YOU CAN!
GO!
PAKT
PAK
PAK
PAK
WHAT IS WRONG WITH YOU DREGS?
YAAHHH!
HE'S GOT ME!
DON'T WORRY, FRIEND!
TOOSH
Must be more Jokerz coming to...
WHOA...

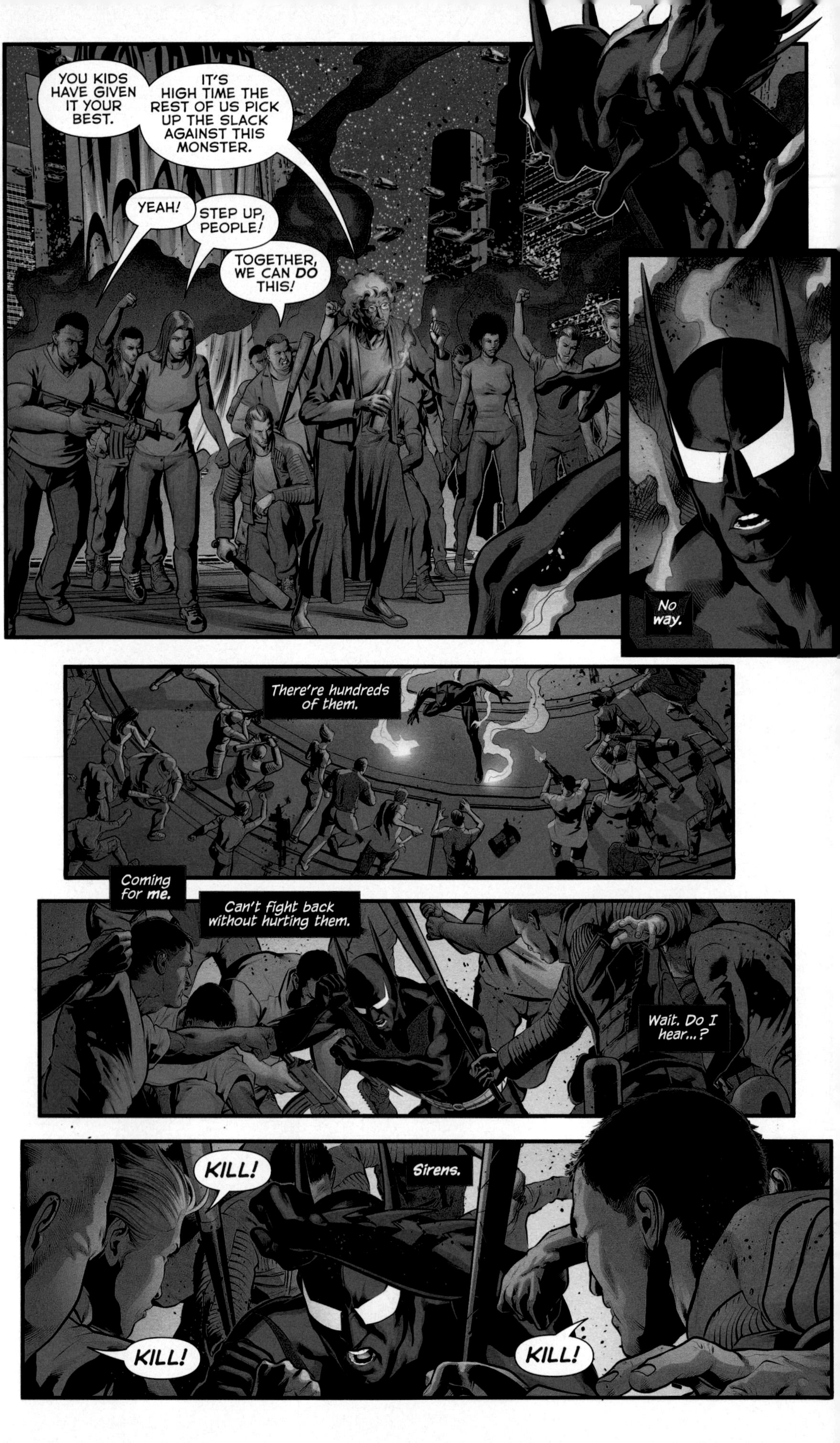
YOU KIDS HAVE GIVEN IT YOUR BEST.
IT'S HIGH TIME THE REST OF US PICK UP THE SLACK AGAINST THIS MONSTER.
YEAH!
STEP UP, PEOPLE!
TOGETHER, WE CAN DO THIS!
No way.
There're hundreds of them.
Coming for me.
Can't fight back without hurting them.
Wait. Do I hear...?
KILL!
Sirens.
KILL!
KILL!

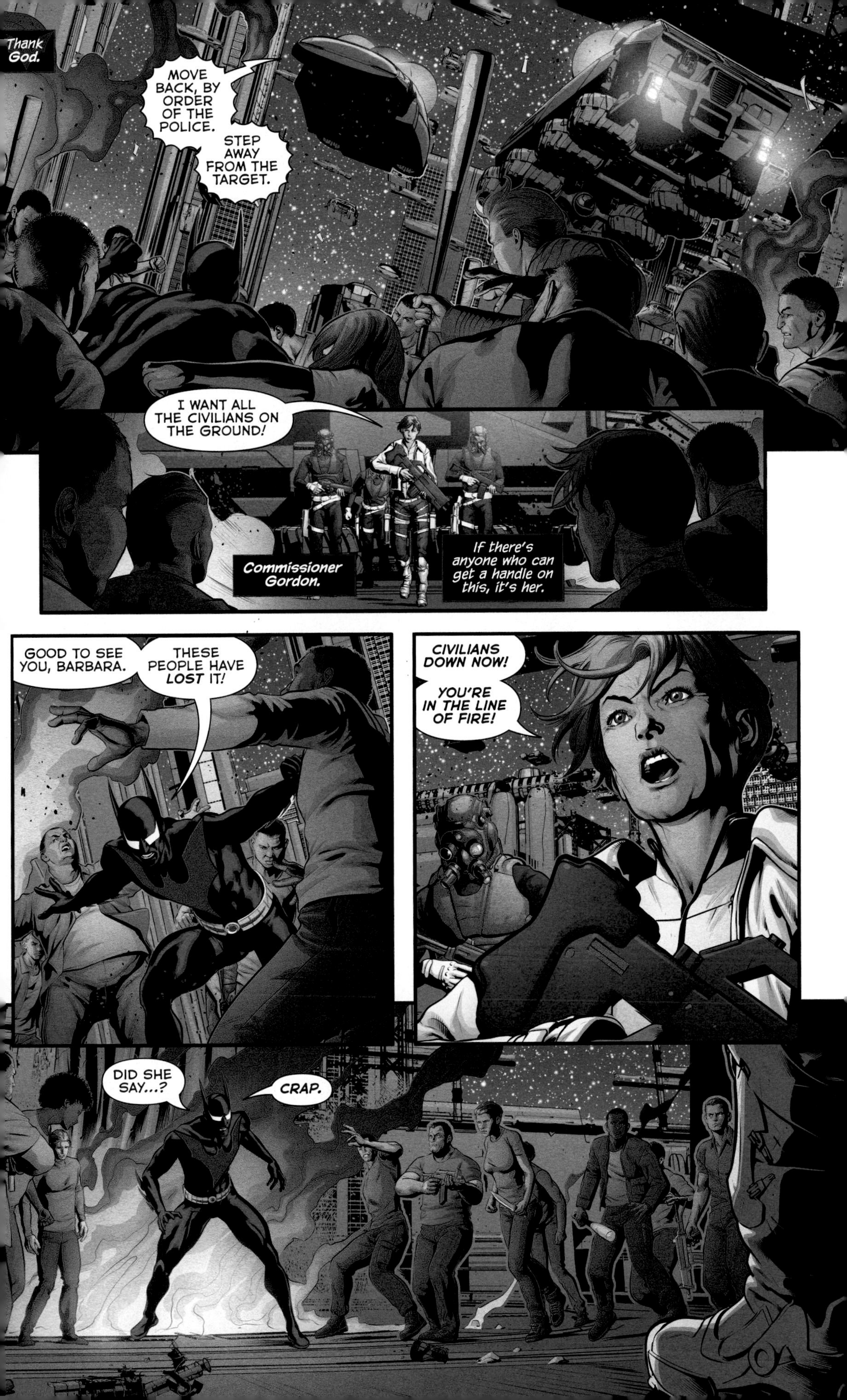
Thank God.
MOVE BACK, BY ORDER OF THE POLICE.
STEP AWAY FROM THE TARGET.
I WANT ALL THE CIVILIANS ON THE GROUND!
Commissioner Gordon.
If there's anyone who can get a handle on this, it's her.
GOOD TO SEE YOU, BARBARA.
THESE PEOPLE HAVE LOST IT!
CIVILIANS DOWN NOW!
YOU'RE IN THE LINE OF FIRE!
DID SHE SAY...?
CRAP.

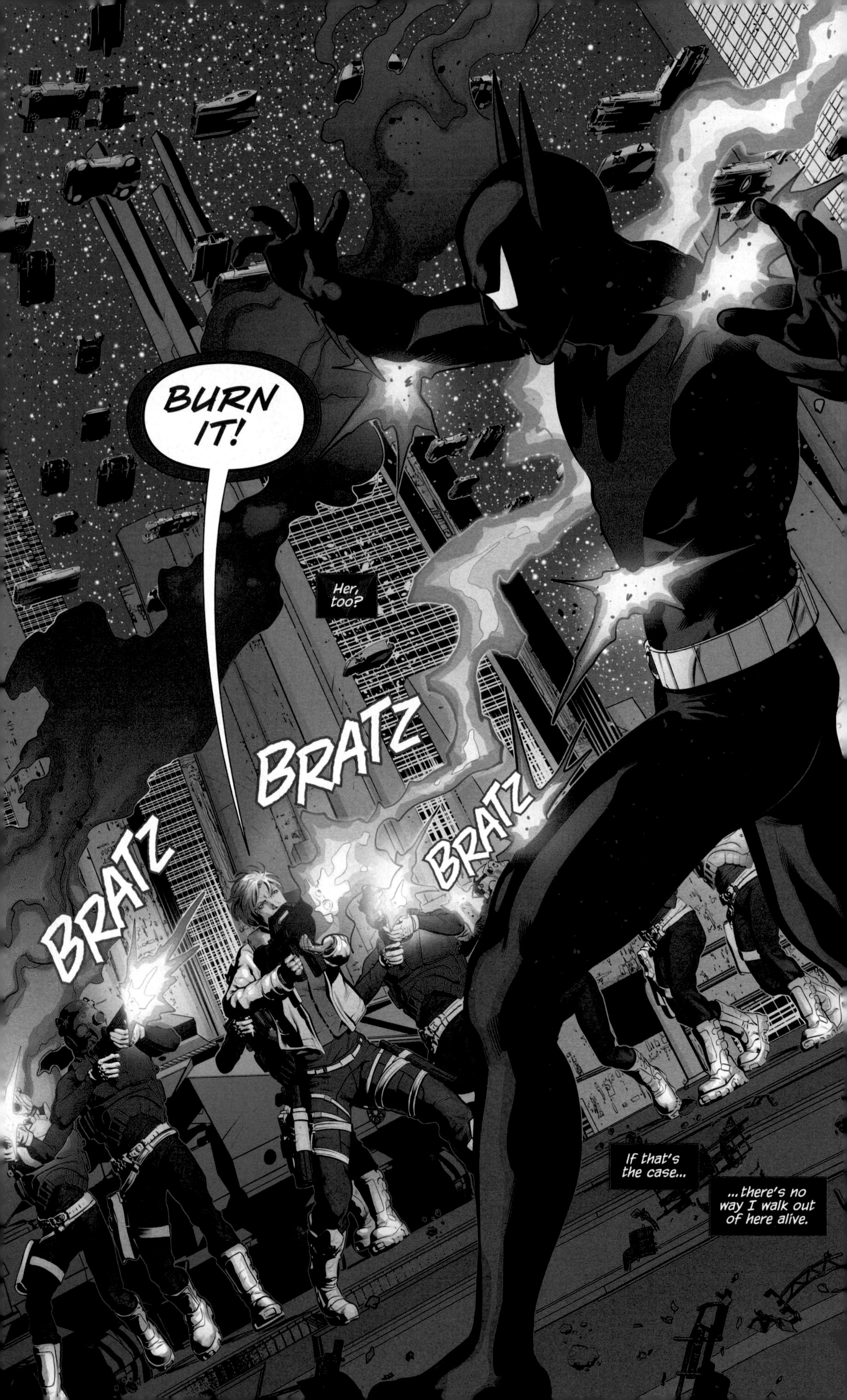
BURN IT!
Her, too?
BRATZ
BRATZ
BRATZ
BRATZ
If that's the case...
...there's no way I walk out of here alive.

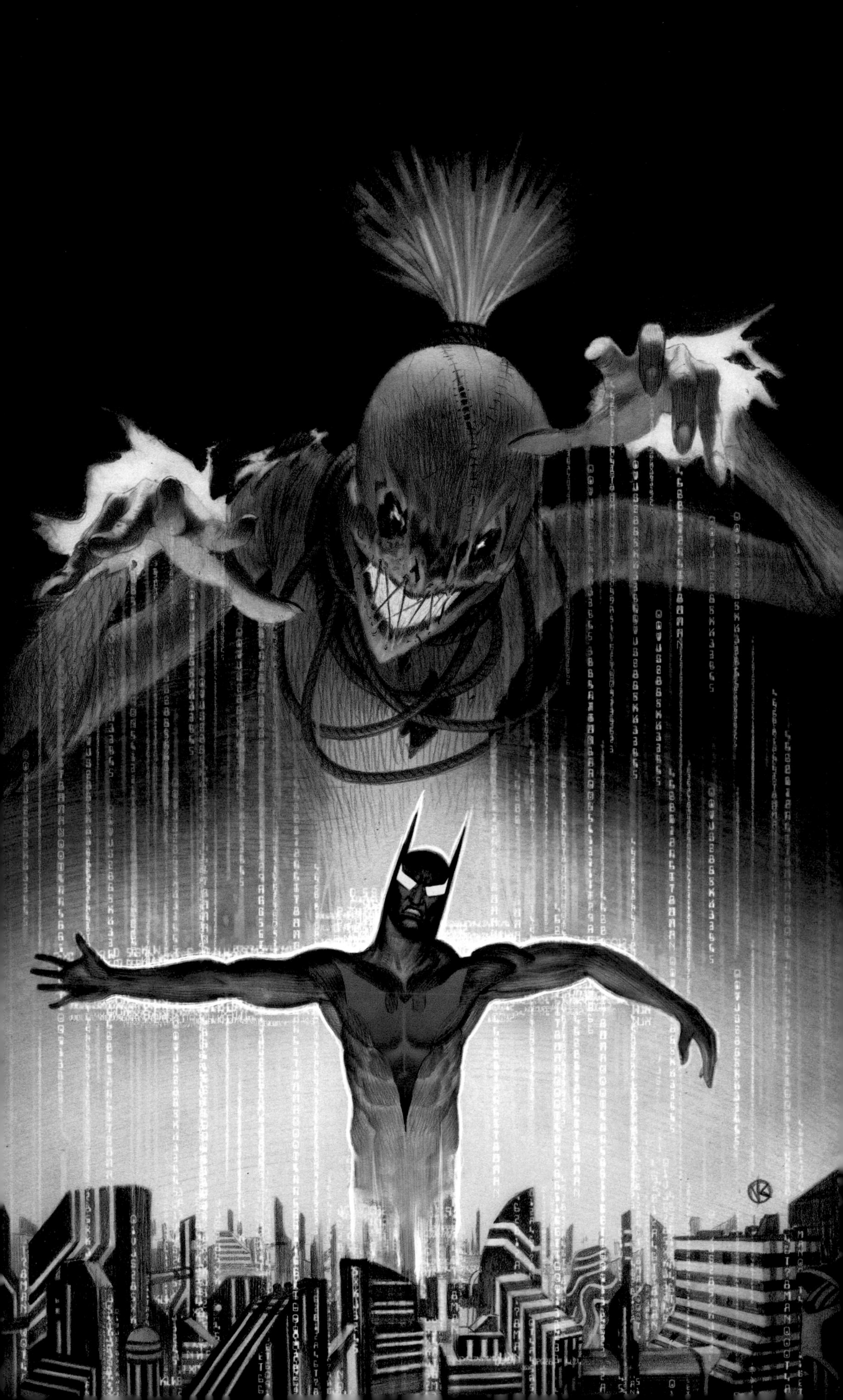

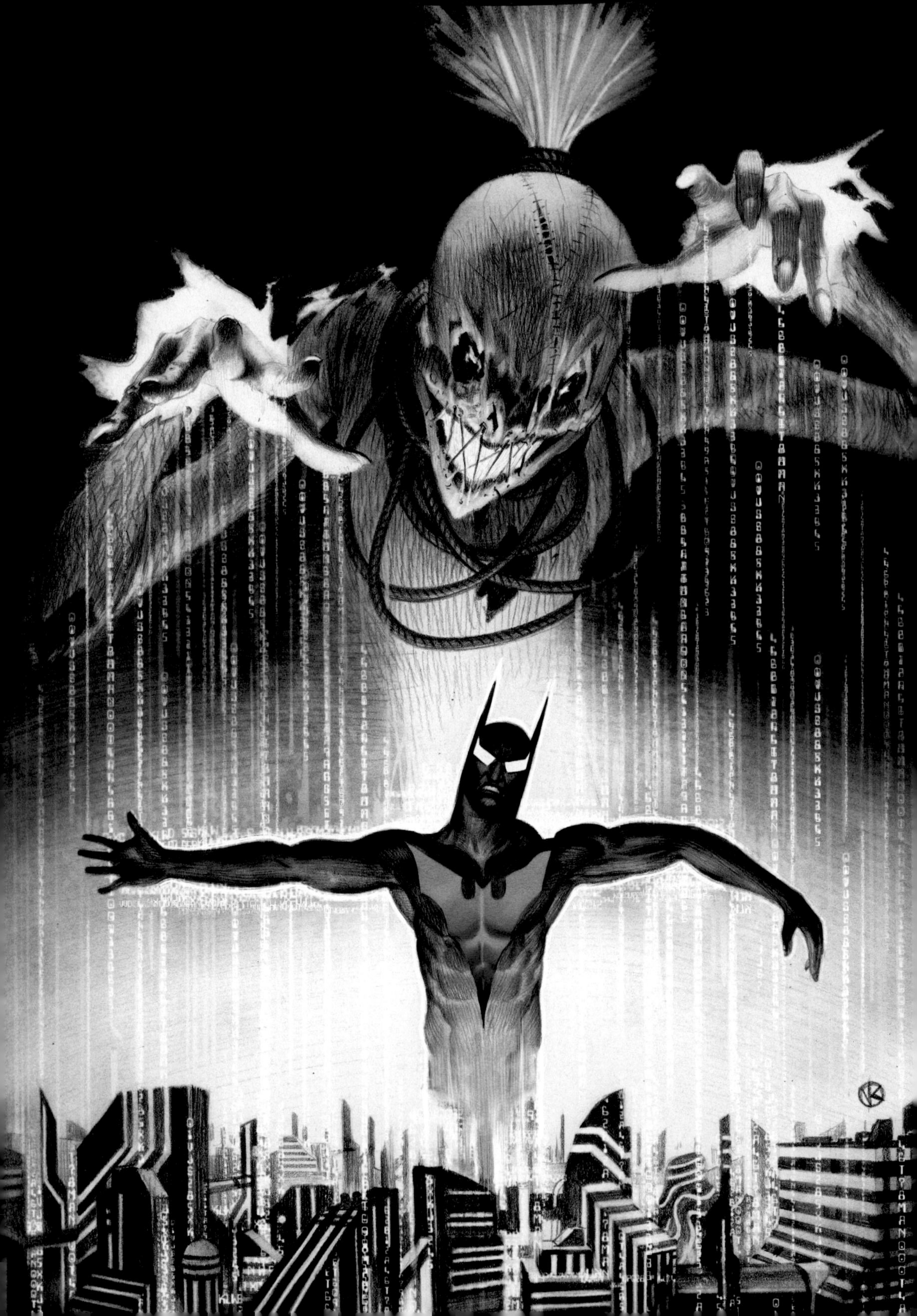

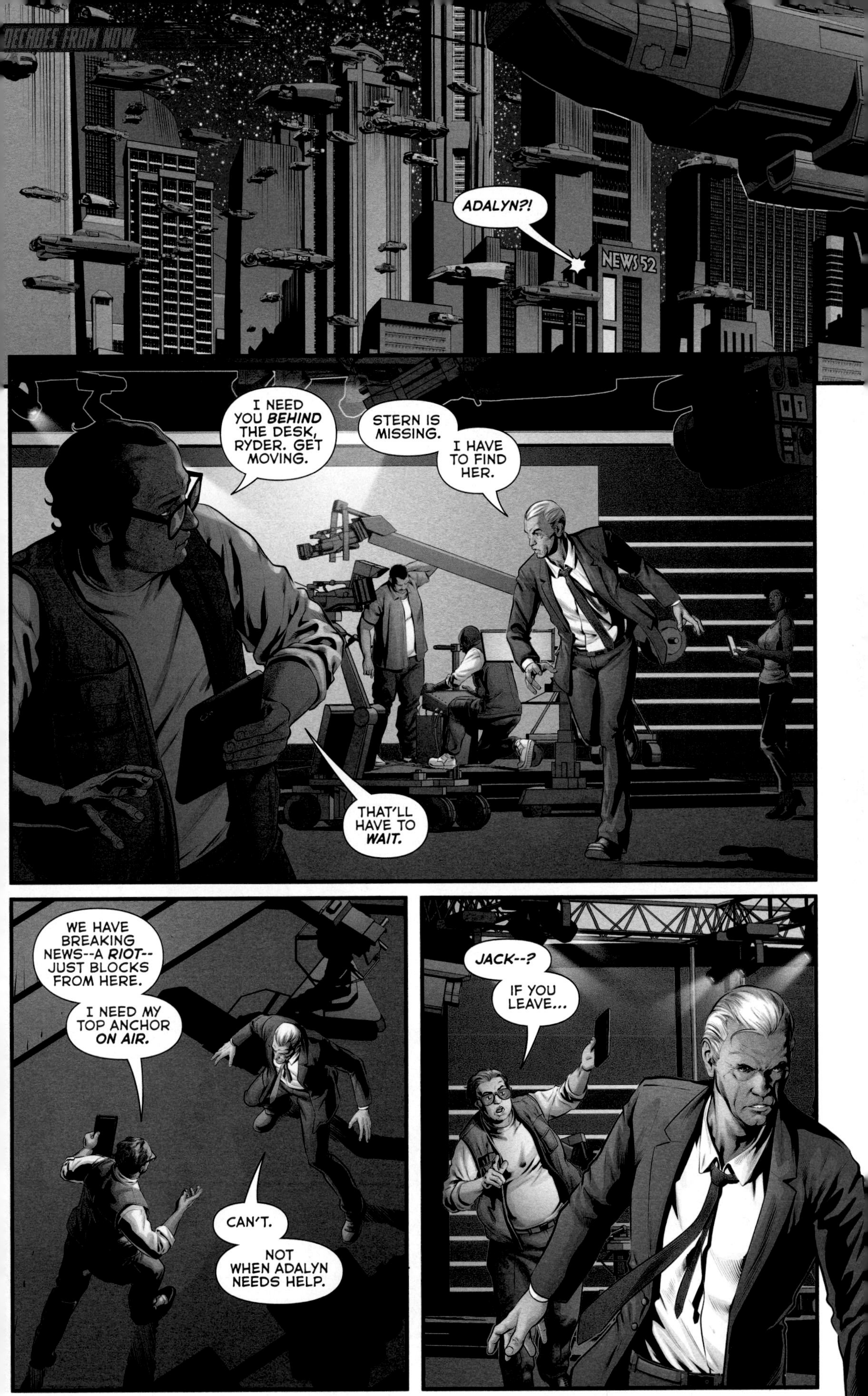
DECADES FROM NOW.
ADALYN?!
NEWS 52
I NEED YOU BEHIND THE DESK, RYDER. GET MOVING.
STERN IS MISSING.
I HAVE TO FIND HER.
THAT'LL HAVE TO WAIT.
WE HAVE BREAKING NEWS--A RIOT--JUST BLOCKS FROM HERE.
I NEED MY TOP ANCHOR ON AIR.
CAN'T.
NOT WHEN ADALYN NEEDS HELP.
JACK--?
IF YOU LEAVE...

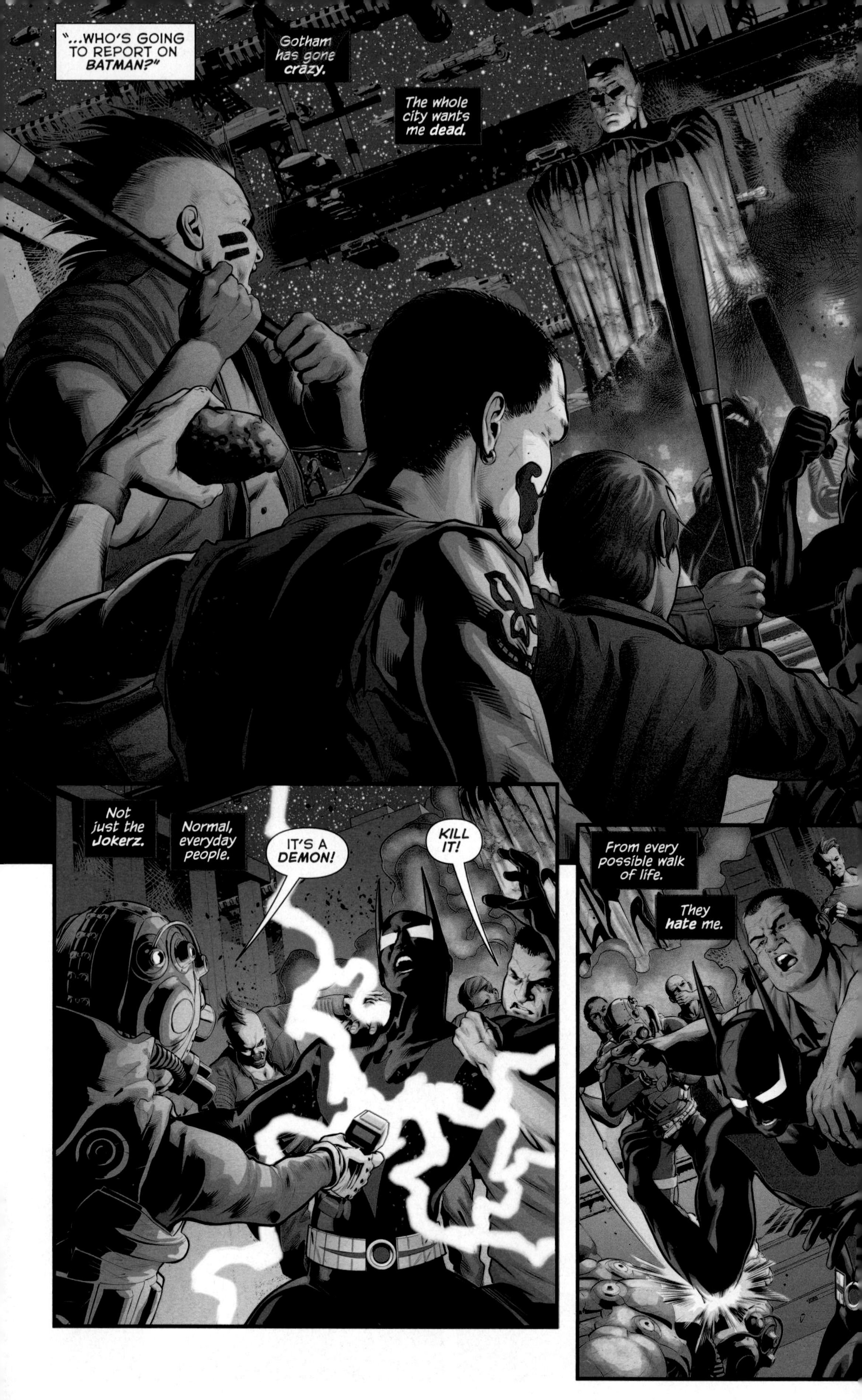
"...WHO'S GOING TO REPORT ON BATMAN?"
Gotham has gone crazy.
The whole city wants me dead.
Not just the Jokerz.
Normal, everyday people.
IT'S A DEMON!
KILL IT!
From every possible walk of life.
They hate me.

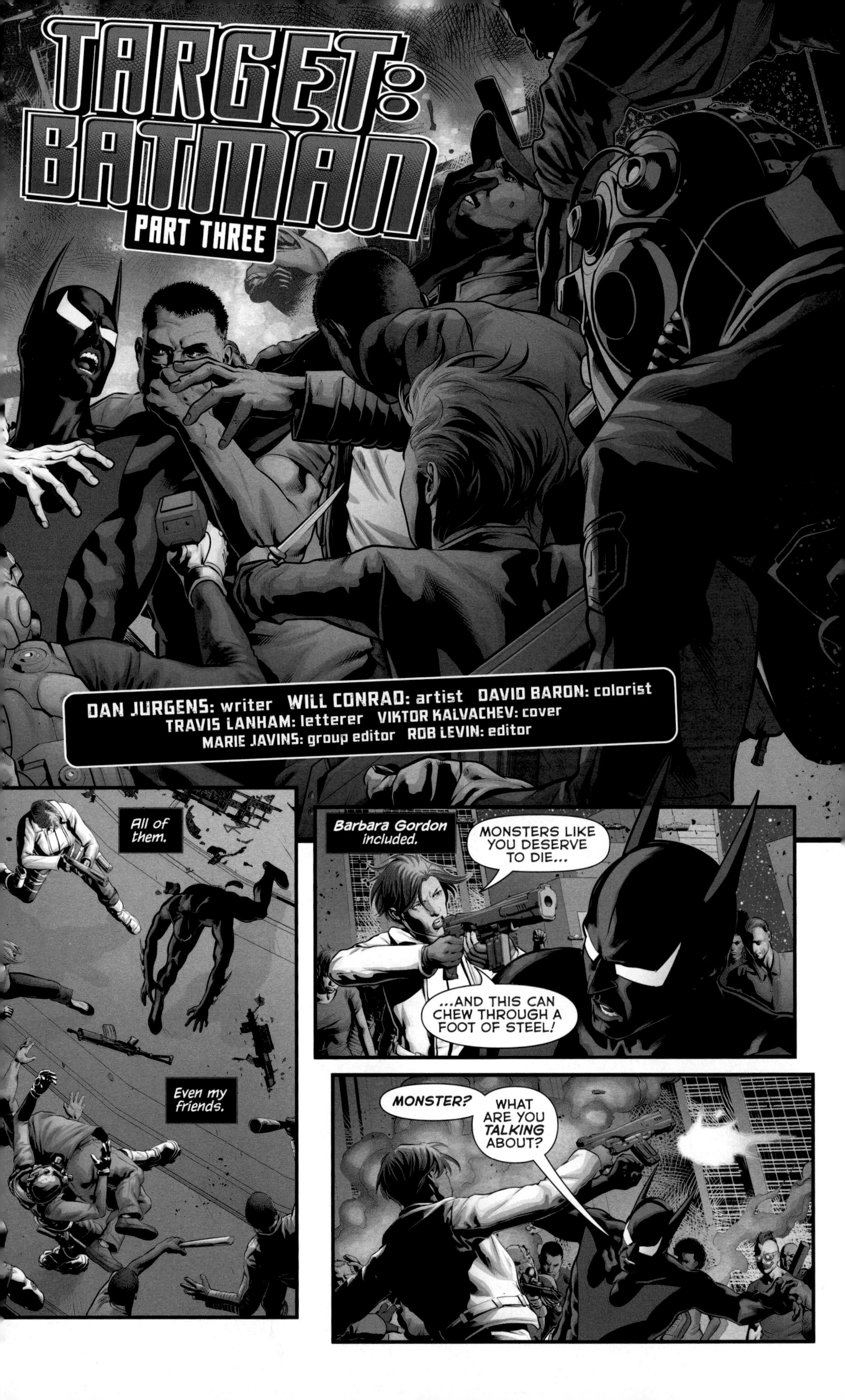

TARGET: BATMAN
PART THREE
DAN JURGENS: writer WILL CONRAD: artist DAVID BARON: colorist
TRAVIS LANHAM: letterer VIKTOR KALVACHEV: cover
MARIE JAVINS: group editor ROB LEVIN: editor
All of them.
Even my friends.
Barbara Gordon included.
MONSTERS LIKE YOU DESERVE TO DIE...
...AND THIS CAN CHEW THROUGH A FOOT OF STEEL!
MONSTER?
WHAT ARE YOU TALKING ABOUT?

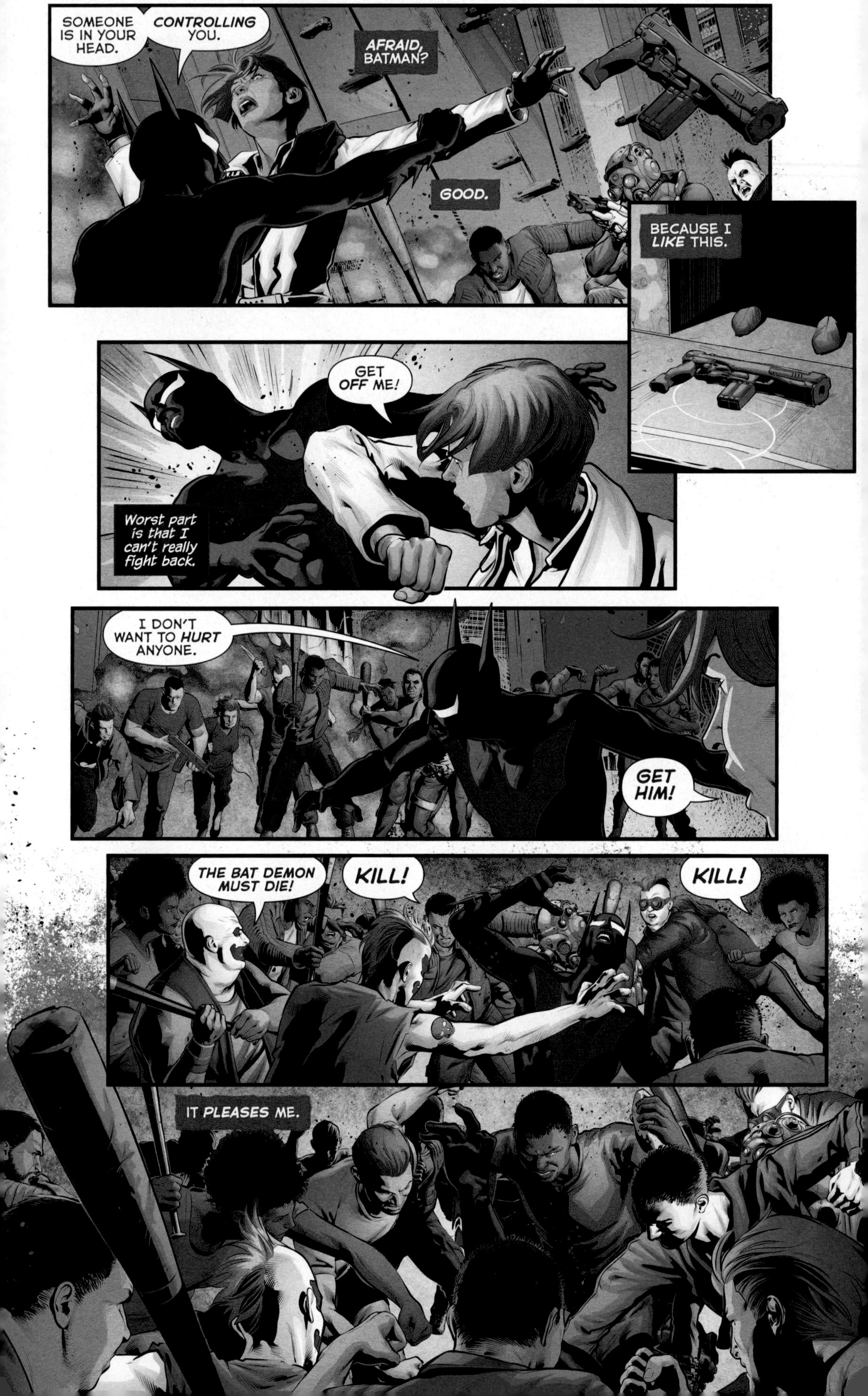
SOMEONE IS IN YOUR HEAD.
CONTROLLING YOU.
AFRAID, BATMAN?
GOOD.
BECAUSE I LIKE THIS.
GET OFF ME!
Worst part is that I can't really fight back.
I DON'T WANT TO HURT ANYONE.
GET HIM!
THE BAT DEMON MUST DIE!
KILL!
KILL!
IT PLEASES ME.

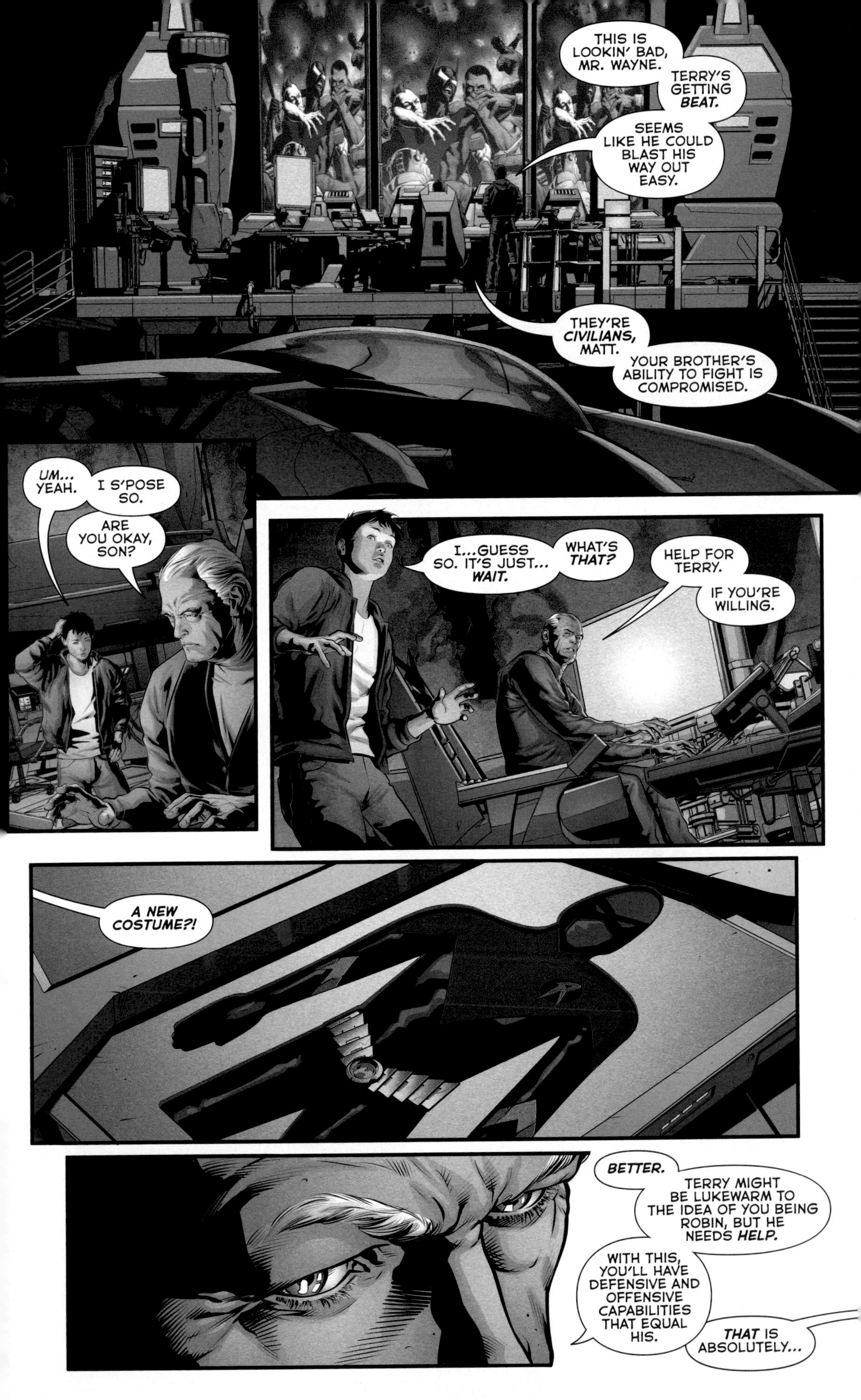
THIS IS LOOKIN' BAD, MR. WAYNE.
TERRY'S GETTING *BEAT.*
SEEMS LIKE HE COULD BLAST HIS WAY OUT EASY.
THEY'RE *CIVILIANS,* MATT.
YOUR BROTHER'S ABILITY TO FIGHT IS COMPROMISED.
UM... YEAH.
I S'POSE SO.
ARE YOU OKAY, SON?
I...GUESS SO. IT'S JUST... *WAIT.*
WHAT'S *THAT?*
HELP FOR TERRY.
IF YOU'RE WILLING.
A NEW COSTUME?!
BETTER.
TERRY MIGHT BE LUKEWARM TO THE IDEA OF YOU BEING ROBIN, BUT HE NEEDS *HELP.*
WITH THIS, YOU'LL HAVE DEFENSIVE AND OFFENSIVE CAPABILITIES THAT EQUAL HIS.
THAT IS ABSOLUTELY...

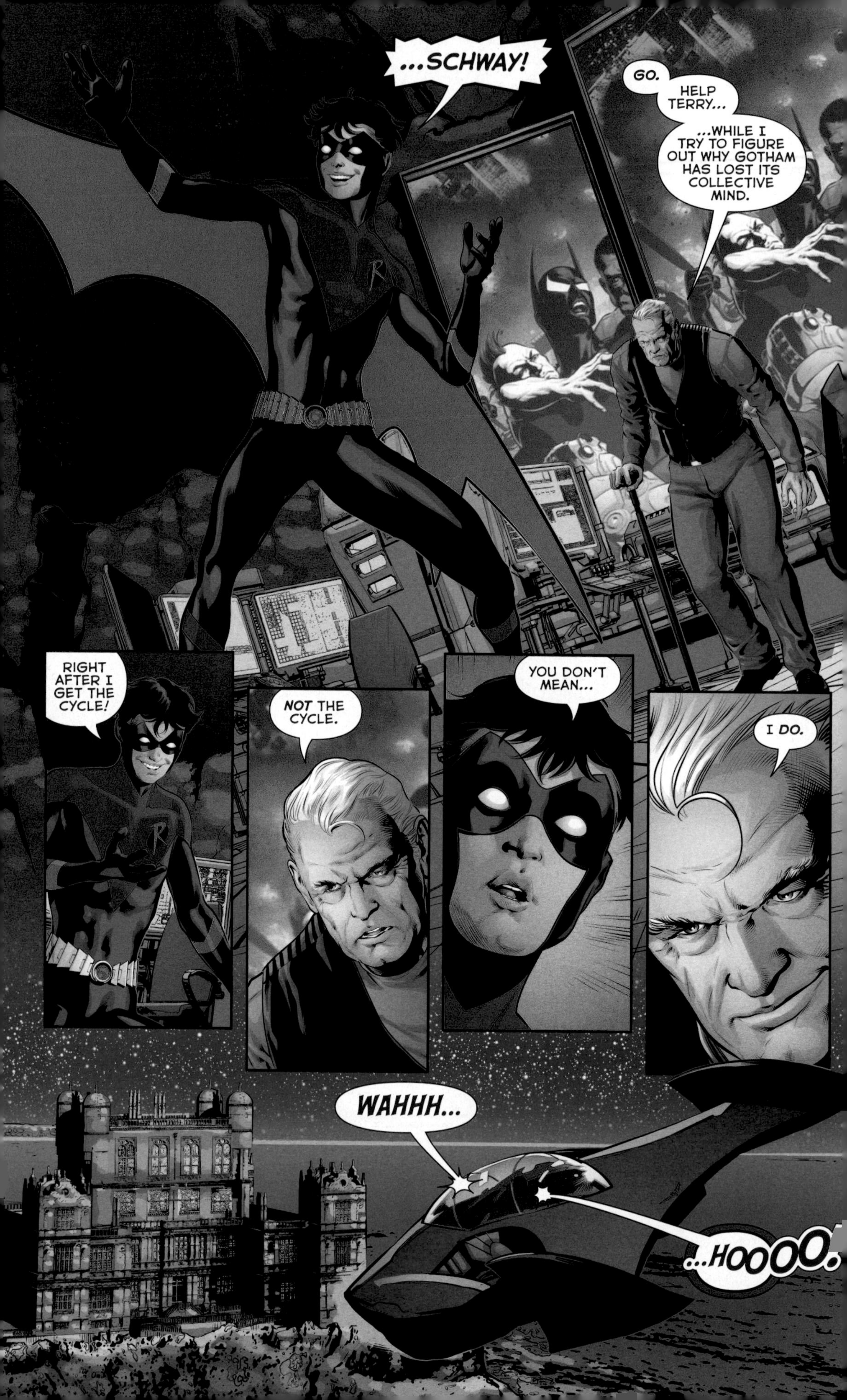
...SCHWAY!
GO.
HELP TERRY...
...WHILE I TRY TO FIGURE OUT WHY GOTHAM HAS LOST ITS COLLECTIVE MIND.
RIGHT AFTER I GET THE CYCLE!
NOT THE CYCLE.
YOU DON'T MEAN...
I DO.
WAHHH...
...HOOOO.

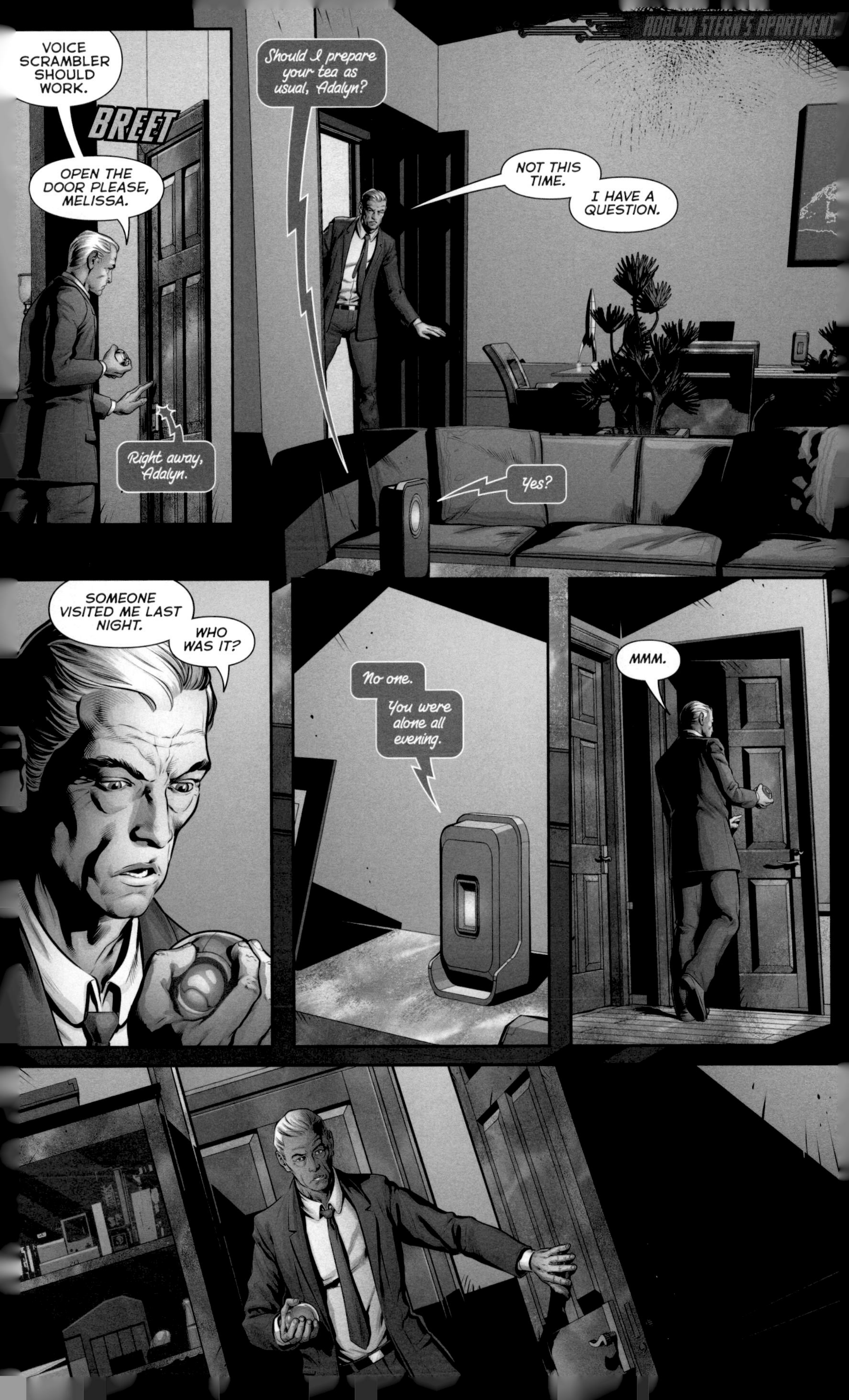
ADALYN STERN'S APARTMENT
VOICE SCRAMBLER SHOULD WORK.
BREET
OPEN THE DOOR PLEASE, MELISSA.
Right away, Adalyn.
Should I prepare your tea as usual, Adalyn?
NOT THIS TIME.
I HAVE A QUESTION.
Yes?
SOMEONE VISITED ME LAST NIGHT.
WHO WAS IT?
No one.
You were alone all evening.
MMM.

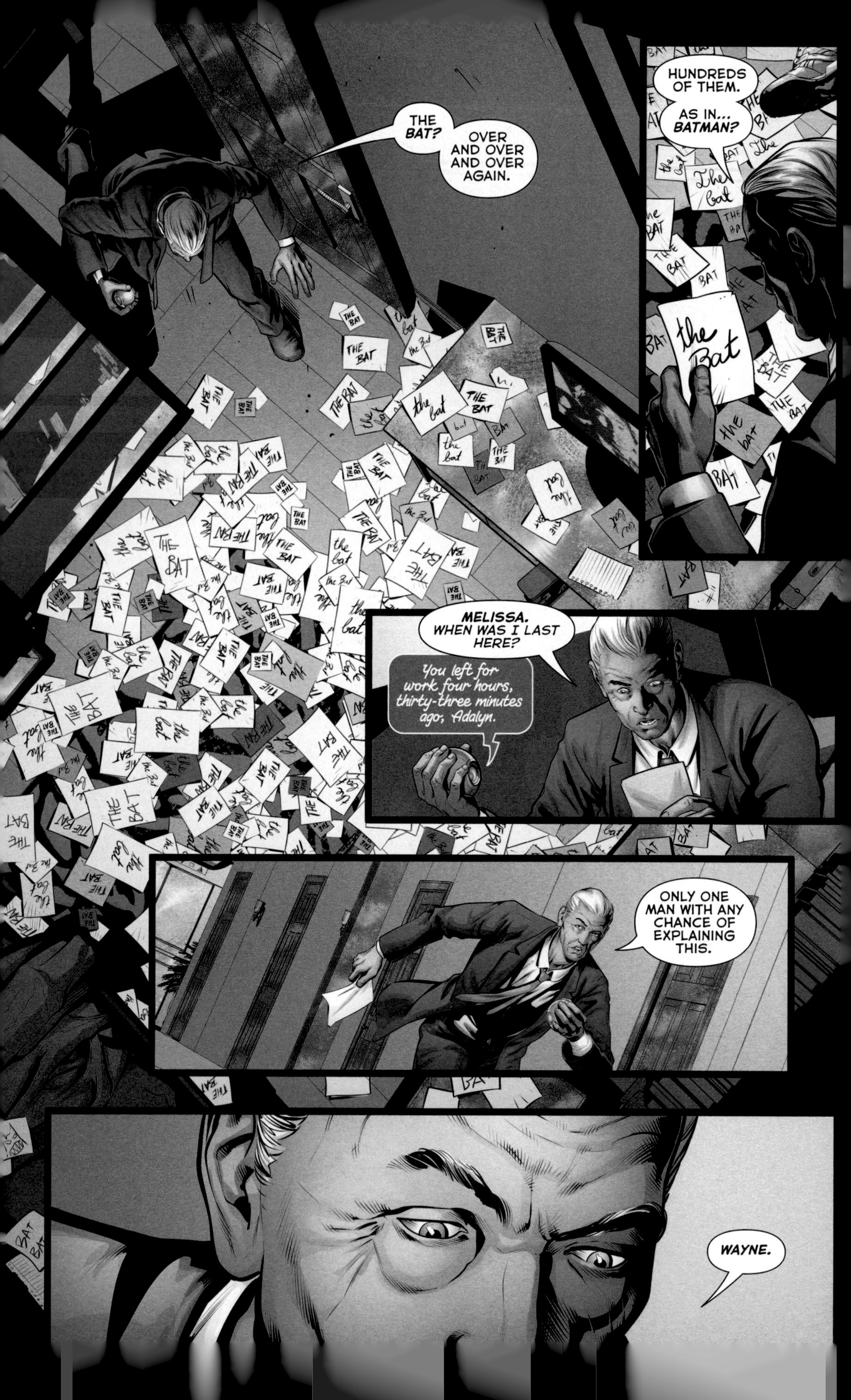
THE BAT?
OVER AND OVER AND OVER AGAIN.
HUNDREDS OF THEM.
AS IN... BATMAN?
MELISSA. WHEN WAS I LAST HERE?
You left for work four hours, thirty-three minutes ago, Adalyn.
ONLY ONE MAN WITH ANY CHANCE OF EXPLAINING THIS.
WAYNE.

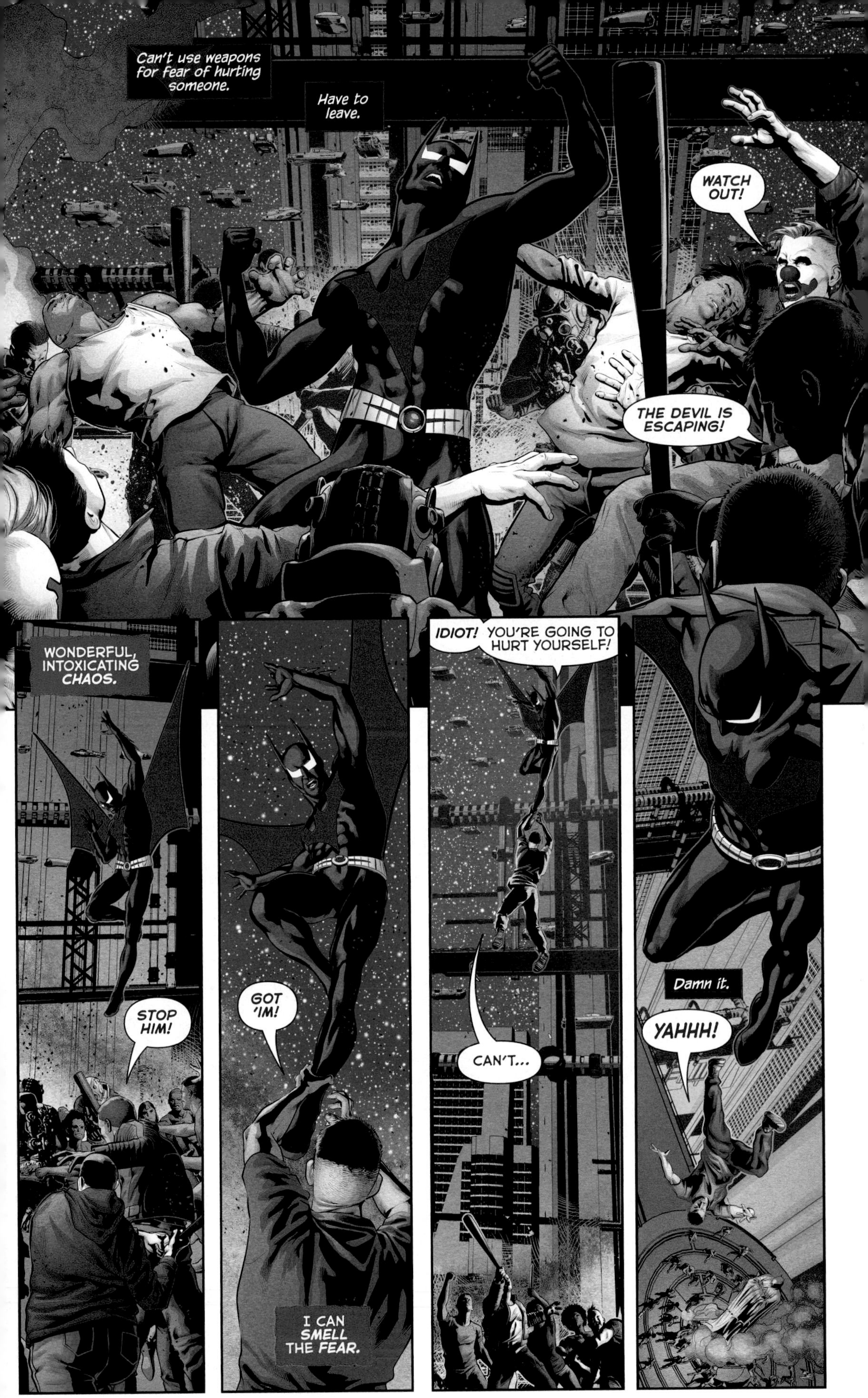

Can't use weapons for fear of hurting someone.
Have to leave.
WATCH OUT!
THE DEVIL IS ESCAPING!
WONDERFUL, INTOXICATING CHAOS.
STOP HIM!
GOT 'IM!
I CAN SMELL THE FEAR.
IDIOT!
YOU'RE GOING TO HURT YOURSELF!
CAN'T...
Damn it.
YAHHH!

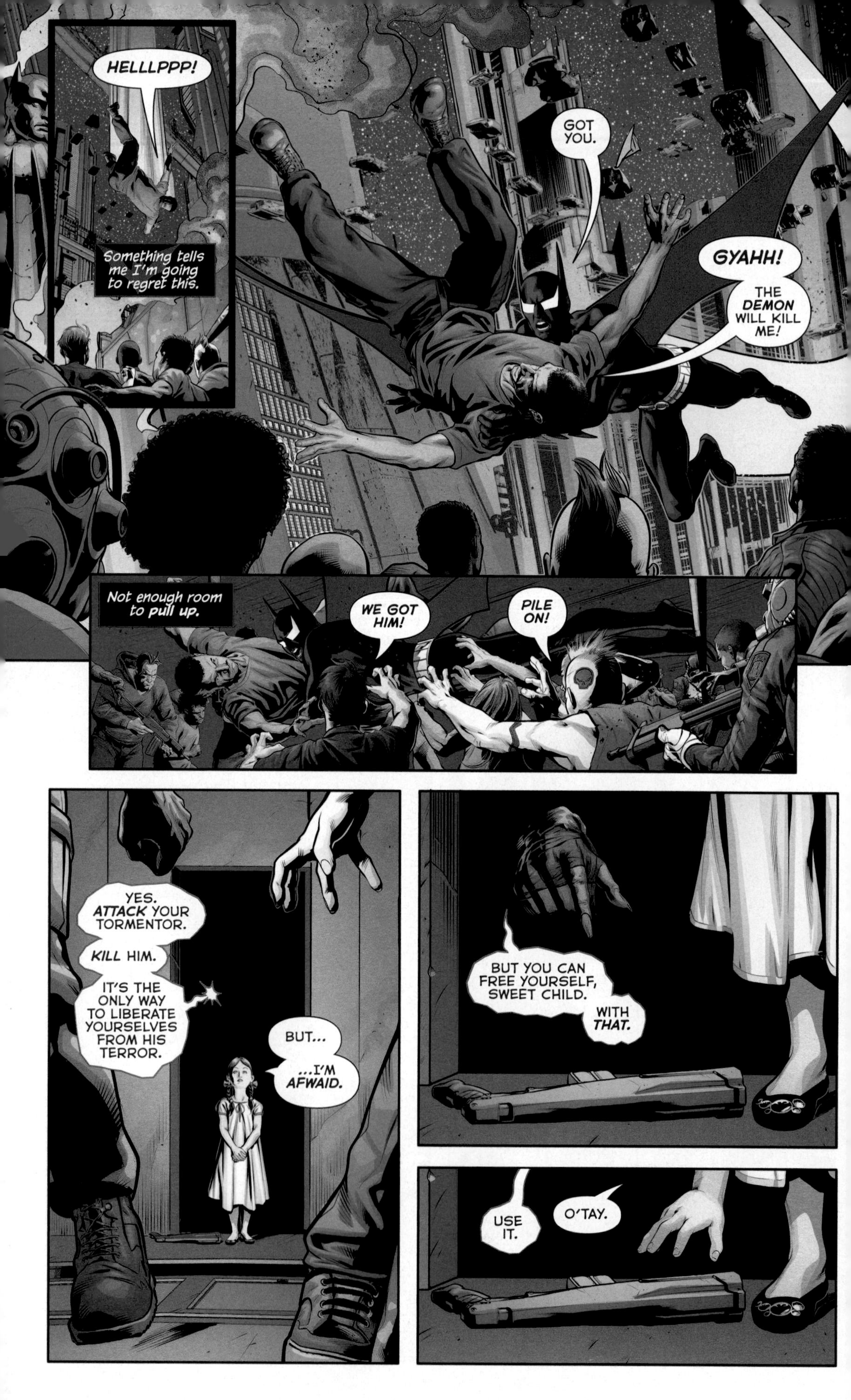
HELLLPPP!
Something tells me I'm going to regret this.
GOT YOU.
GYAHH!
THE DEMON WILL KILL ME!
Not enough room to pull up.
WE GOT HIM!
PILE ON!
YES. ATTACK YOUR TORMENTOR.
KILL HIM.
IT'S THE ONLY WAY TO LIBERATE YOURSELVES FROM HIS TERROR.
BUT...
...I'M AFWAID.
BUT YOU CAN FREE YOURSELF, SWEET CHILD.
WITH THAT.
USE IT.
O'TAY.

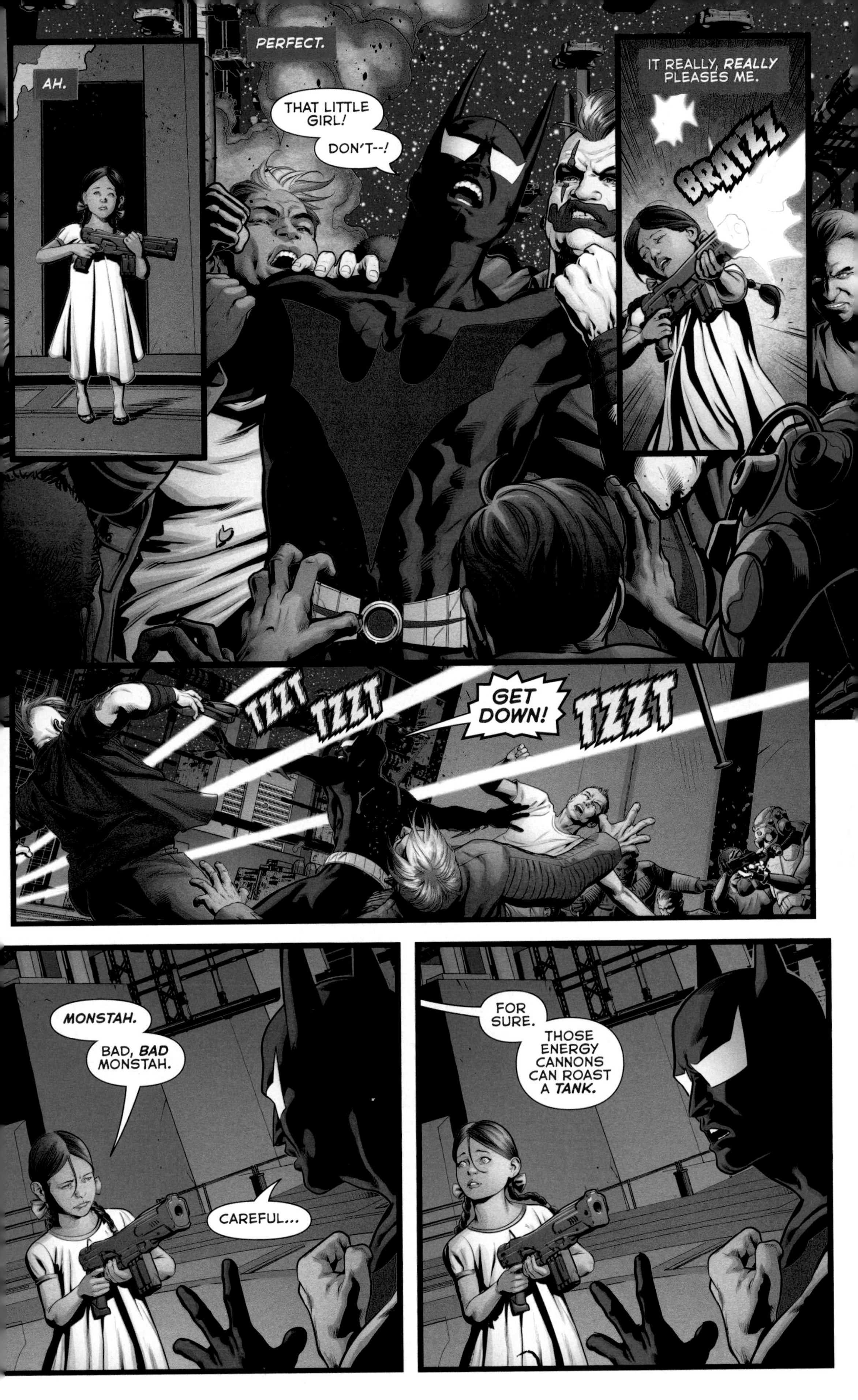
AH.
PERFECT.
THAT LITTLE GIRL!
DON'T--!
IT REALLY, REALLY PLEASES ME.
BRATZZ
TZZT
TZZT
GET DOWN!
TZZT
MONSTAH.
BAD, BAD MONSTAH.
CAREFUL...
FOR SURE.
THOSE ENERGY CANNONS CAN ROAST A TANK.

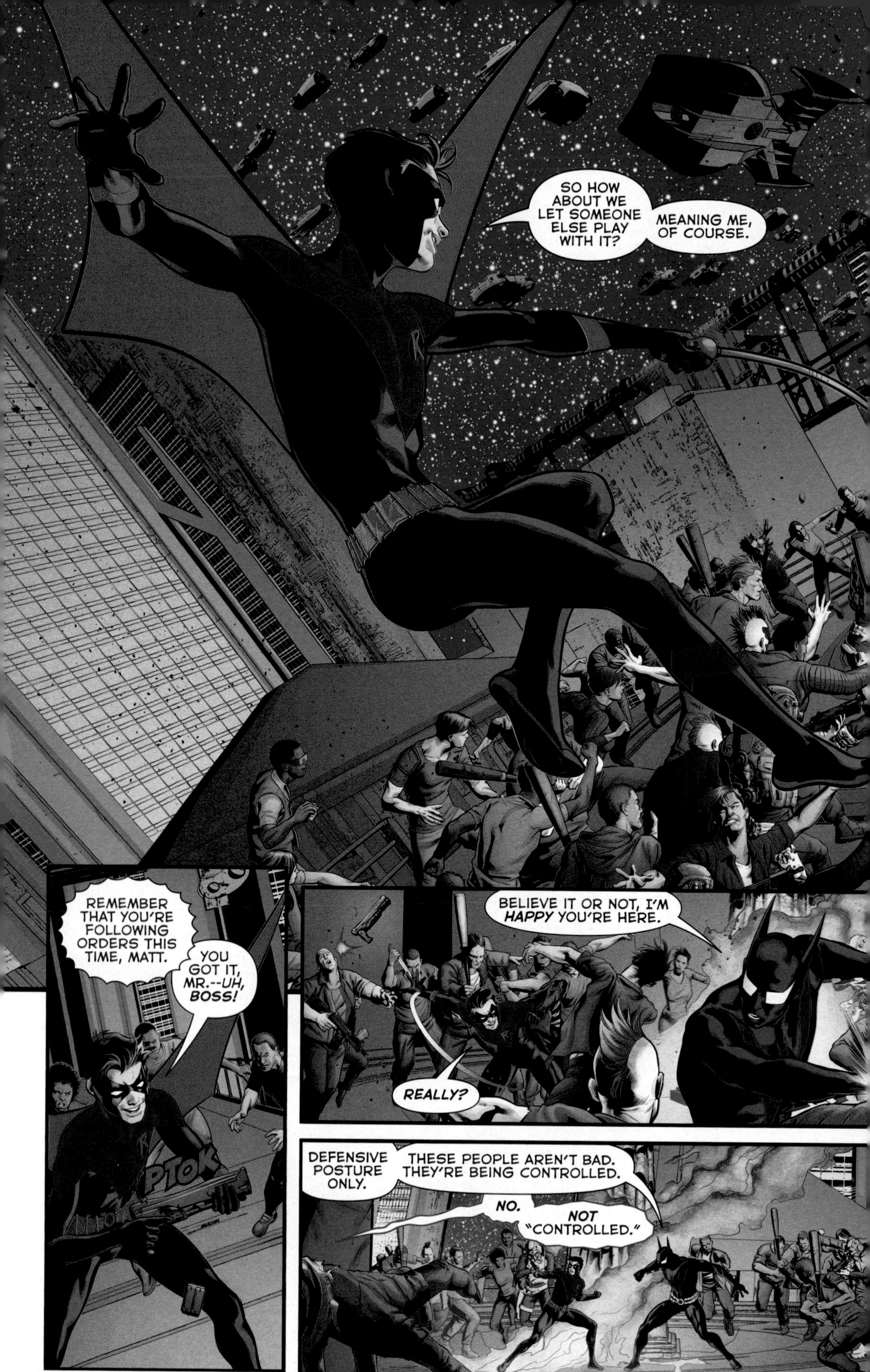
SO HOW ABOUT WE LET SOMEONE ELSE PLAY WITH IT?
MEANING ME, OF COURSE.
REMEMBER THAT YOU'RE FOLLOWING ORDERS THIS TIME, MATT.
YOU GOT IT, MR.--UH, BOSS!
PTOK
BELIEVE IT OR NOT, I'M HAPPY YOU'RE HERE.
REALLY?
DEFENSIVE POSTURE ONLY.
THESE PEOPLE AREN'T BAD. THEY'RE BEING CONTROLLED.
NO.
NOT "CONTROLLED."

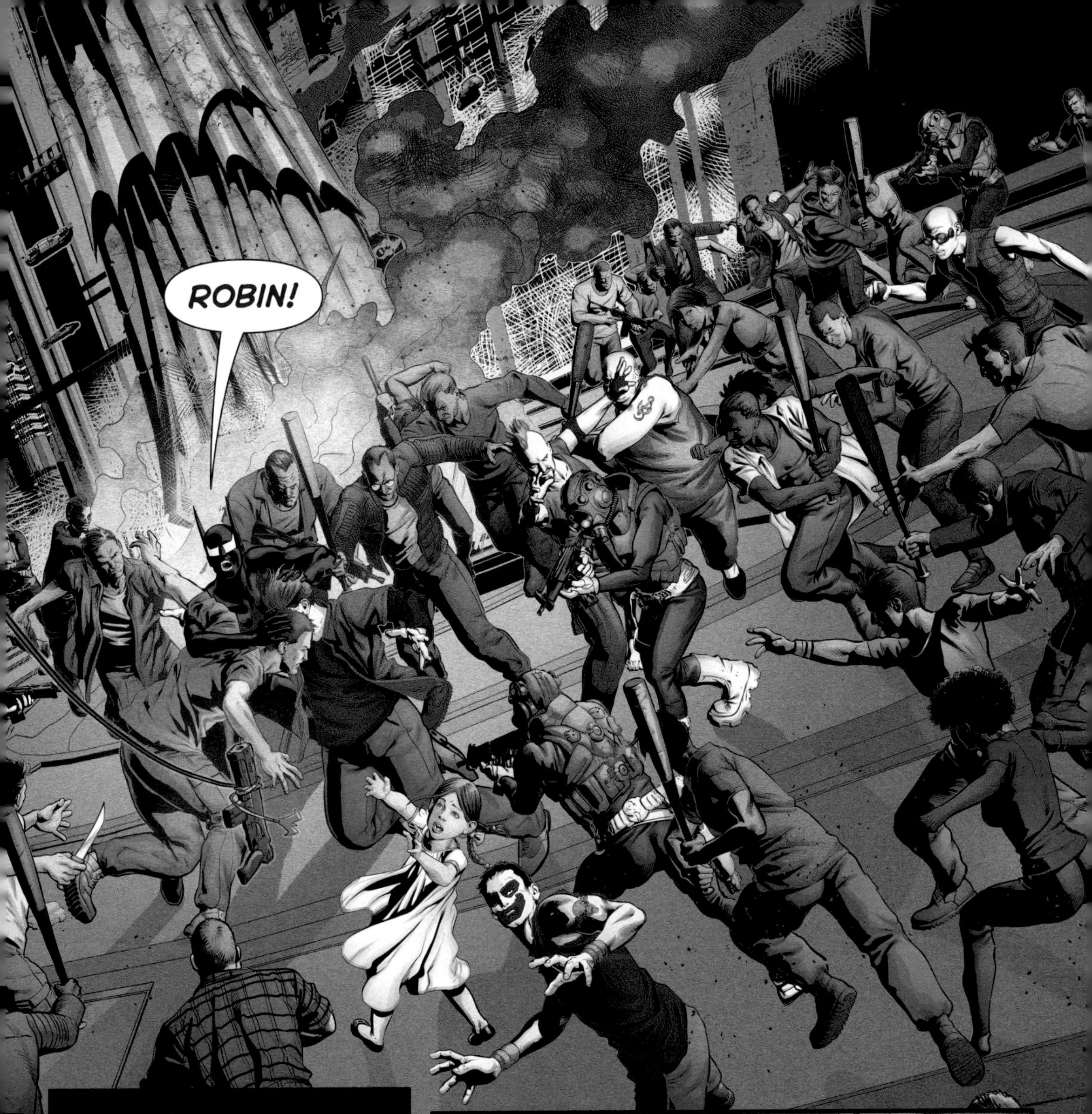
ROBIN!

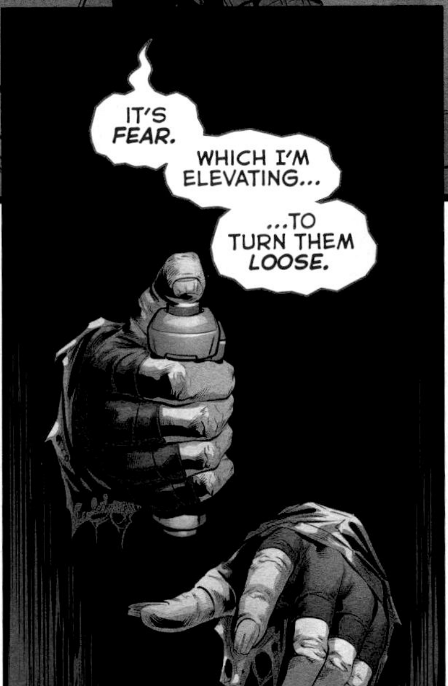
IT'S *FEAR.*
WHICH I'M ELEVATING...
...TO TURN THEM *LOOSE.*

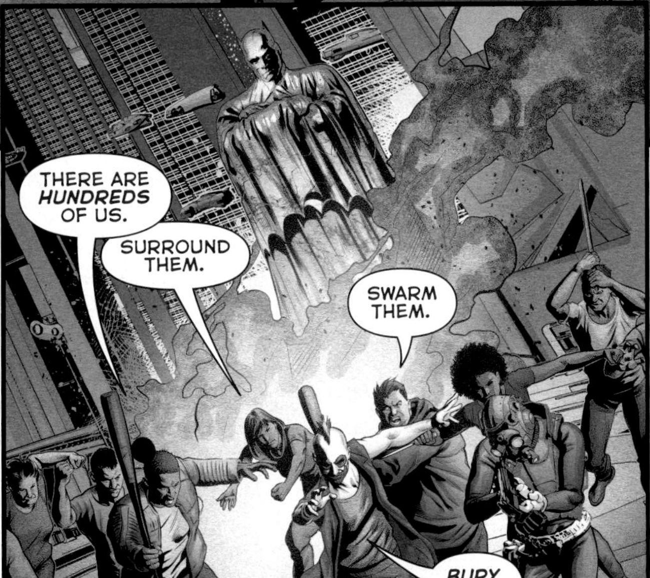
THERE ARE *HUNDREDS* OF US.
SURROUND THEM.
SWARM THEM.
BURY THEM.

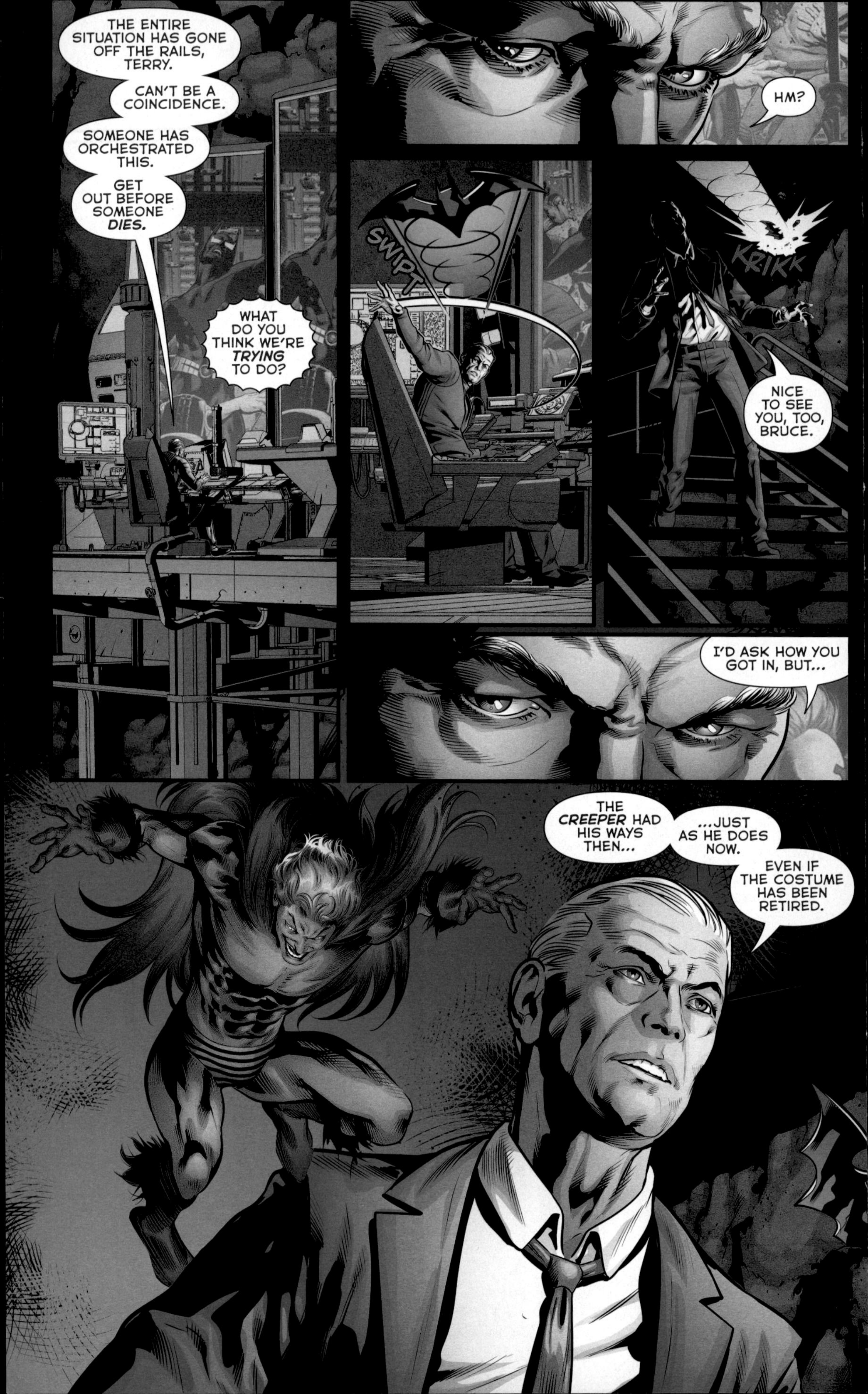
THE ENTIRE SITUATION HAS GONE OFF THE RAILS, TERRY.
CAN'T BE A COINCIDENCE.
SOMEONE HAS ORCHESTRATED THIS.
GET OUT BEFORE SOMEONE DIES.
WHAT DO YOU THINK WE'RE TRYING TO DO?
HM?
SWIPT
KRIKK
NICE TO SEE YOU, TOO, BRUCE.
I'D ASK HOW YOU GOT IN, BUT...
THE CREEPER HAD HIS WAYS THEN...
...JUST AS HE DOES NOW.
EVEN IF THE COSTUME HAS BEEN RETIRED.

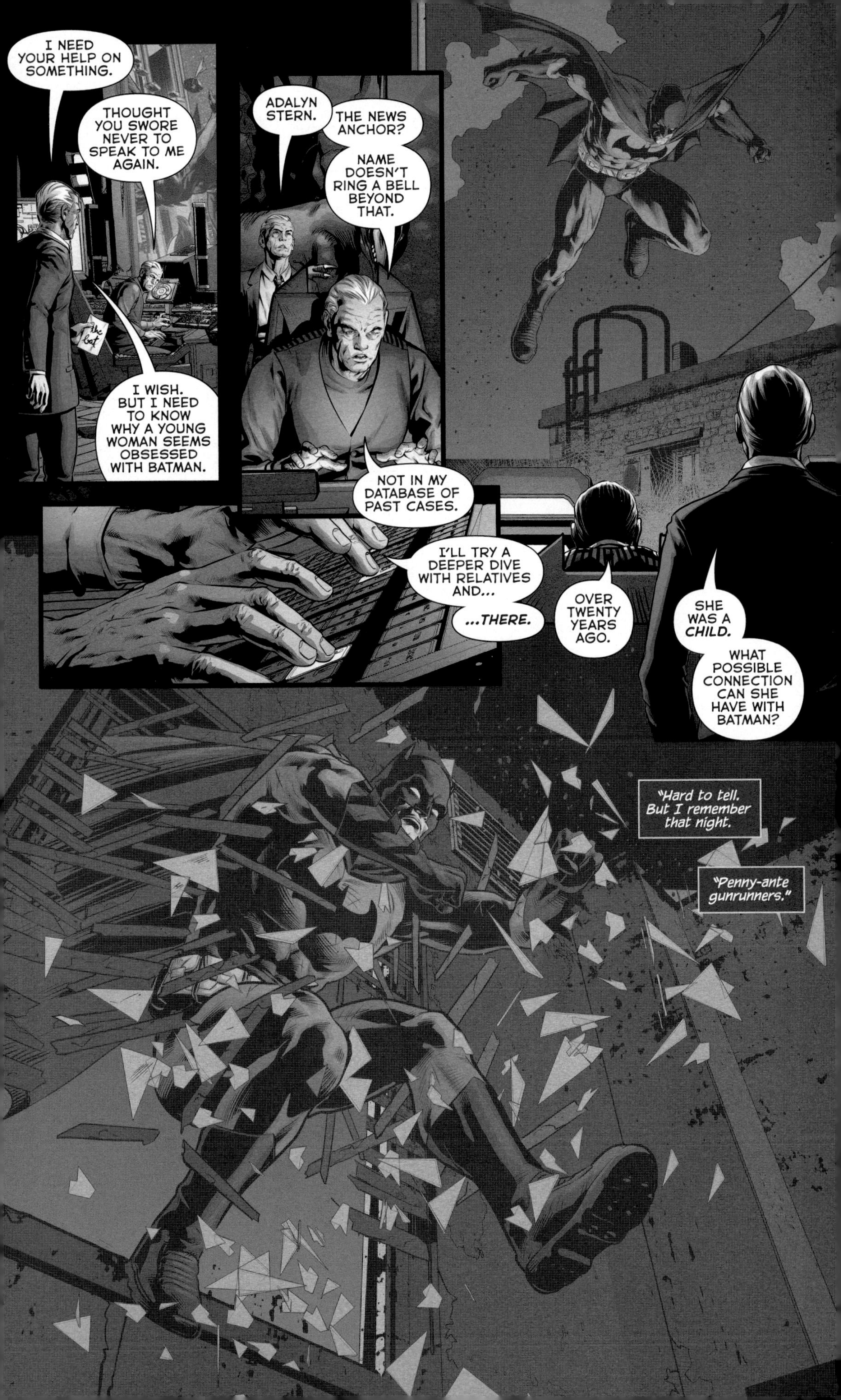

I NEED YOUR HELP ON SOMETHING.
THOUGHT YOU SWORE NEVER TO SPEAK TO ME AGAIN.
I WISH. BUT I NEED TO KNOW WHY A YOUNG WOMAN SEEMS OBSESSED WITH BATMAN.
ADALYN STERN.
THE NEWS ANCHOR?
NAME DOESN'T RING A BELL BEYOND THAT.
NOT IN MY DATABASE OF PAST CASES.
I'LL TRY A DEEPER DIVE WITH RELATIVES AND...
...THERE.
OVER TWENTY YEARS AGO.
SHE WAS A CHILD.
WHAT POSSIBLE CONNECTION CAN SHE HAVE WITH BATMAN?
"Hard to tell. But I remember that night.
"Penny-ante gunrunners."

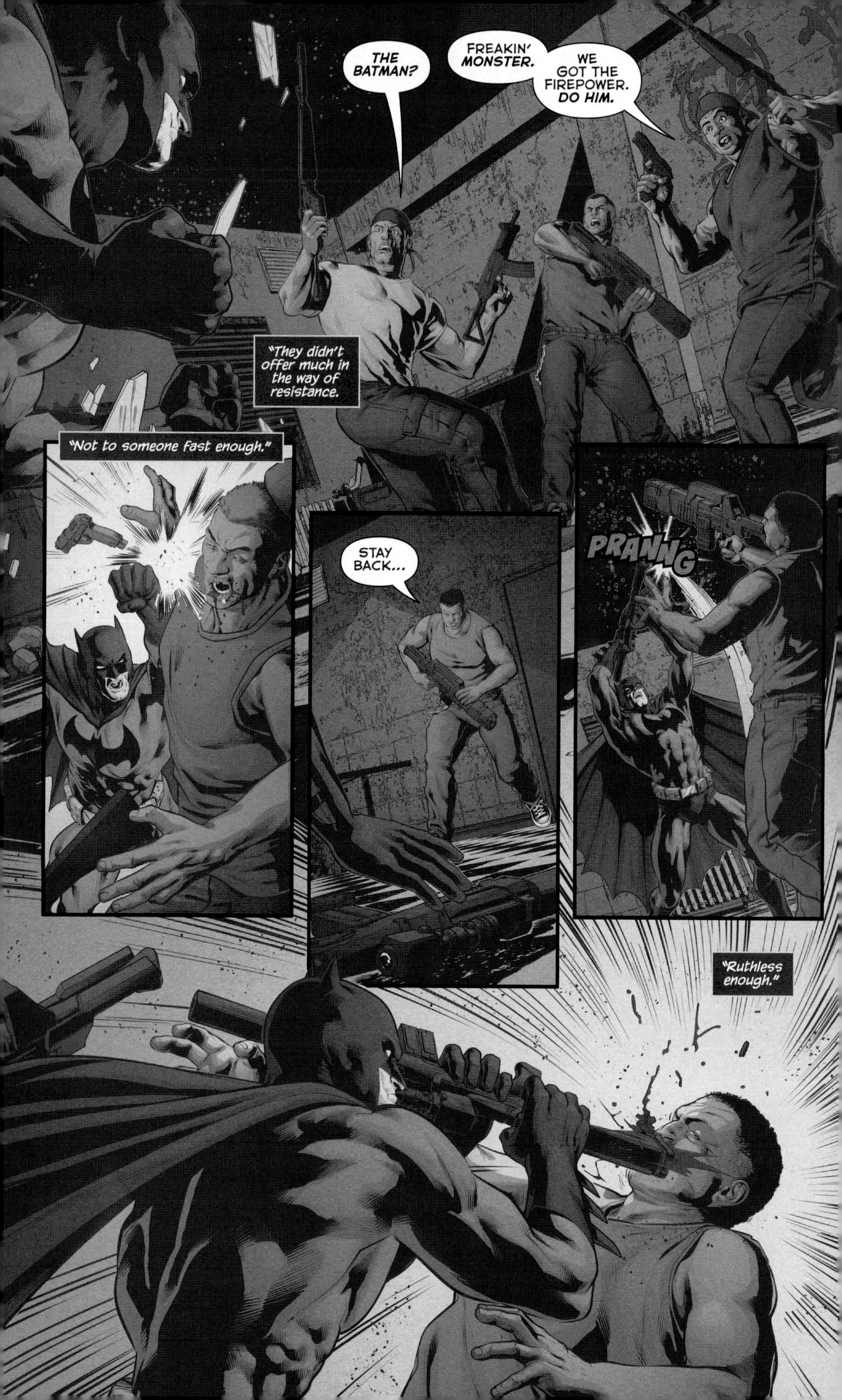
THE BATMAN?
FREAKIN' MONSTER.
WE GOT THE FIREPOWER. DO HIM.
"They didn't offer much in the way of resistance.
"Not to someone fast enough."
STAY BACK...
PRANNG
"Ruthless enough."

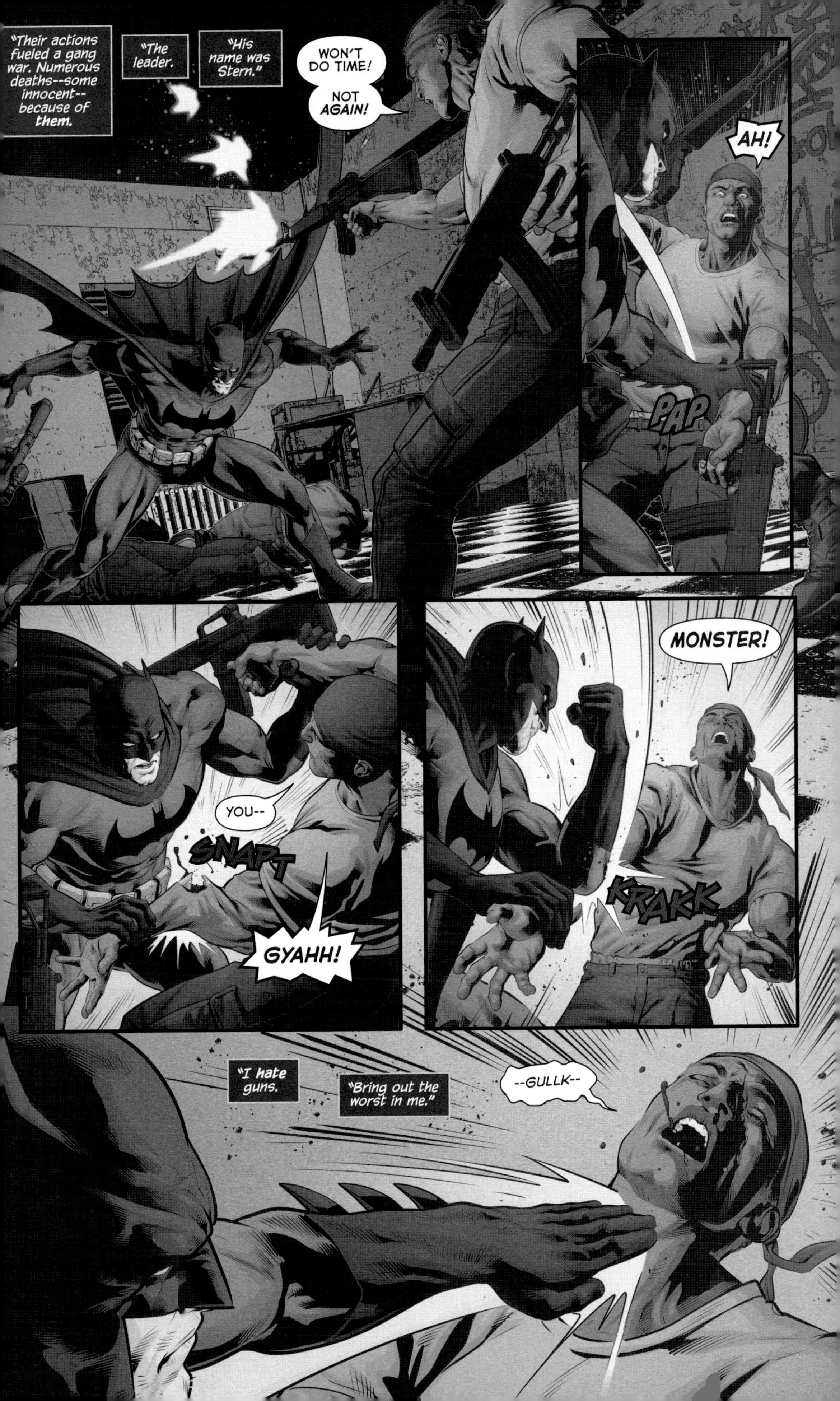
"Their actions fueled a gang war. Numerous deaths--some innocent--because of them.
"The leader.
"His name was Stern."
WON'T DO TIME!
NOT AGAIN!
AH!
PAP
YOU--
SNAPT
GYAHH!
MONSTER!
KRAKK
"I hate guns.
"Bring out the worst in me."
--GULLK--

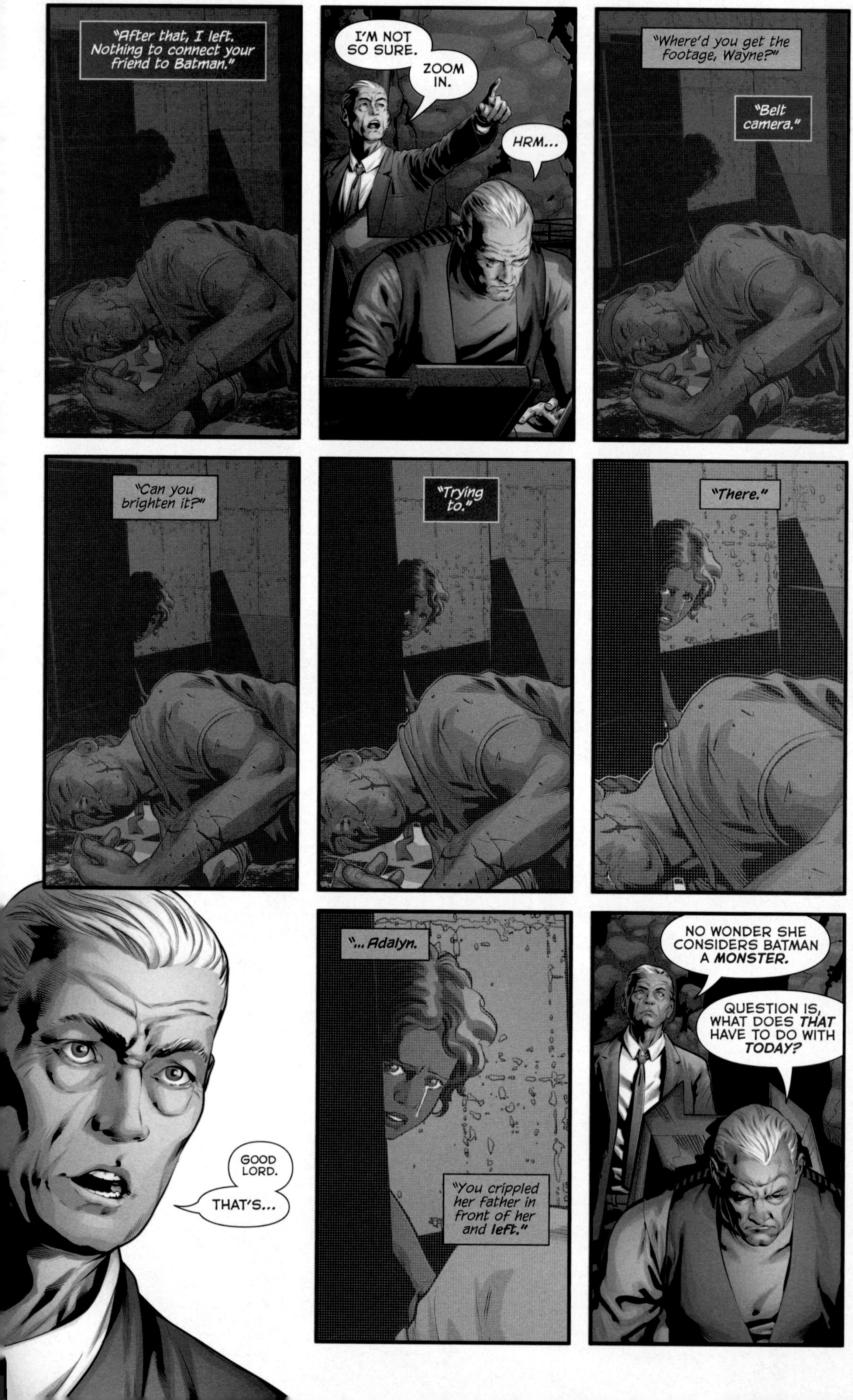
"After that, I left. Nothing to connect your friend to Batman."
I'M NOT SO SURE.
ZOOM IN.
HRM...
"Where'd you get the footage, Wayne?"
"Belt camera."
"Can you brighten it?"
"Trying to."
"There."
GOOD LORD.
THAT'S...
"...Adalyn.
"You crippled her father in front of her and left."
NO WONDER SHE CONSIDERS BATMAN A MONSTER.
QUESTION IS, WHAT DOES THAT HAVE TO DO WITH TODAY?

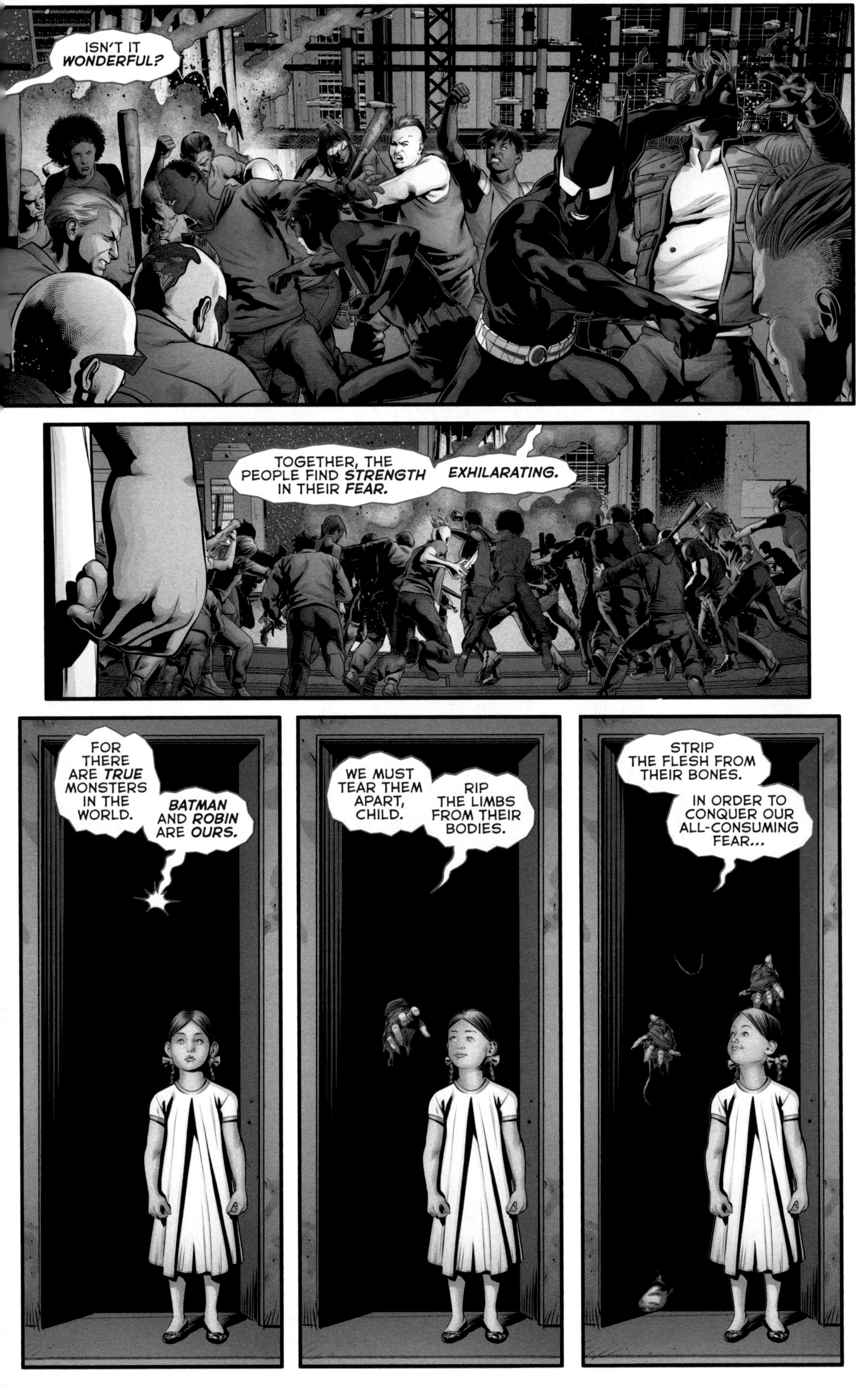
ISN'T IT WONDERFUL?
TOGETHER, THE PEOPLE FIND STRENGTH IN THEIR FEAR.
EXHILARATING.
FOR THERE ARE TRUE MONSTERS IN THE WORLD.
BATMAN AND ROBIN ARE OURS.
WE MUST TEAR THEM APART, CHILD.
RIP THE LIMBS FROM THEIR BODIES.
STRIP THE FLESH FROM THEIR BONES.
IN ORDER TO CONQUER OUR ALL-CONSUMING FEAR...

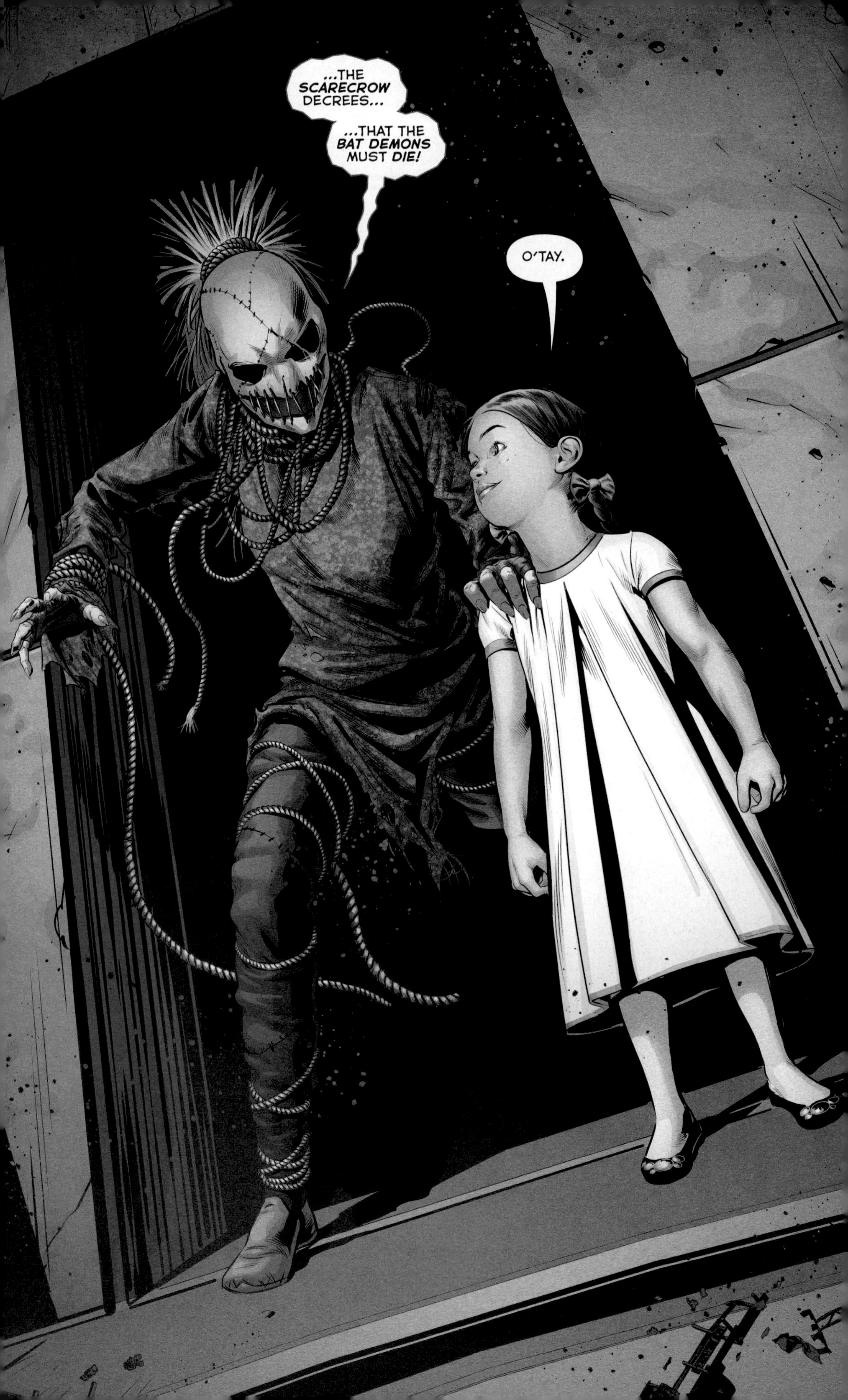
...THE SCARECROW DECREES...
...THAT THE BAT DEMONS MUST DIE!
O'TAY.

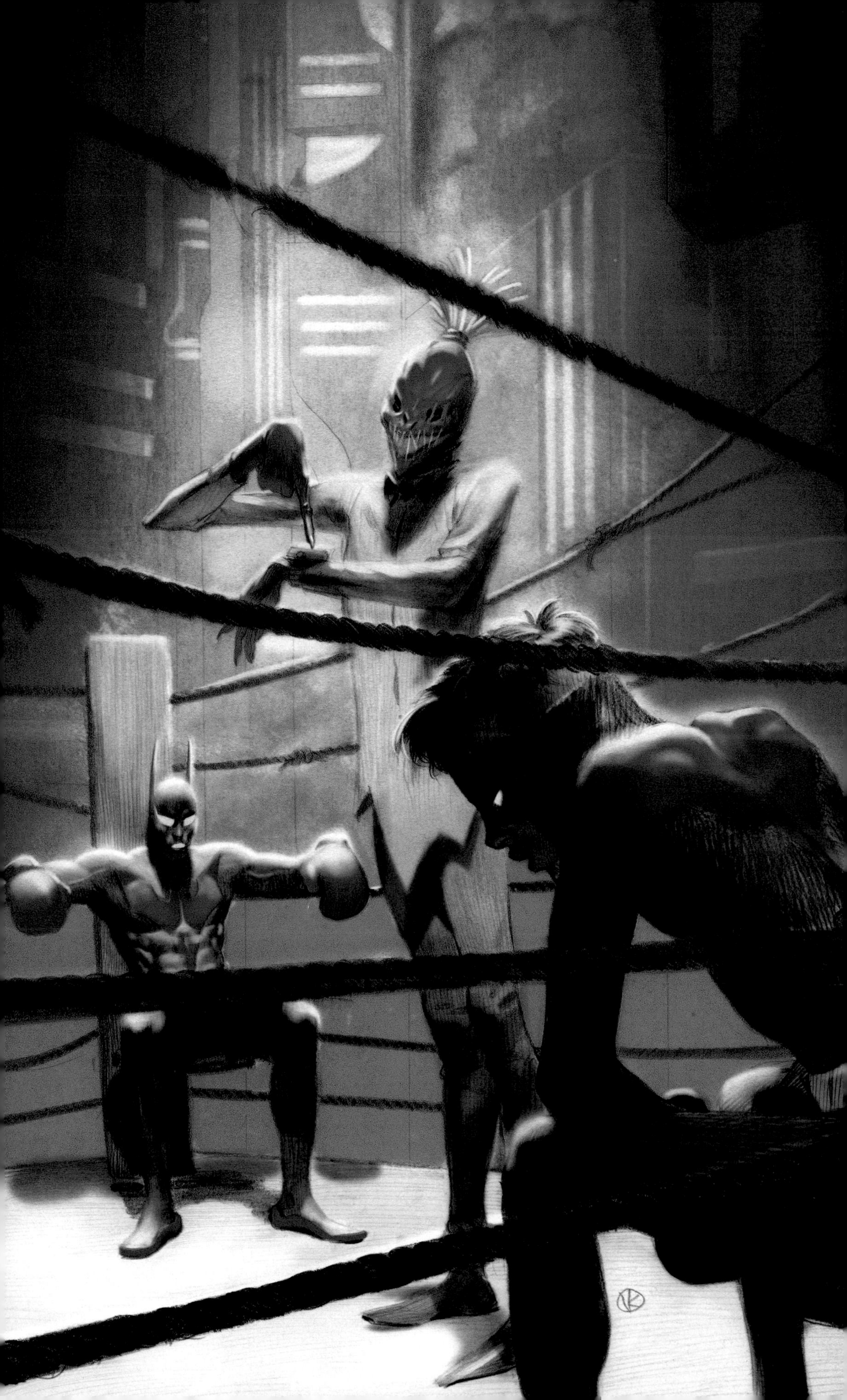

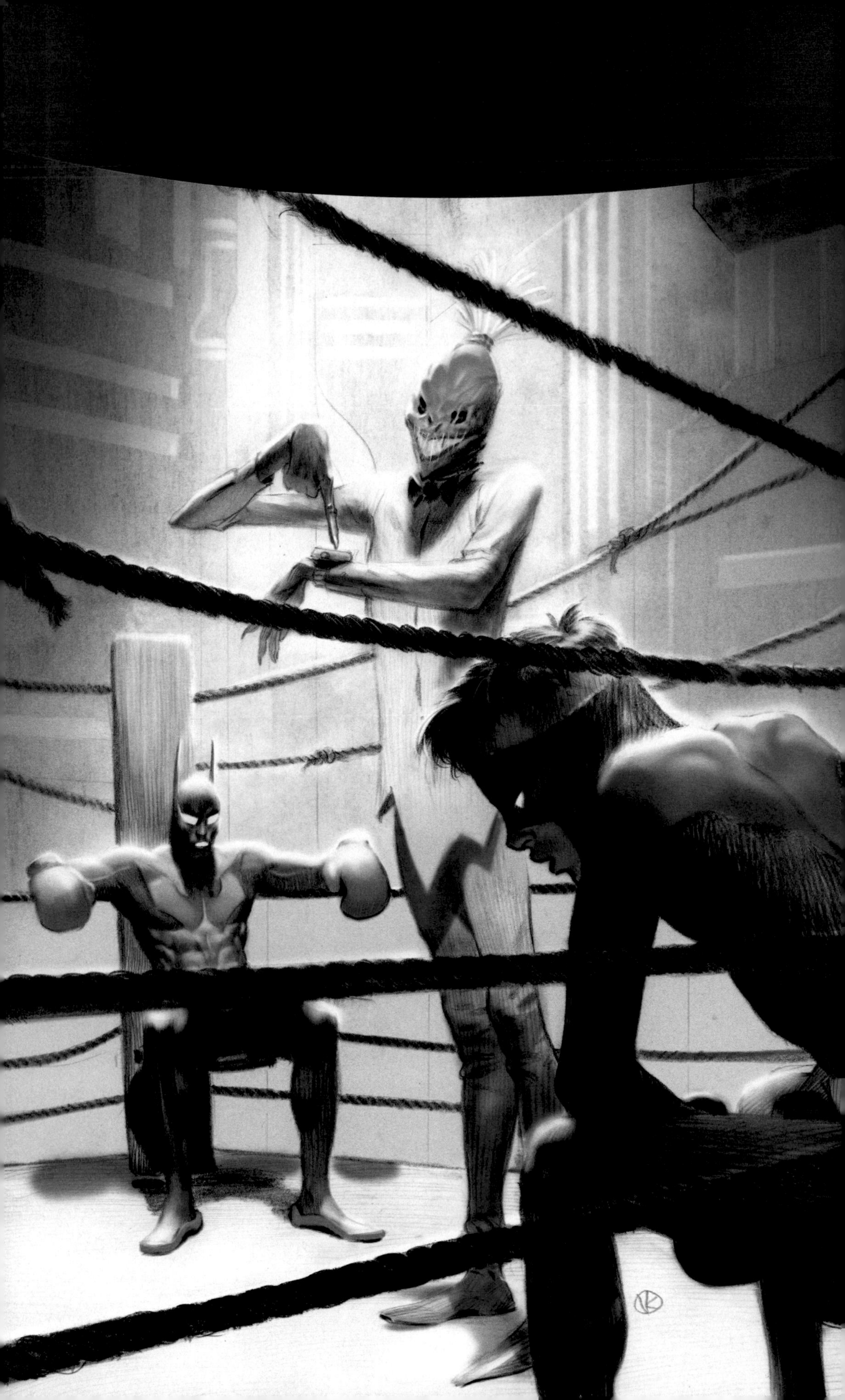

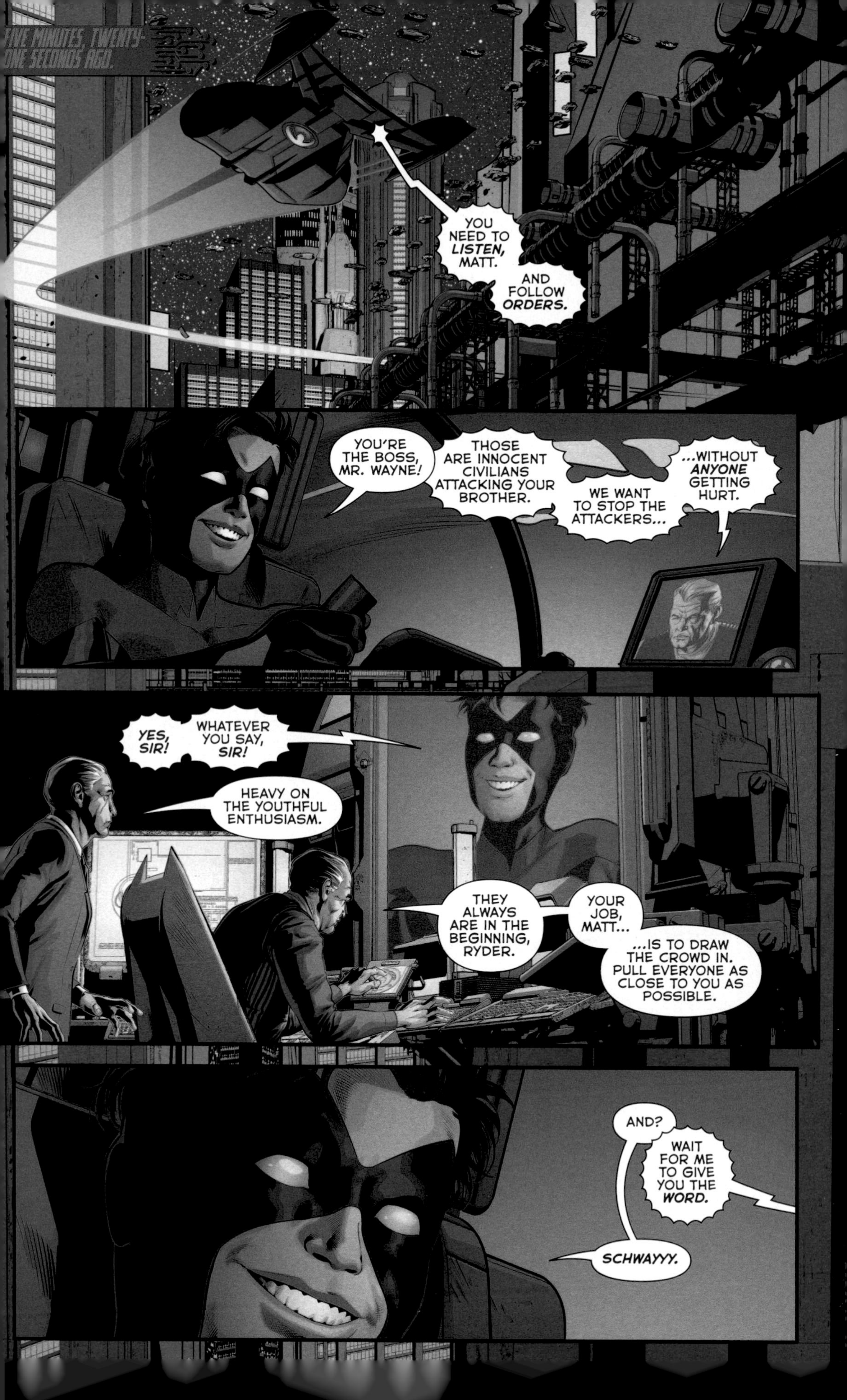
FIVE MINUTES, TWENTY-ONE SECONDS AGO.
YOU NEED TO LISTEN, MATT.
AND FOLLOW ORDERS.
YOU'RE THE BOSS, MR. WAYNE!
THOSE ARE INNOCENT CIVILIANS ATTACKING YOUR BROTHER.
WE WANT TO STOP THE ATTACKERS...
...WITHOUT ANYONE GETTING HURT.
YES, SIR!
WHATEVER YOU SAY, SIR!
HEAVY ON THE YOUTHFUL ENTHUSIASM.
THEY ALWAYS ARE IN THE BEGINNING, RYDER.
YOUR JOB, MATT...
...IS TO DRAW THE CROWD IN. PULL EVERYONE AS CLOSE TO YOU AS POSSIBLE.
AND?
WAIT FOR ME TO GIVE YOU THE WORD.
SCHWAYYY.

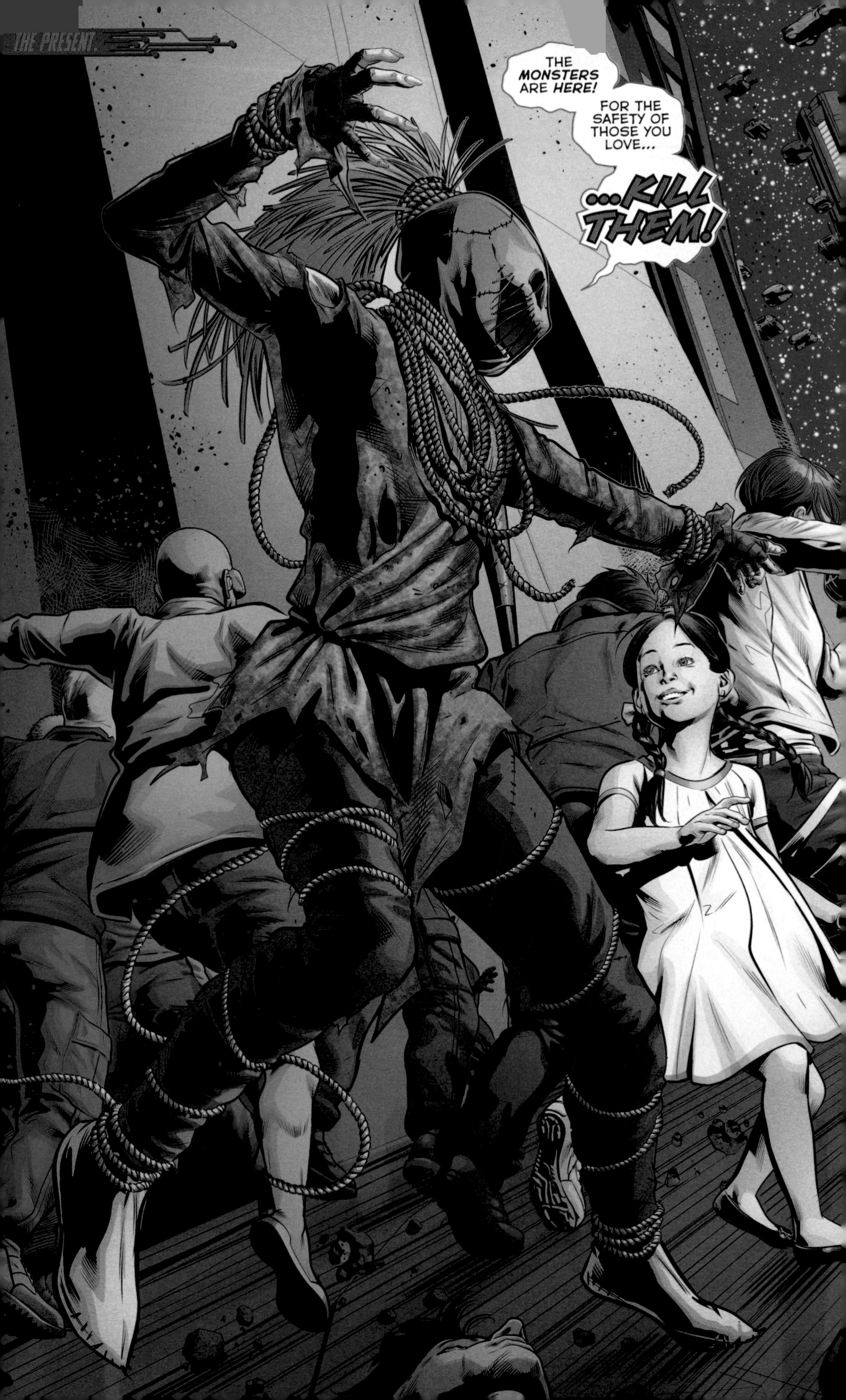
THE PRESENT.
THE MONSTERS ARE HERE!
FOR THE SAFETY OF THOSE YOU LOVE...
...KILL THEM!

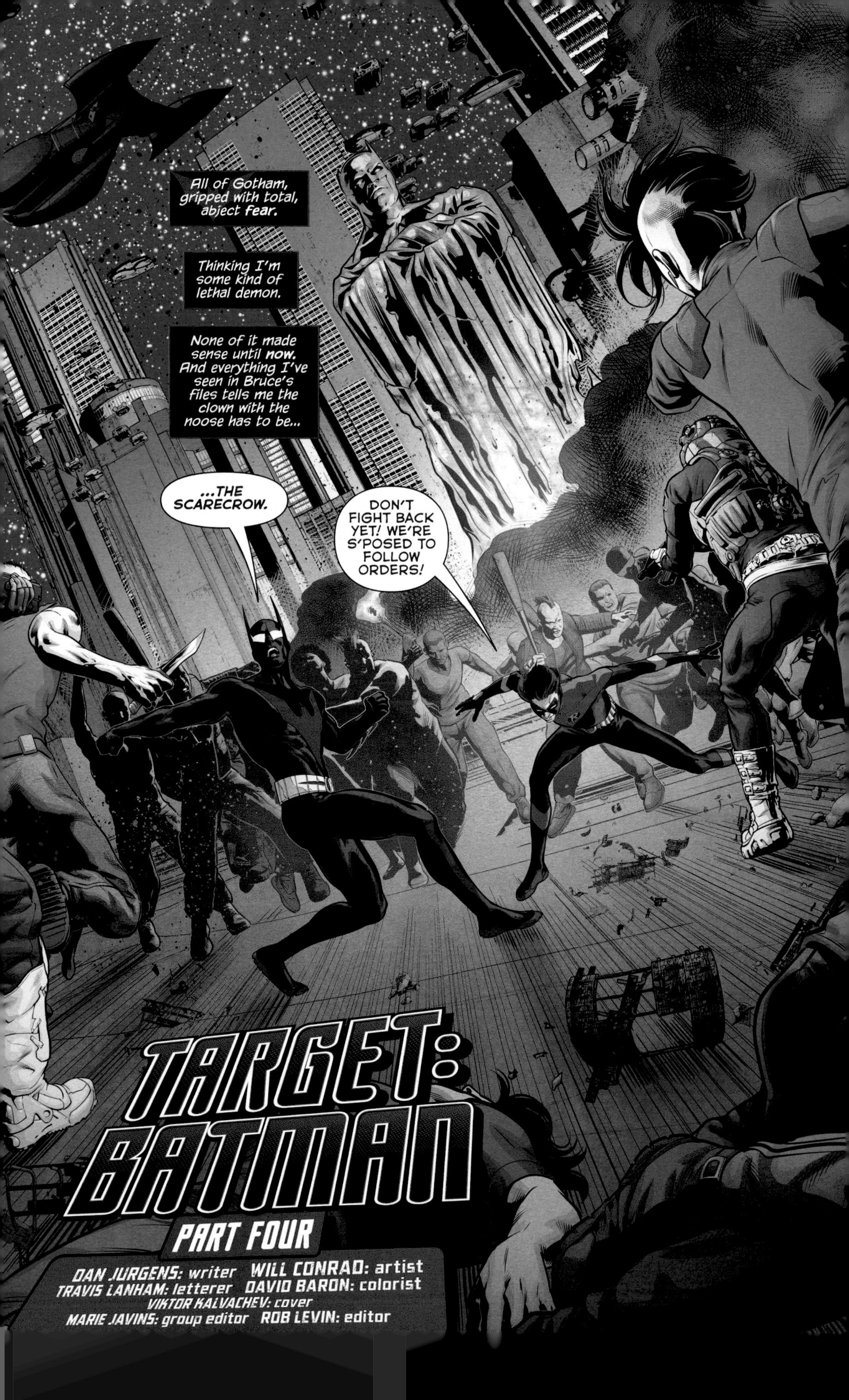

All of Gotham, gripped with total, abject fear.
Thinking I'm some kind of lethal demon.
None of it made sense until now. And everything I've seen in Bruce's files tells me the clown with the noose has to be...
...THE SCARECROW.
DON'T FIGHT BACK YET! WE'RE S'POSED TO FOLLOW ORDERS!
TARGET: BATMAN
PART FOUR
DAN JURGENS: writer WILL CONRAD: artist
TRAVIS LANHAM: letterer DAVID BARON: colorist
VIKTOR KALVACHEV: cover
MARIE JAVINS: group editor ROB LEVIN: editor

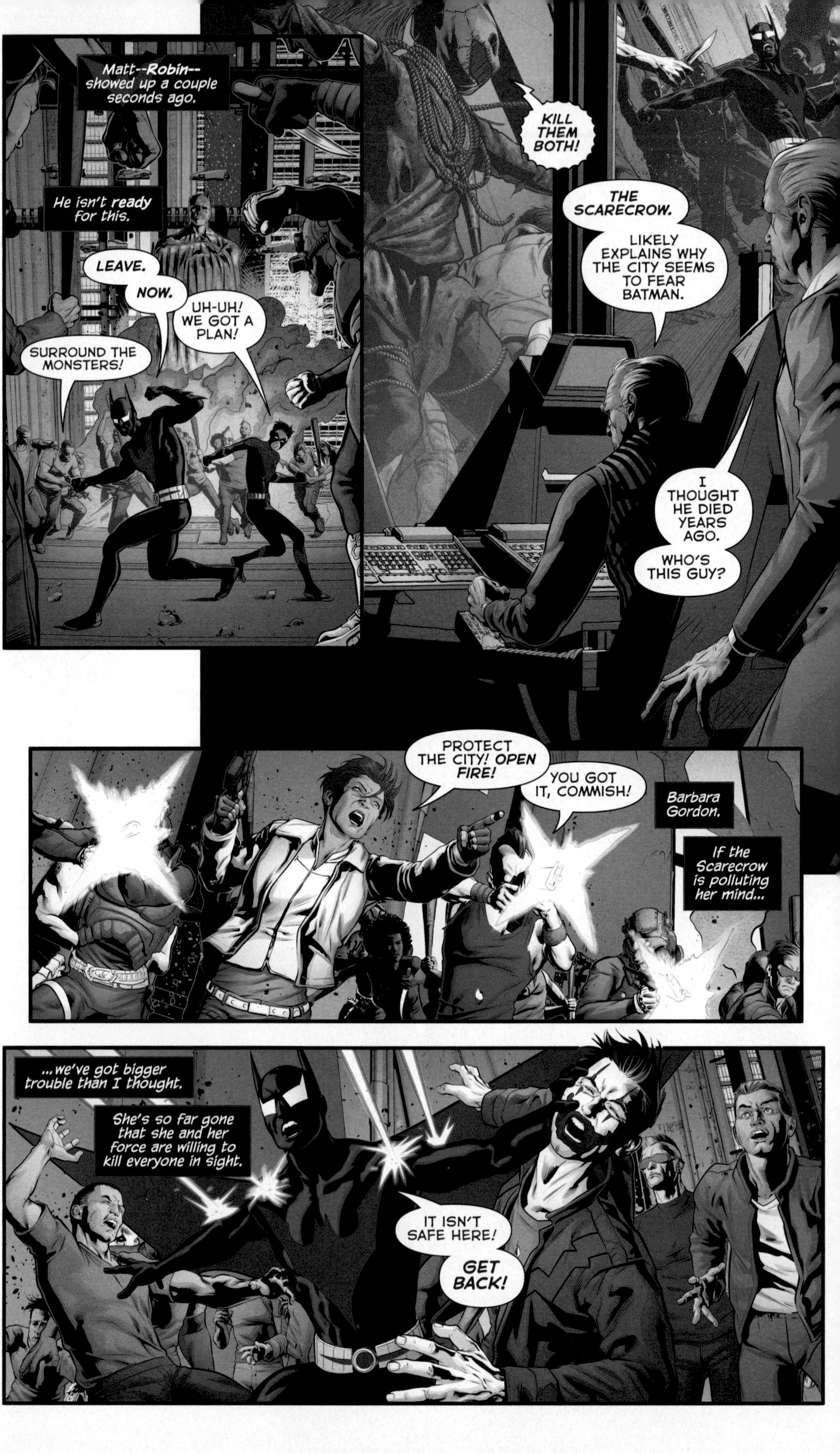
Matt--Robin-- showed up a couple seconds ago.
He isn't ready for this.
LEAVE.
NOW.
UH-UH! WE GOT A PLAN!
SURROUND THE MONSTERS!
KILL THEM BOTH!
THE SCARECROW.
LIKELY EXPLAINS WHY THE CITY SEEMS TO FEAR BATMAN.
I THOUGHT HE DIED YEARS AGO.
WHO'S THIS GUY?
PROTECT THE CITY! OPEN FIRE!
YOU GOT IT, COMMISH!
Barbara Gordon.
If the Scarecrow is polluting her mind...
...we've got bigger trouble than I thought.
She's so far gone that she and her force are willing to kill everyone in sight.
IT ISN'T SAFE HERE!
GET BACK!

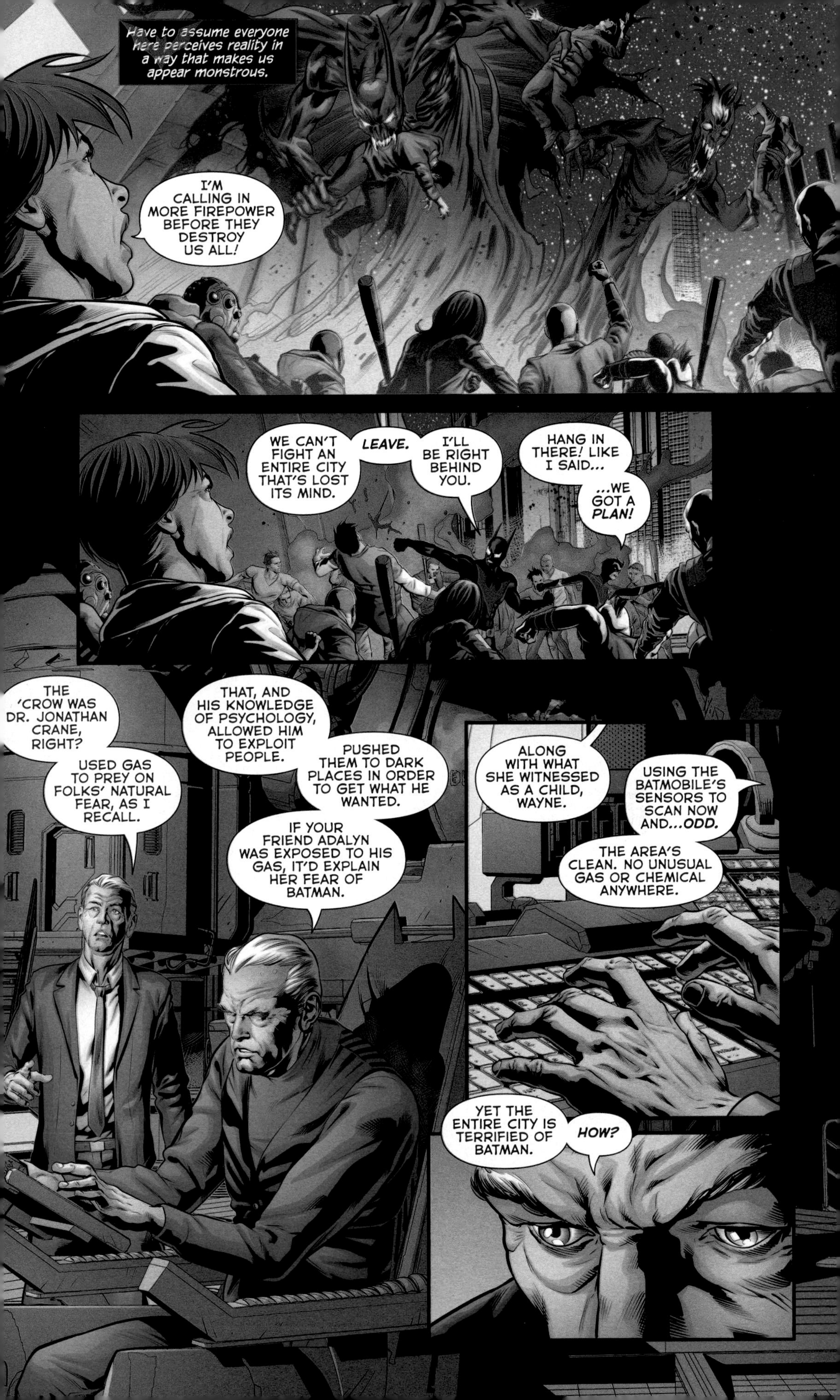

Have to assume everyone here perceives reality in a way that makes us appear monstrous.
I'M CALLING IN MORE FIREPOWER BEFORE THEY DESTROY US ALL!
WE CAN'T FIGHT AN ENTIRE CITY THAT'S LOST ITS MIND.
LEAVE.
I'LL BE RIGHT BEHIND YOU.
HANG IN THERE! LIKE I SAID...
...WE GOT A PLAN!
THE 'CROW WAS DR. JONATHAN CRANE, RIGHT?
USED GAS TO PREY ON FOLKS' NATURAL FEAR, AS I RECALL.
THAT, AND HIS KNOWLEDGE OF PSYCHOLOGY, ALLOWED HIM TO EXPLOIT PEOPLE.
PUSHED THEM TO DARK PLACES IN ORDER TO GET WHAT HE WANTED.
IF YOUR FRIEND ADALYN WAS EXPOSED TO HIS GAS, IT'D EXPLAIN HER FEAR OF BATMAN.
ALONG WITH WHAT SHE WITNESSED AS A CHILD, WAYNE.
USING THE BATMOBILE'S SENSORS TO SCAN NOW AND...ODD.
THE AREA'S CLEAN. NO UNUSUAL GAS OR CHEMICAL ANYWHERE.
YET THE ENTIRE CITY IS TERRIFIED OF BATMAN.
HOW?

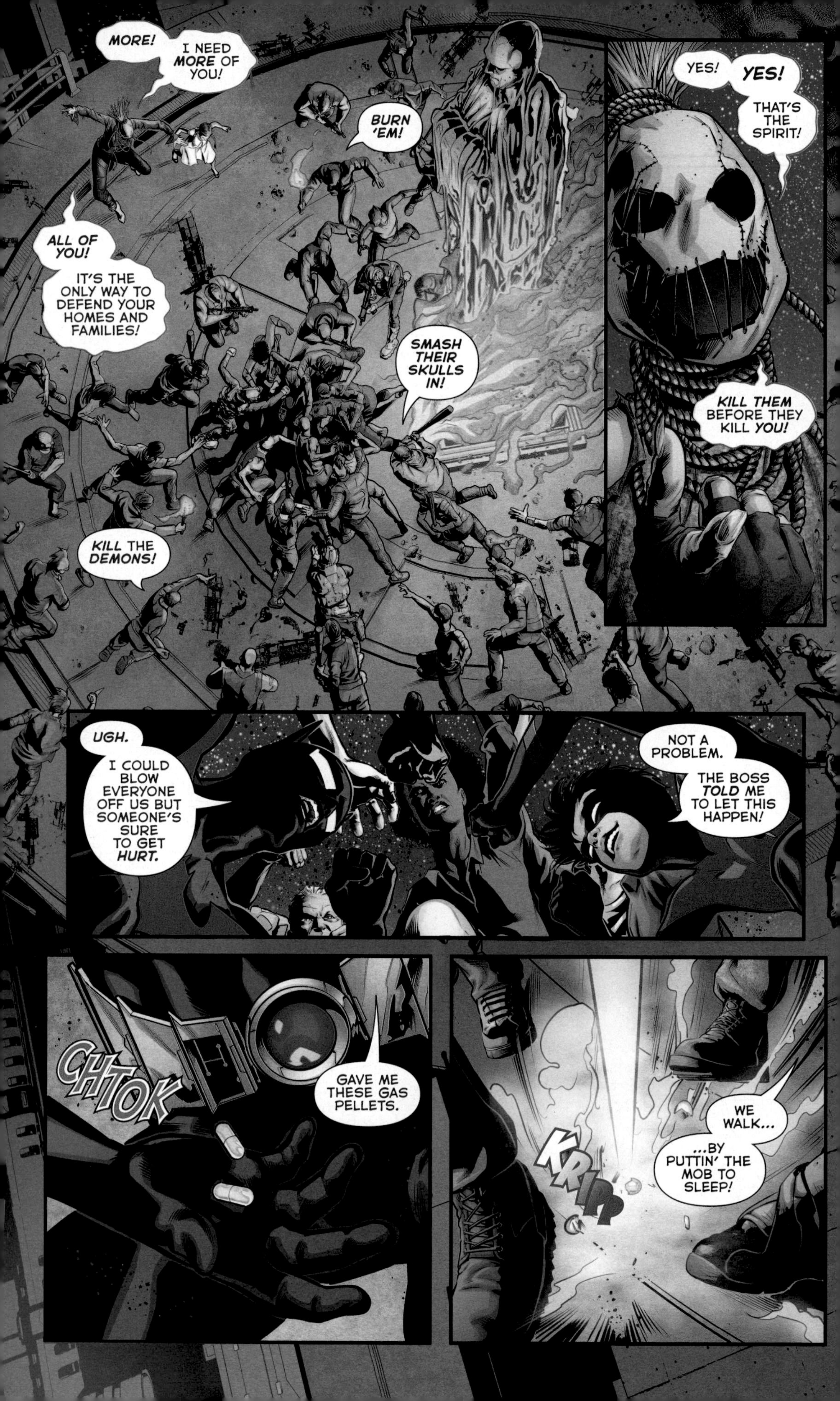
MORE!
I NEED MORE OF YOU!
BURN 'EM!
ALL OF YOU!
IT'S THE ONLY WAY TO DEFEND YOUR HOMES AND FAMILIES!
SMASH THEIR SKULLS IN!
KILL THE DEMONS!
YES!
YES!
THAT'S THE SPIRIT!
KILL THEM BEFORE THEY KILL YOU!
UGH.
I COULD BLOW EVERYONE OFF US BUT SOMEONE'S SURE TO GET HURT.
NOT A PROBLEM.
THE BOSS TOLD ME TO LET THIS HAPPEN!
CHTOK
GAVE ME THESE GAS PELLETS.
KRIPP
WE WALK...
...BY PUTTIN' THE MOB TO SLEEP!

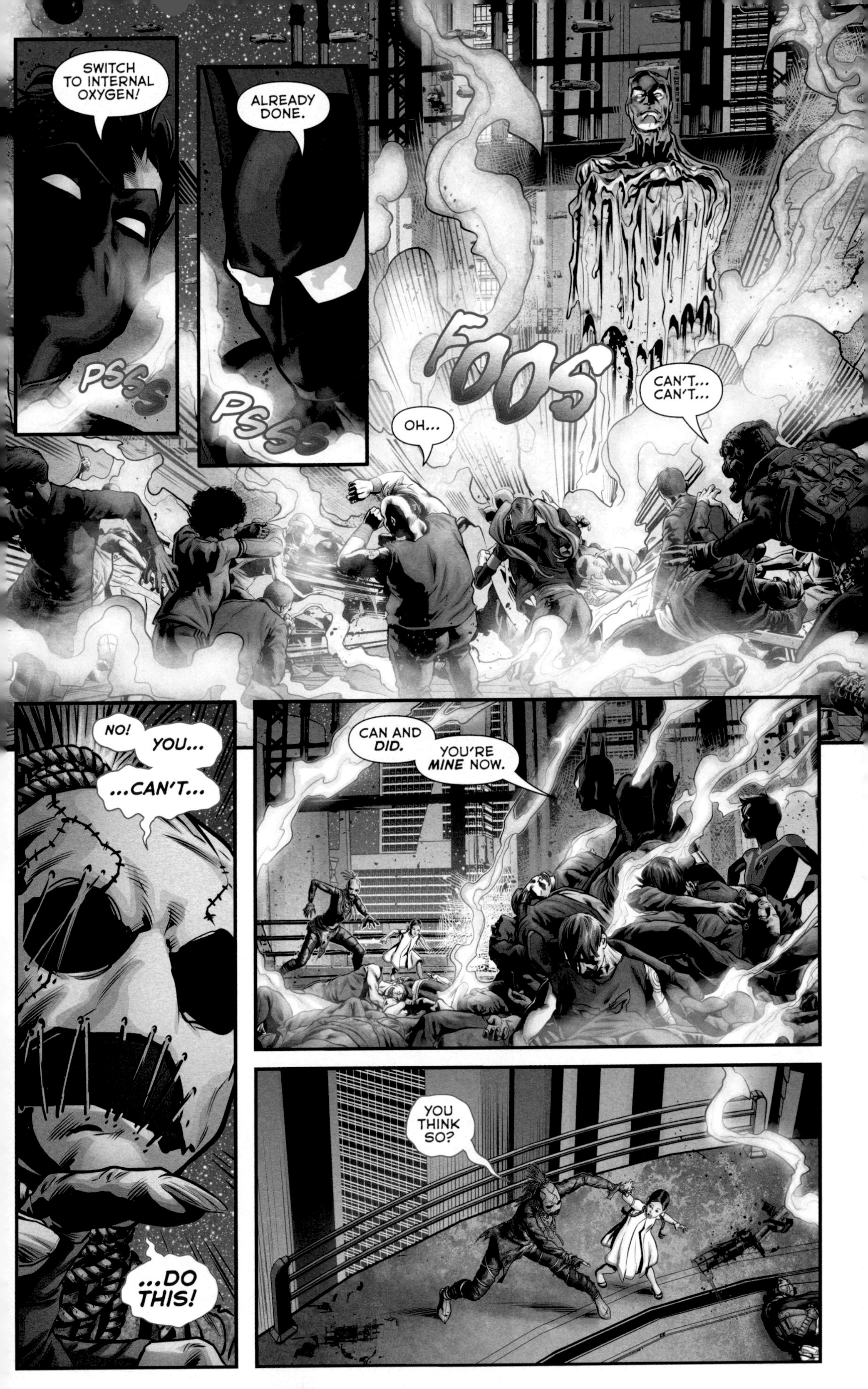
SWITCH TO INTERNAL OXYGEN!
PSSS
ALREADY DONE.
PSSS
FOOS
OH...
CAN'T... CAN'T...
NO!
YOU...
...CAN'T...
...DO THIS!
CAN AND DID.
YOU'RE MINE NOW.
YOU THINK SO?

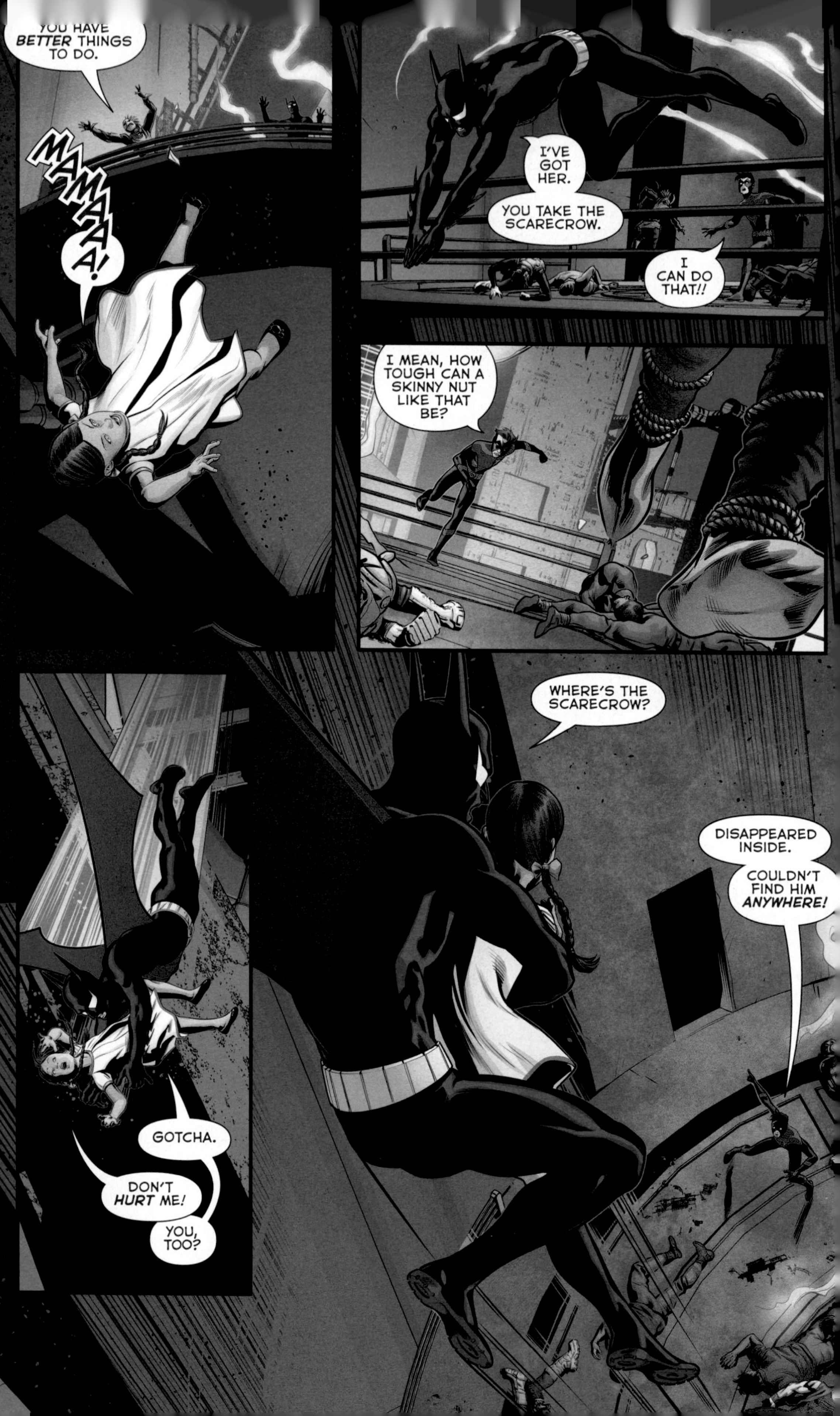
YOU HAVE BETTER THINGS TO DO.
MAMAAA!
I'VE GOT HER.
YOU TAKE THE SCARECROW.
I CAN DO THAT!!
I MEAN, HOW TOUGH CAN A SKINNY NUT LIKE THAT BE?
GOTCHA.
DON'T HURT ME!
YOU, TOO?
WHERE'S THE SCARECROW?
DISAPPEARED INSIDE.
COULDN'T FIND HIM ANYWHERE!

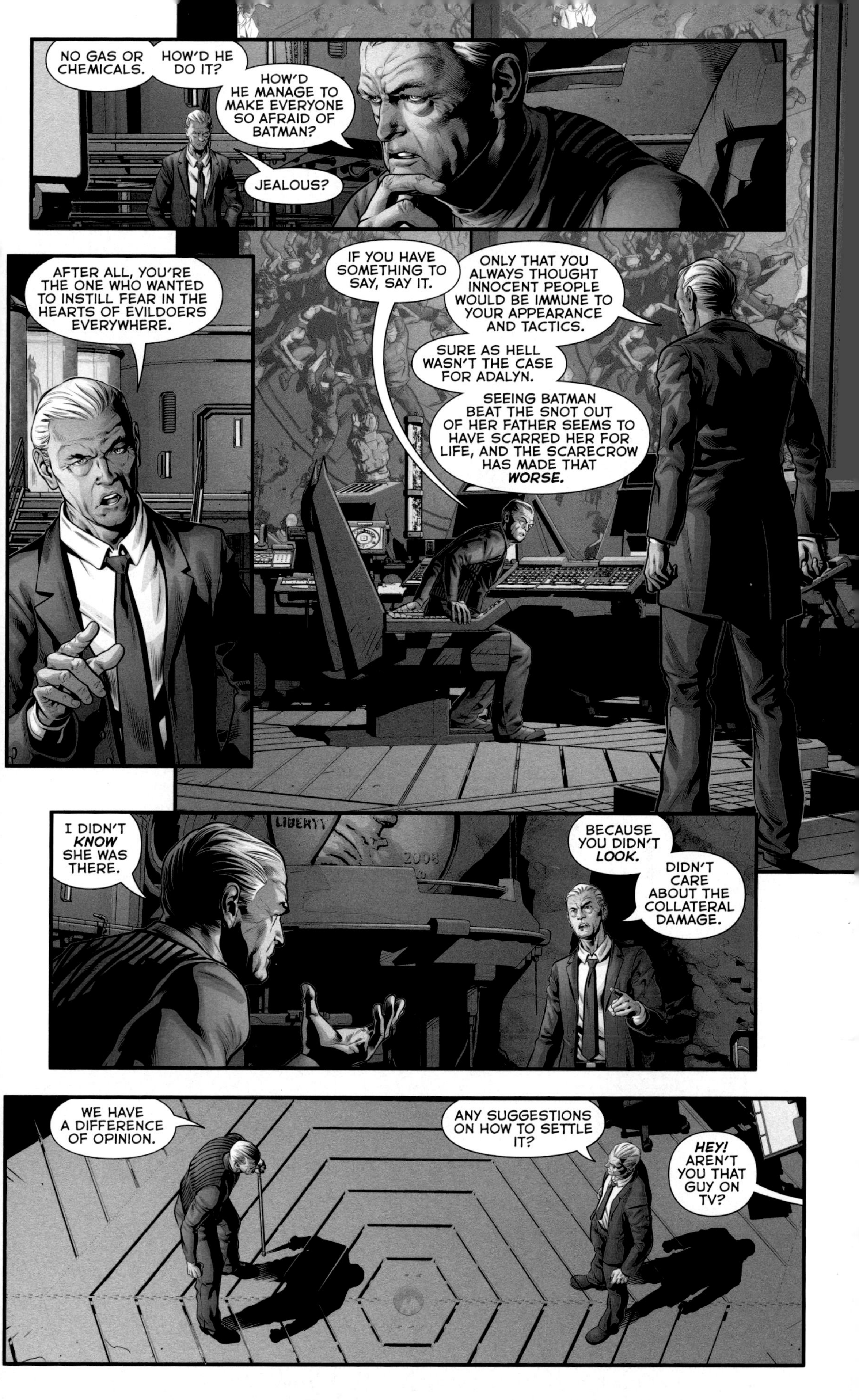
NO GAS OR CHEMICALS.
HOW'D HE DO IT?
HOW'D HE MANAGE TO MAKE EVERYONE SO AFRAID OF BATMAN?
JEALOUS?
AFTER ALL, YOU'RE THE ONE WHO WANTED TO INSTILL FEAR IN THE HEARTS OF EVILDOERS EVERYWHERE.
IF YOU HAVE SOMETHING TO SAY, SAY IT.
ONLY THAT YOU ALWAYS THOUGHT INNOCENT PEOPLE WOULD BE IMMUNE TO YOUR APPEARANCE AND TACTICS.
SURE AS HELL WASN'T THE CASE FOR ADALYN.
SEEING BATMAN BEAT THE SNOT OUT OF HER FATHER SEEMS TO HAVE SCARRED HER FOR LIFE, AND THE SCARECROW HAS MADE THAT ***WORSE.***
I DIDN'T ***KNOW*** SHE WAS THERE.
BECAUSE YOU DIDN'T ***LOOK.***
DIDN'T CARE ABOUT THE COLLATERAL DAMAGE.
WE HAVE A DIFFERENCE OF OPINION.
ANY SUGGESTIONS ON HOW TO SETTLE IT?
HEY! AREN'T YOU THAT GUY ON TV?

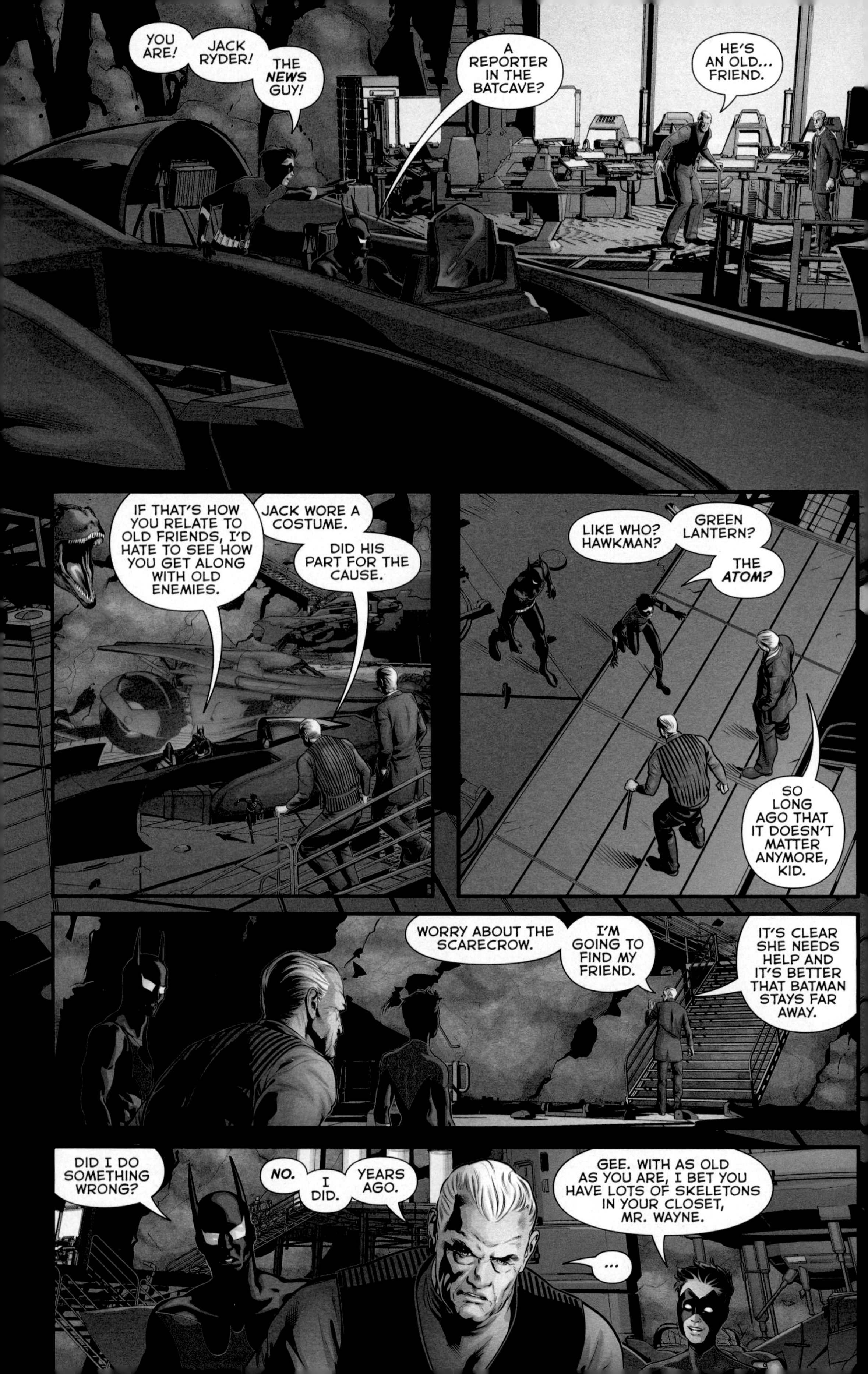
YOU ARE!
JACK RYDER!
THE NEWS GUY!
A REPORTER IN THE BATCAVE?
HE'S AN OLD... FRIEND.
IF THAT'S HOW YOU RELATE TO OLD FRIENDS, I'D HATE TO SEE HOW YOU GET ALONG WITH OLD ENEMIES.
JACK WORE A COSTUME.
DID HIS PART FOR THE CAUSE.
LIKE WHO? HAWKMAN?
GREEN LANTERN?
THE ATOM?
SO LONG AGO THAT IT DOESN'T MATTER ANYMORE, KID.
WORRY ABOUT THE SCARECROW.
I'M GOING TO FIND MY FRIEND.
IT'S CLEAR SHE NEEDS HELP AND IT'S BETTER THAT BATMAN STAYS FAR AWAY.
DID I DO SOMETHING WRONG?
NO.
I DID.
YEARS AGO.
GEE. WITH AS OLD AS YOU ARE, I BET YOU HAVE LOTS OF SKELETONS IN YOUR CLOSET, MR. WAYNE.
...

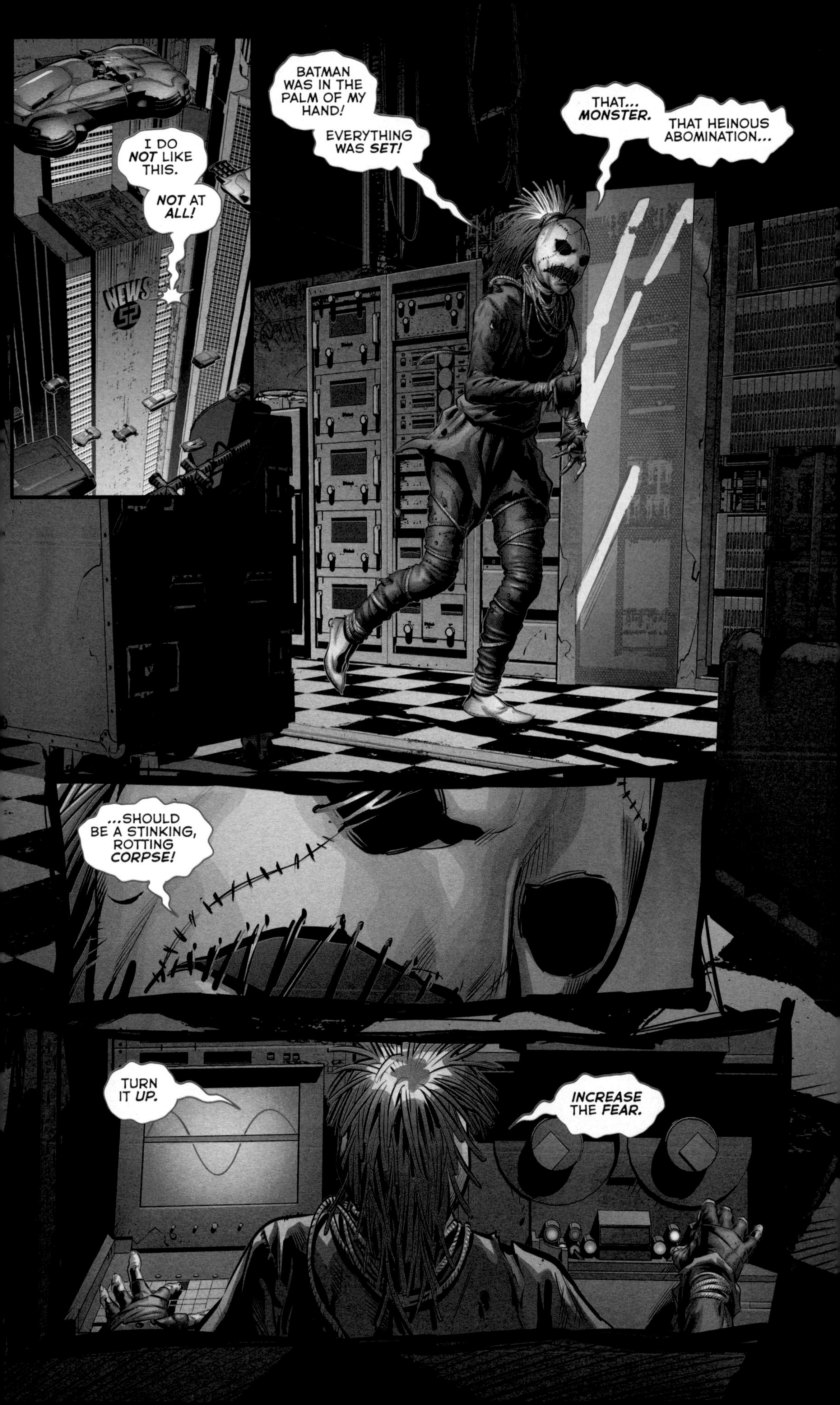
I DO NOT LIKE THIS.
NOT AT ALL!
NEWS 52
BATMAN WAS IN THE PALM OF MY HAND!
EVERYTHING WAS SET!
THAT... MONSTER.
THAT HEINOUS ABOMINATION...
...SHOULD BE A STINKING, ROTTING CORPSE!
TURN IT UP.
INCREASE THE FEAR.

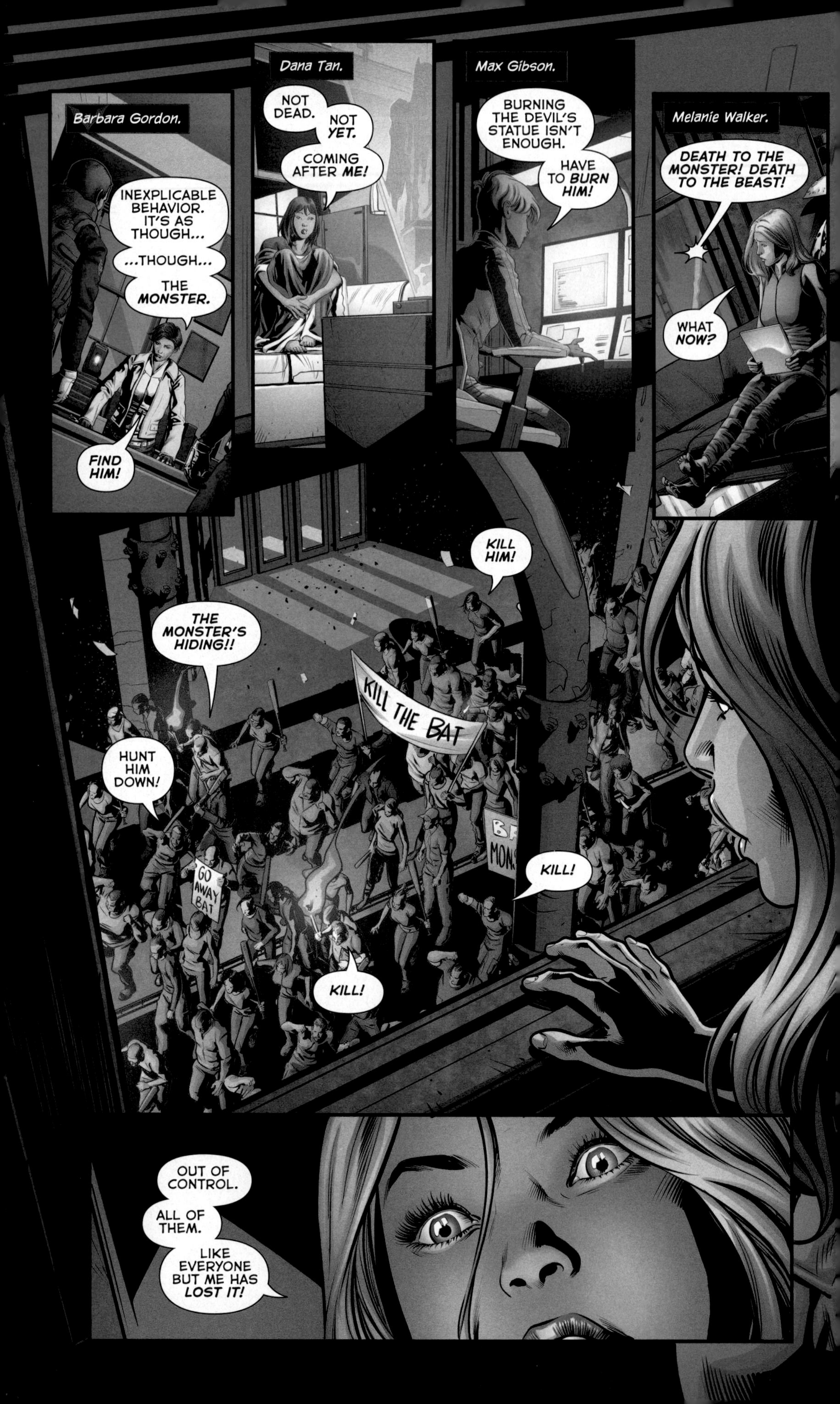

Barbara Gordon.
INEXPLICABLE BEHAVIOR. IT'S AS THOUGH...
...THOUGH...
THE MONSTER.
FIND HIM!
Dana Tan.
NOT DEAD.
NOT YET.
COMING AFTER ME!
Max Gibson.
BURNING THE DEVIL'S STATUE ISN'T ENOUGH.
HAVE TO BURN HIM!
Melanie Walker.
DEATH TO THE MONSTER! DEATH TO THE BEAST!
WHAT NOW?
KILL HIM!
THE MONSTER'S HIDING!!
KILL THE BAT
HUNT HIM DOWN!
GO AWAY BAT
KILL!
KILL!
OUT OF CONTROL.
ALL OF THEM.
LIKE EVERYONE BUT ME HAS LOST IT!

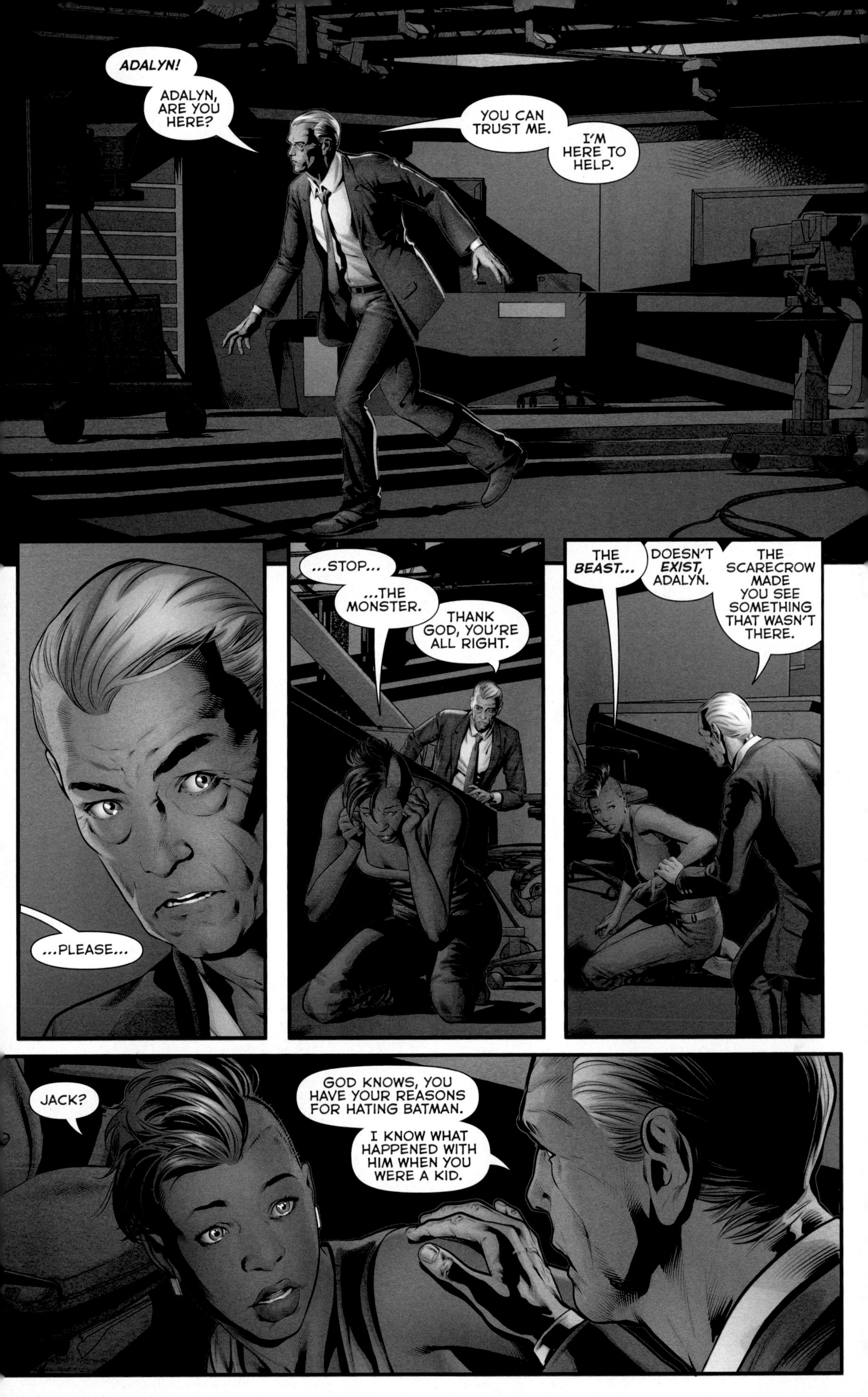
ADALYN!
ADALYN, ARE YOU HERE?
YOU CAN TRUST ME.
I'M HERE TO HELP.
...PLEASE...
...STOP...
...THE MONSTER.
THANK GOD, YOU'RE ALL RIGHT.
THE BEAST...
DOESN'T EXIST, ADALYN.
THE SCARECROW MADE YOU SEE SOMETHING THAT WASN'T THERE.
JACK?
GOD KNOWS, YOU HAVE YOUR REASONS FOR HATING BATMAN.
I KNOW WHAT HAPPENED WITH HIM WHEN YOU WERE A KID.

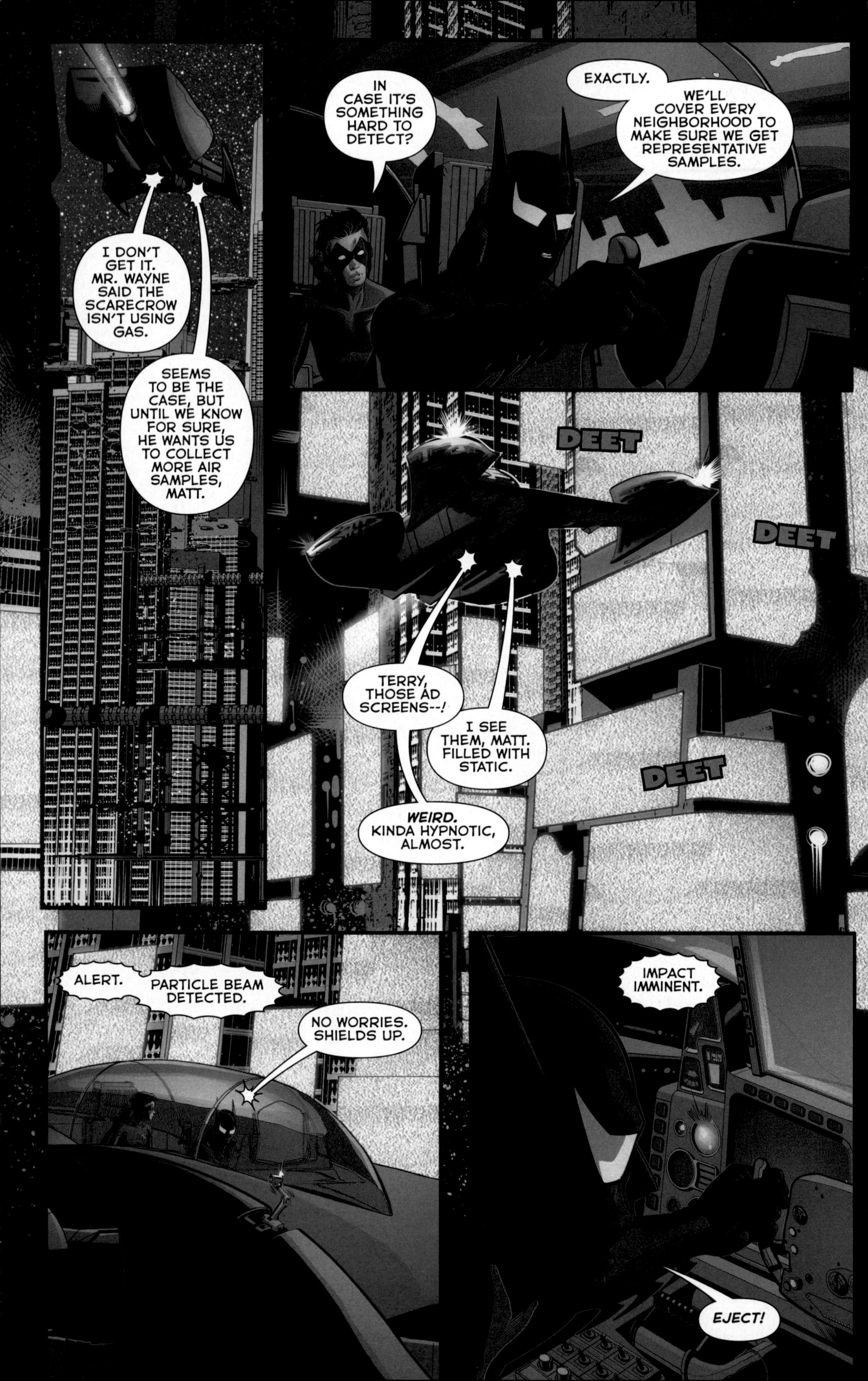
I DON'T GET IT. MR. WAYNE SAID THE SCARECROW ISN'T USING GAS.
SEEMS TO BE THE CASE, BUT UNTIL WE KNOW FOR SURE, HE WANTS US TO COLLECT MORE AIR SAMPLES, MATT.
IN CASE IT'S SOMETHING HARD TO DETECT?
EXACTLY.
WE'LL COVER EVERY NEIGHBORHOOD TO MAKE SURE WE GET REPRESENTATIVE SAMPLES.
DEET
DEET
DEET
TERRY, THOSE AD SCREENS--!
I SEE THEM, MATT. FILLED WITH STATIC.
WEIRD. KINDA HYPNOTIC, ALMOST.
ALERT.
PARTICLE BEAM DETECTED.
NO WORRIES. SHIELDS UP.
IMPACT IMMINENT.
EJECT!

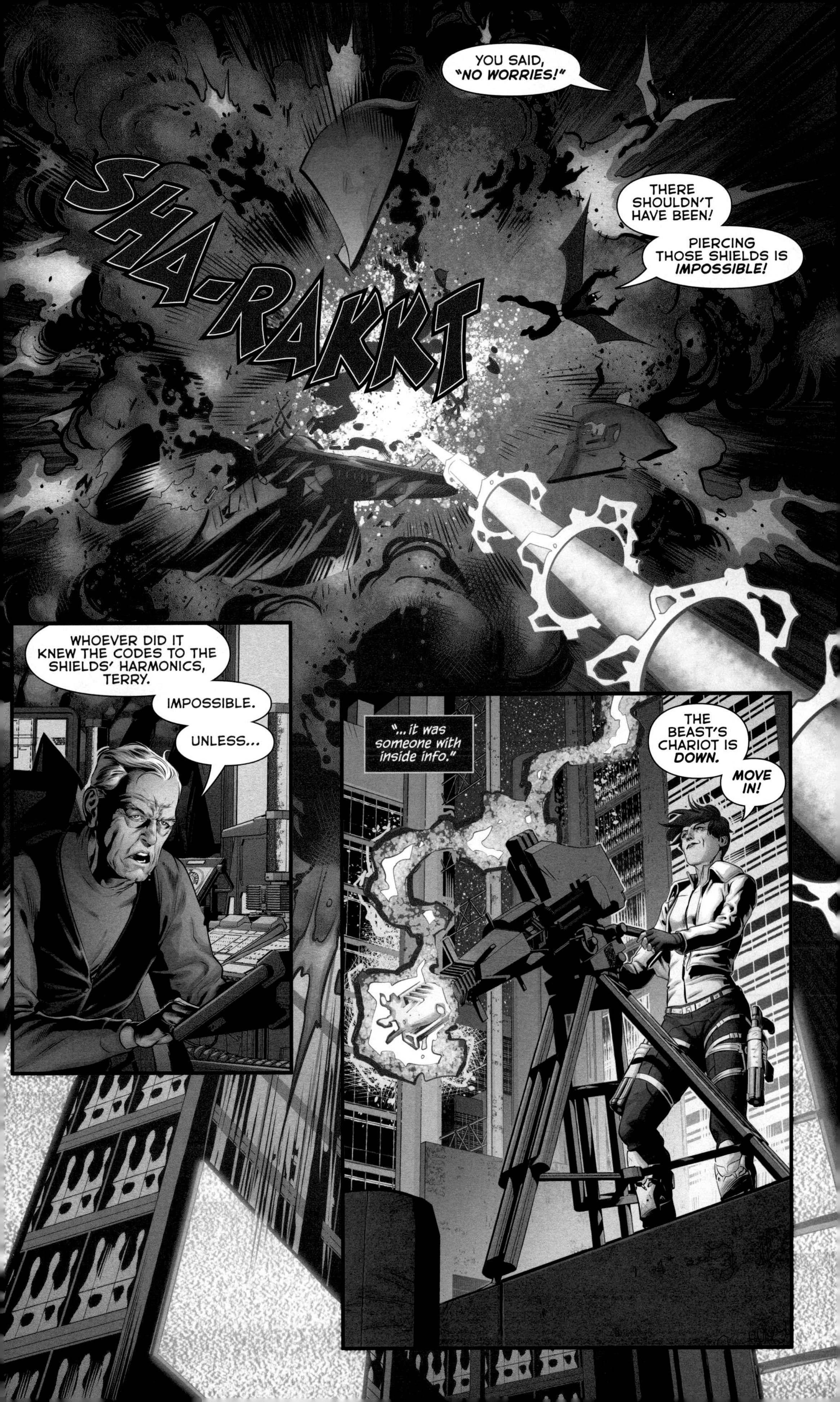
YOU SAID, "NO WORRIES!"
SHA-RAKKT
THERE SHOULDN'T HAVE BEEN!
PIERCING THOSE SHIELDS IS IMPOSSIBLE!
WHOEVER DID IT KNEW THE CODES TO THE SHIELDS' HARMONICS, TERRY.
IMPOSSIBLE.
UNLESS...
"...it was someone with inside info."
THE BEAST'S CHARIOT IS DOWN.
MOVE IN!

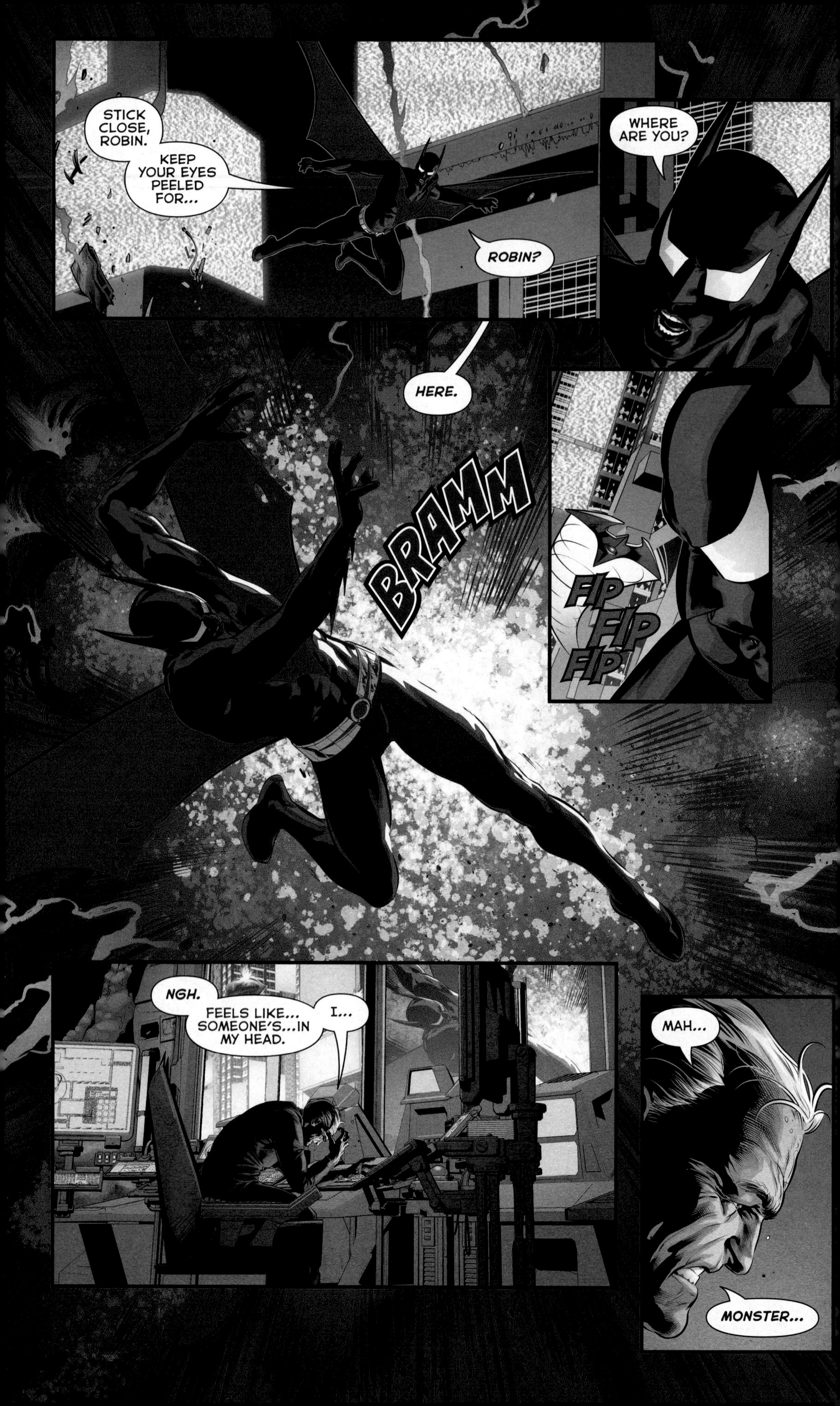
STICK CLOSE, ROBIN.
KEEP YOUR EYES PEELED FOR...
ROBIN?
WHERE ARE YOU?
HERE.
BRAMM
FIP FIP FIP
NGH.
FEELS LIKE... SOMEONE'S...IN MY HEAD.
I...
MAH...
MONSTER...

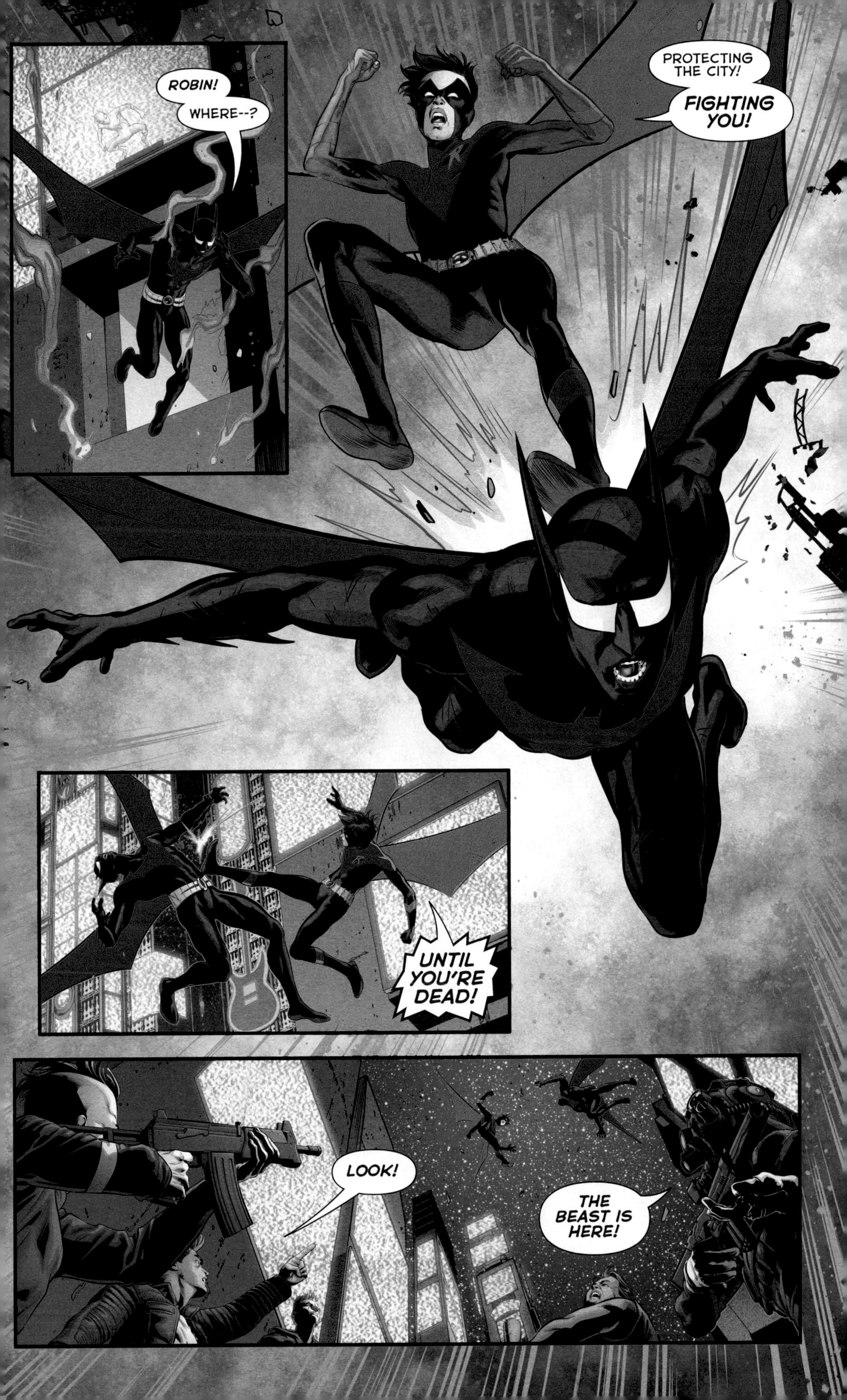
ROBIN!
WHERE--?
PROTECTING THE CITY!
FIGHTING YOU!
UNTIL YOU'RE DEAD!
LOOK!
THE BEAST IS HERE!

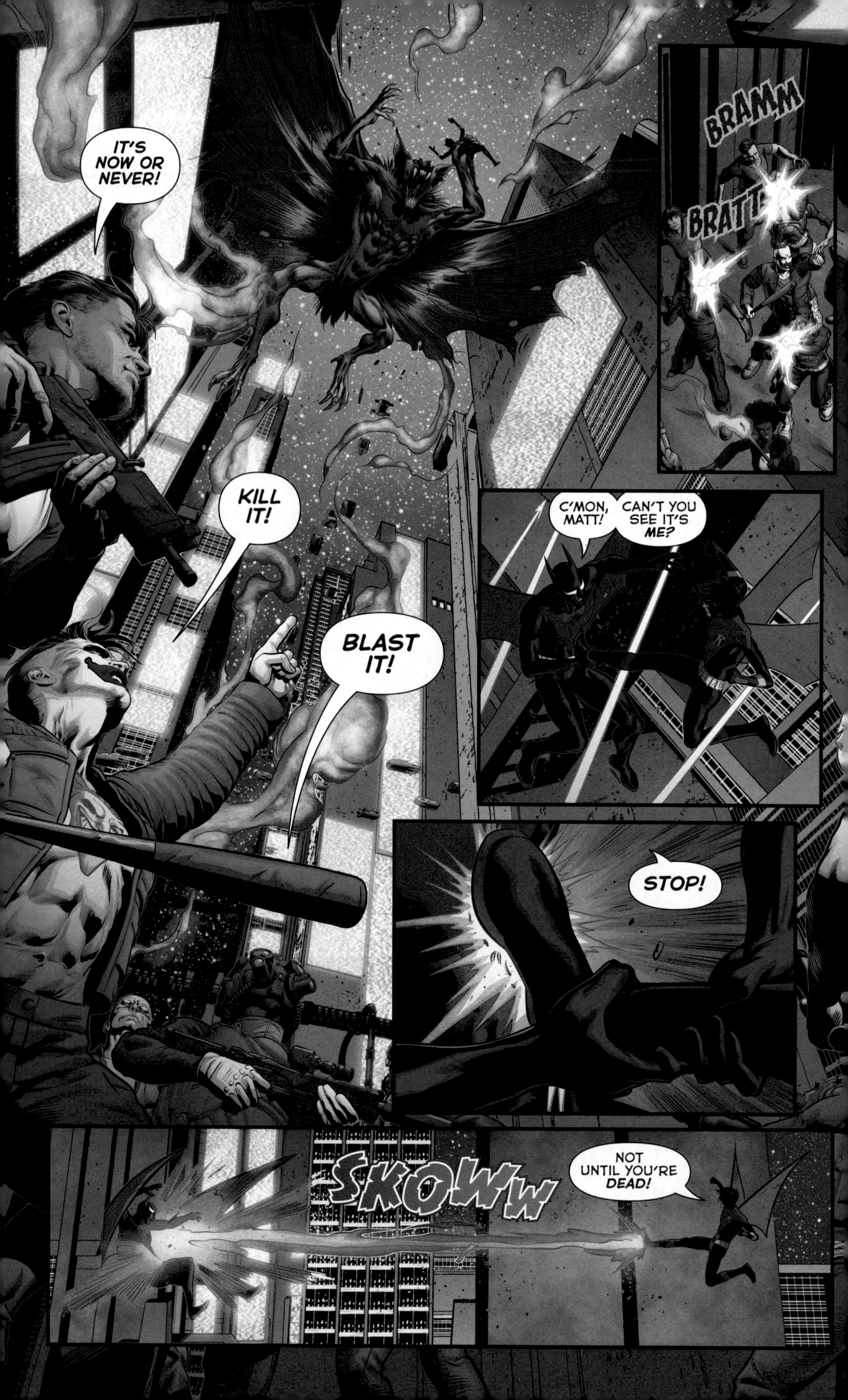
IT'S NOW OR NEVER!
KILL IT!
BLAST IT!
BRAMM
BRATT
C'MON, MATT!
CAN'T YOU SEE IT'S ME?
STOP!
SKOWW
NOT UNTIL YOU'RE DEAD!

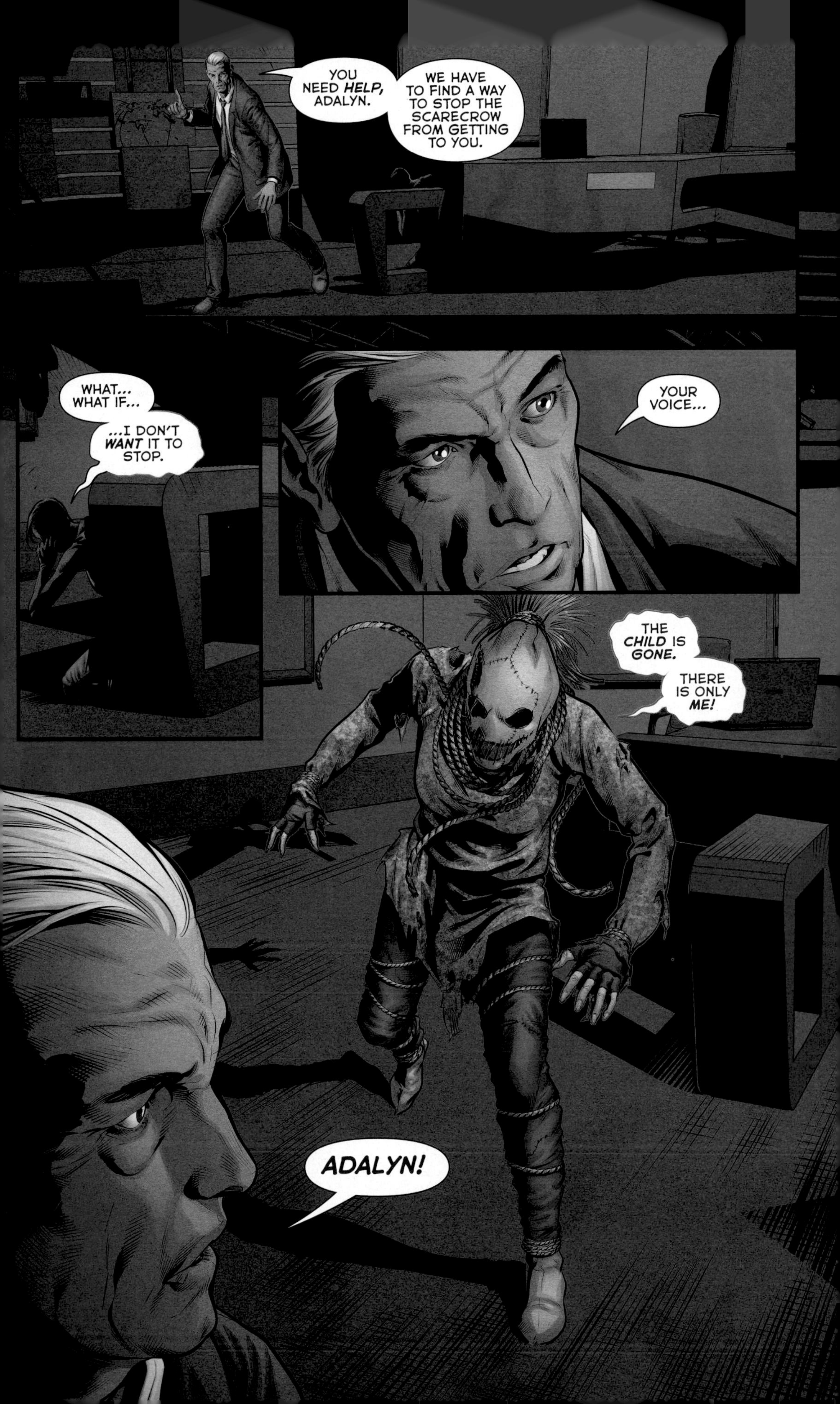
YOU NEED HELP, ADALYN.
WE HAVE TO FIND A WAY TO STOP THE SCARECROW FROM GETTING TO YOU.
WHAT... WHAT IF...
...I DON'T WANT IT TO STOP.
YOUR VOICE...
THE CHILD IS GONE.
THERE IS ONLY ME!
ADALYN!

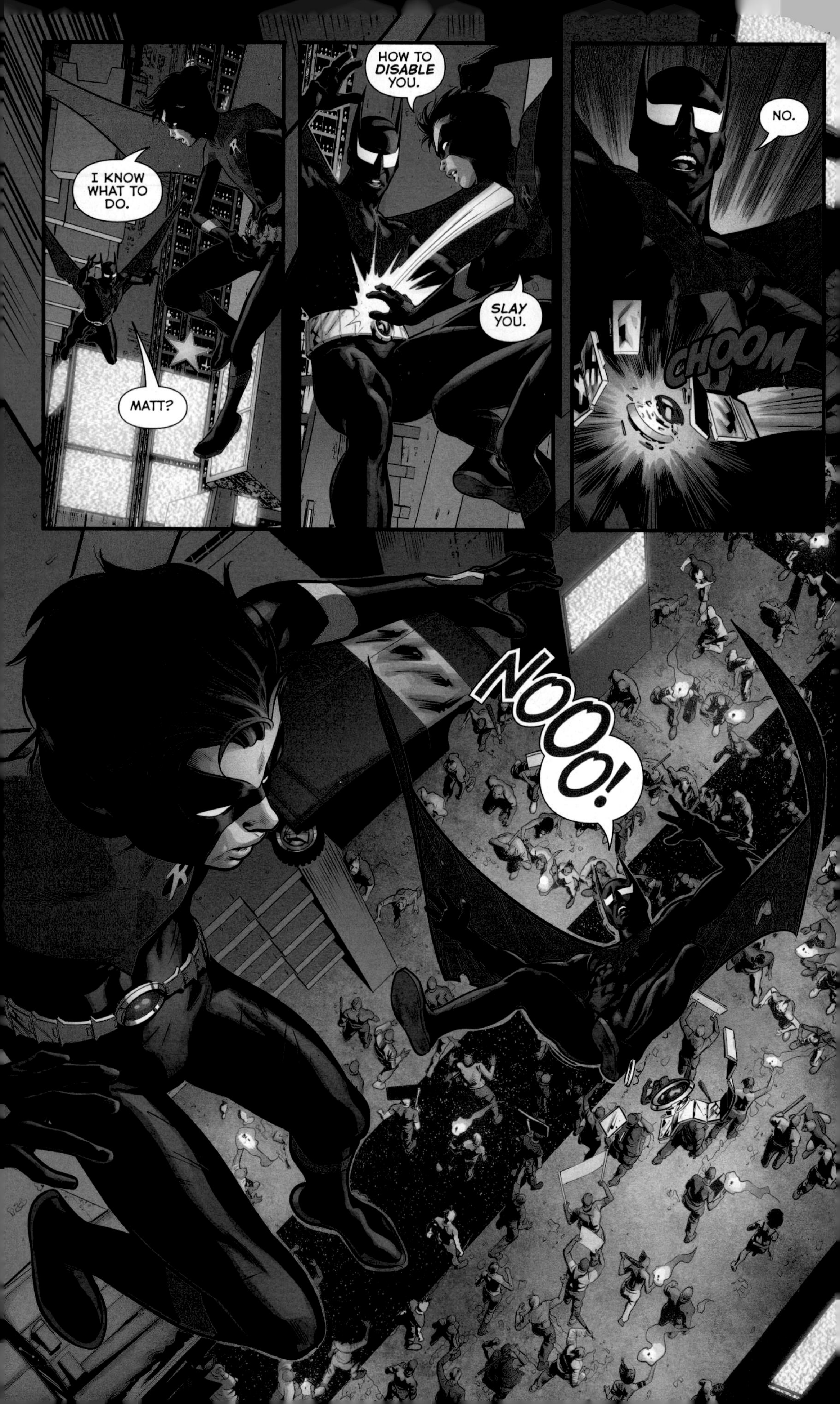
I KNOW WHAT TO DO.
MATT?
HOW TO DISABLE YOU.
SLAY YOU.
NO.
CHOOM
NOOO!

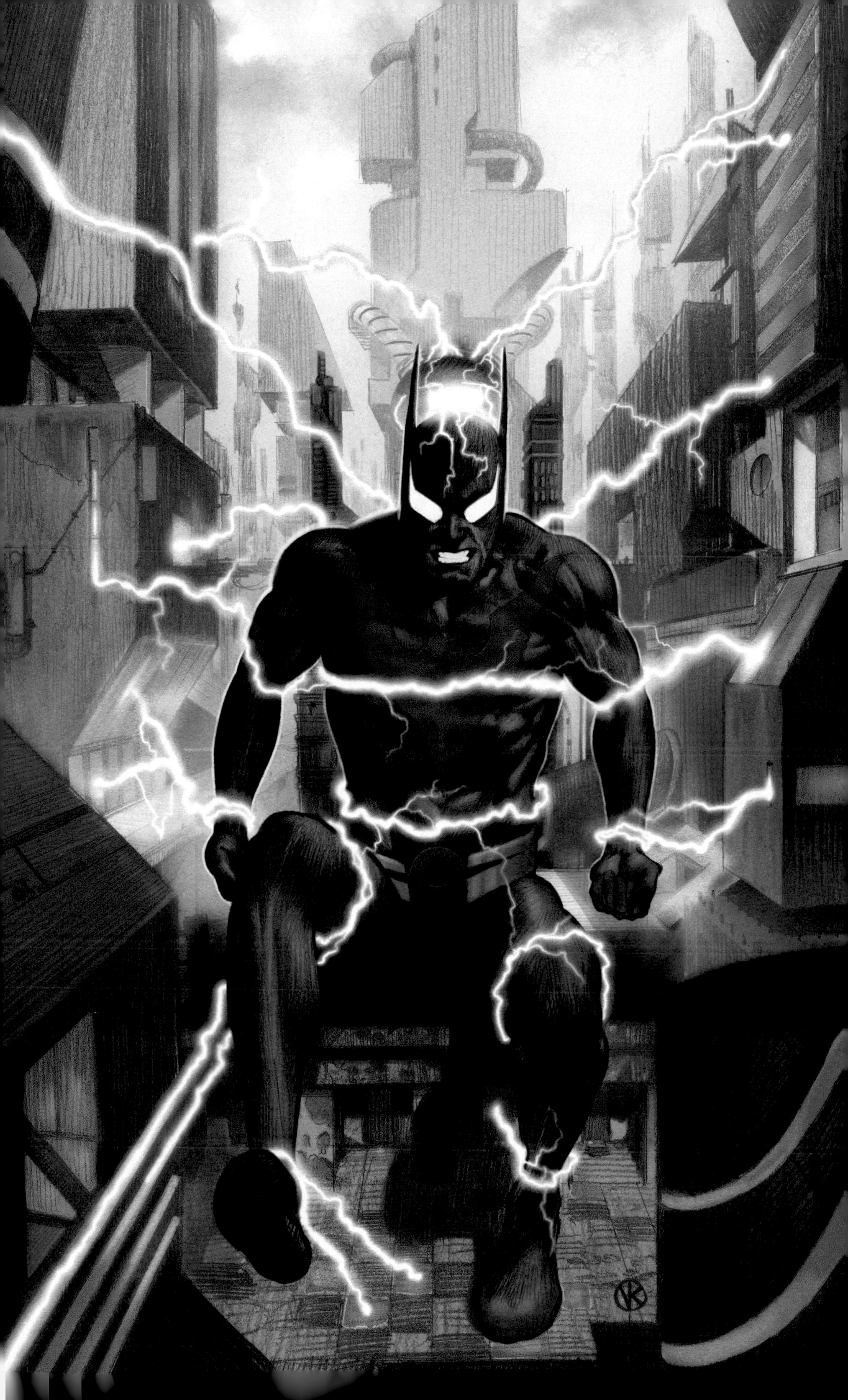

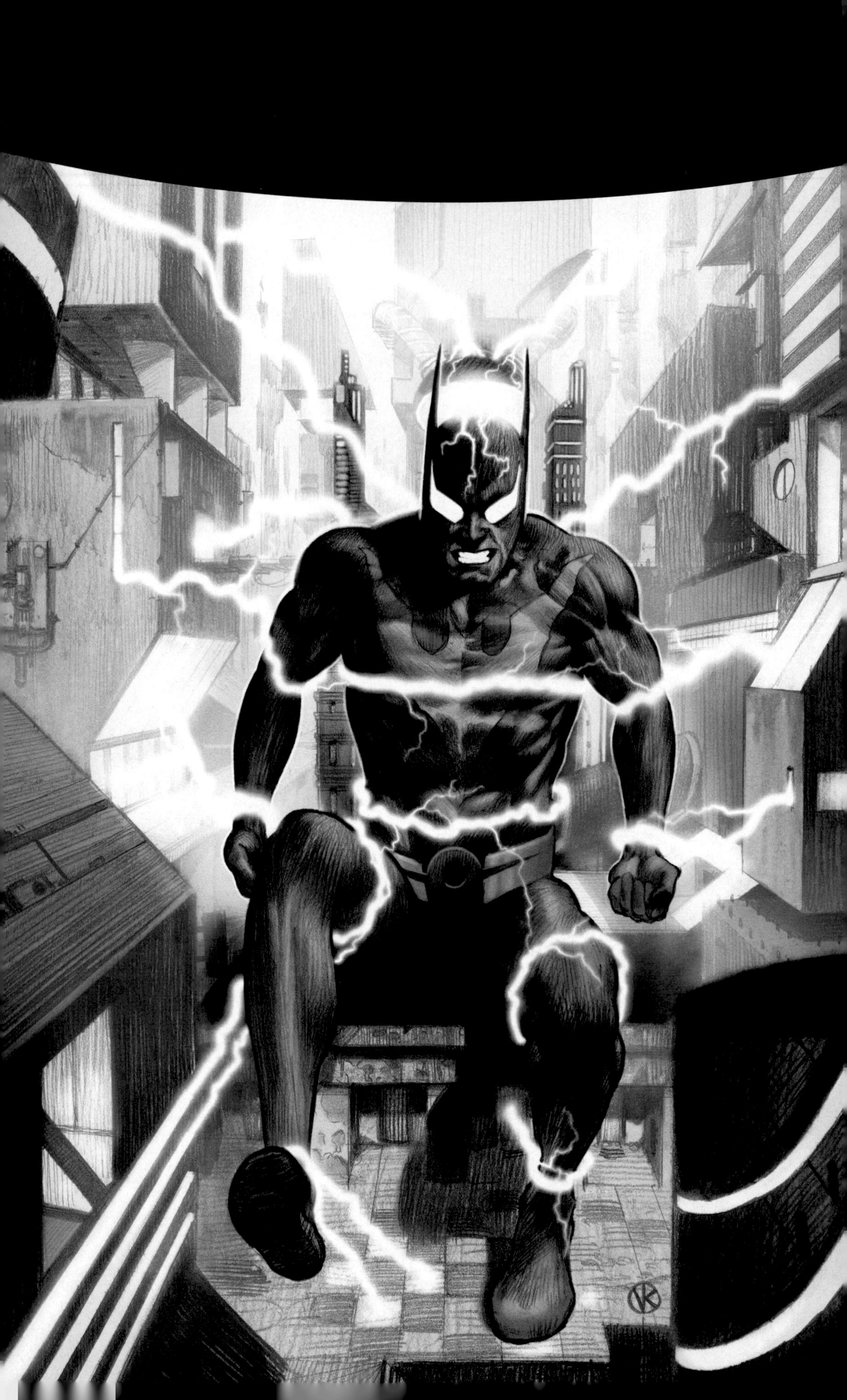

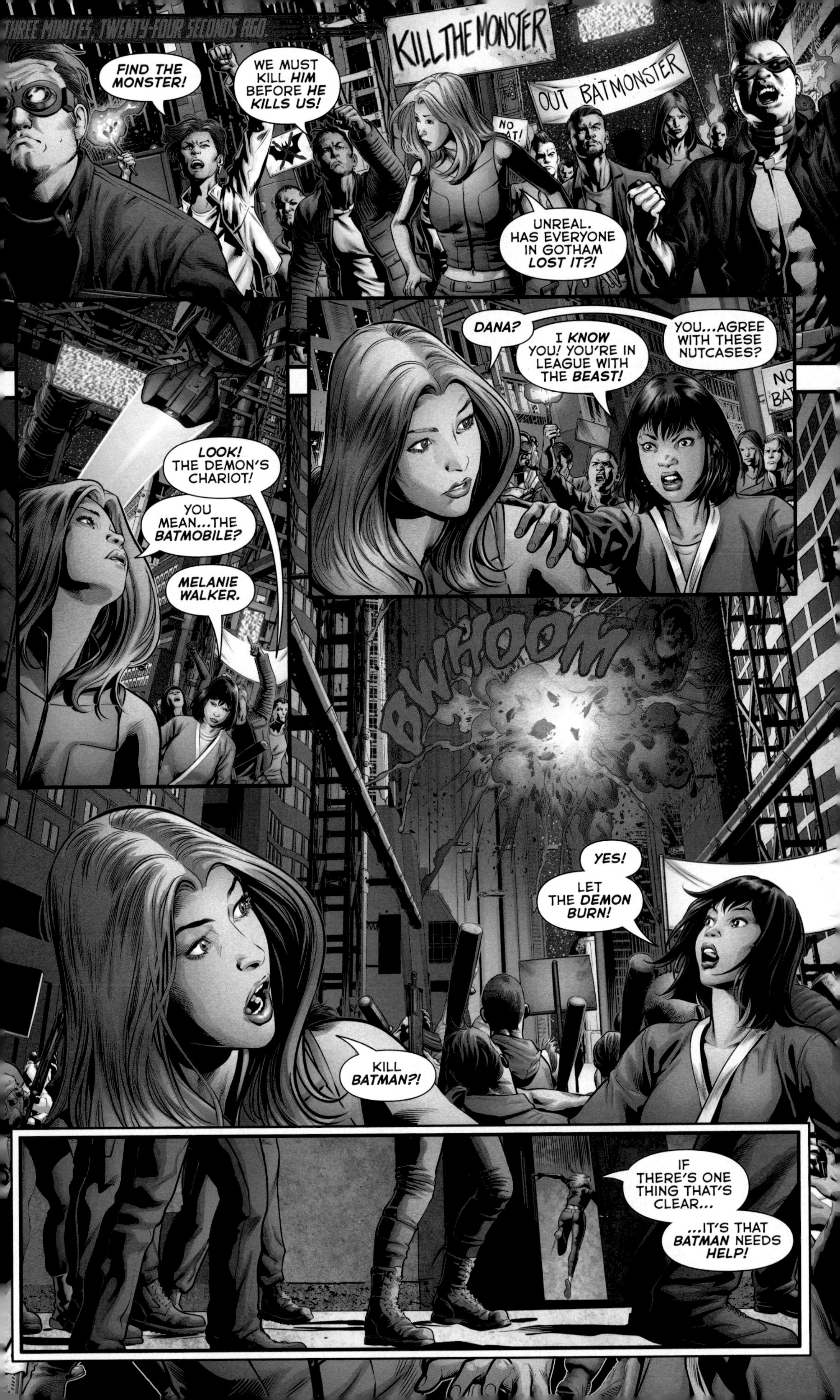
THREE MINUTES, TWENTY-FOUR SECONDS AGO.
KILL THE MONSTER
OUT BATMONSTER
FIND THE MONSTER!
WE MUST KILL HIM BEFORE HE KILLS US!
UNREAL. HAS EVERYONE IN GOTHAM LOST IT?!
DANA?
I KNOW YOU! YOU'RE IN LEAGUE WITH THE BEAST!
YOU...AGREE WITH THESE NUTCASES?
LOOK! THE DEMON'S CHARIOT!
YOU MEAN...THE BATMOBILE?
MELANIE WALKER.
BWHOOM
YES!
LET THE DEMON BURN!
KILL BATMAN?!
IF THERE'S ONE THING THAT'S CLEAR...
...IT'S THAT BATMAN NEEDS HELP!

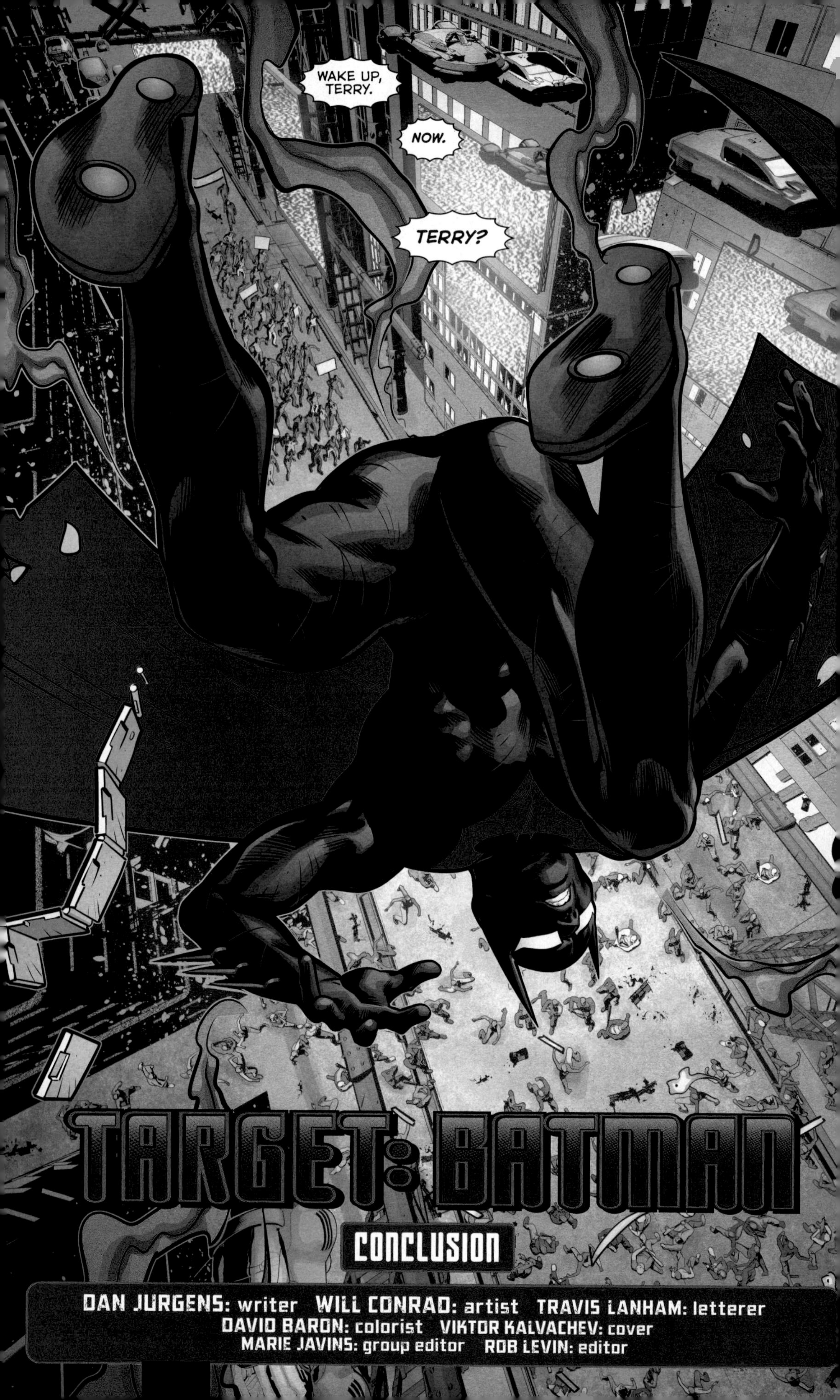
WAKE UP, TERRY.
NOW.
TERRY?
TARGET: BATMAN
CONCLUSION
DAN JURGENS: writer WILL CONRAD: artist TRAVIS LANHAM: letterer
DAVID BARON: colorist VIKTOR KALVACHEV: cover
MARIE JAVINS: group editor ROB LEVIN: editor

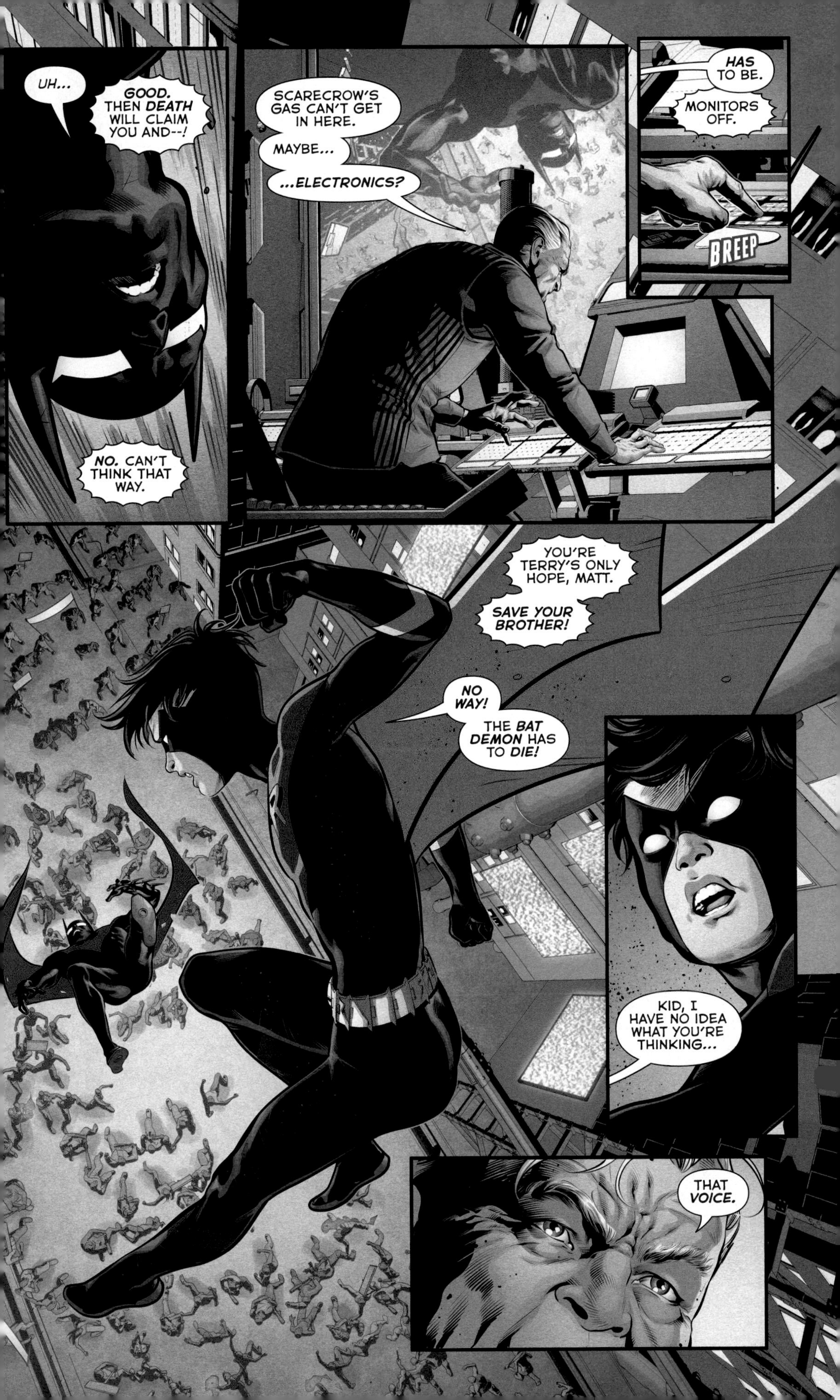

UH...
GOOD. THEN DEATH WILL CLAIM YOU AND--!
NO. CAN'T THINK THAT WAY.
SCARECROW'S GAS CAN'T GET IN HERE.
MAYBE...
...ELECTRONICS?
HAS TO BE.
MONITORS OFF.
BREEP
YOU'RE TERRY'S ONLY HOPE, MATT.
SAVE YOUR BROTHER!
NO WAY!
THE BAT DEMON HAS TO DIE!
KID, I HAVE NO IDEA WHAT YOU'RE THINKING...
THAT VOICE.

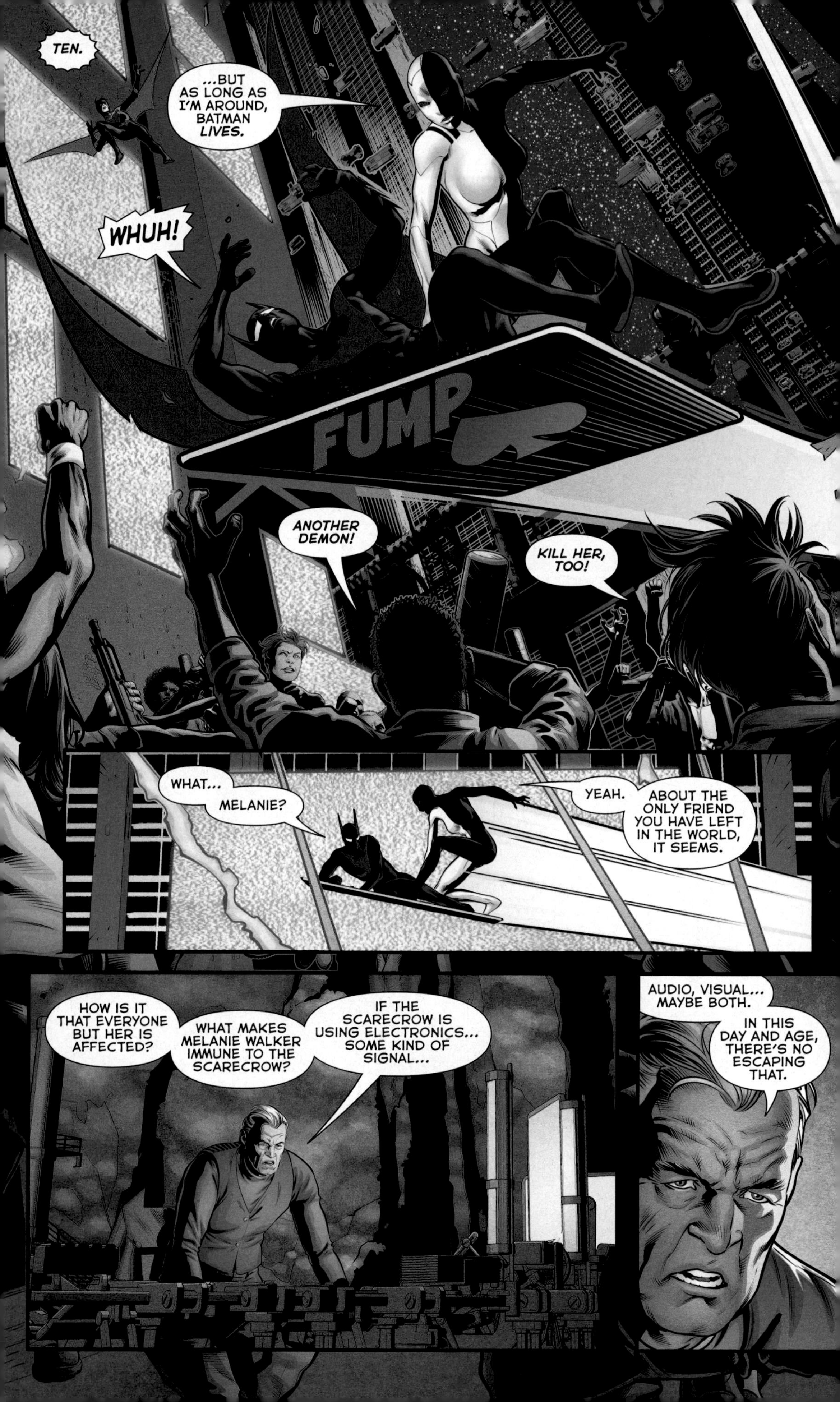
TEN.
...BUT AS LONG AS I'M AROUND, BATMAN *LIVES.*
WHUH!
FUMP
ANOTHER DEMON!
KILL HER, TOO!
WHAT...
MELANIE?
YEAH.
ABOUT THE ONLY FRIEND YOU HAVE LEFT IN THE WORLD, IT SEEMS.
HOW IS IT THAT EVERYONE BUT HER IS AFFECTED?
WHAT MAKES MELANIE WALKER IMMUNE TO THE SCARECROW?
IF THE SCARECROW IS USING ELECTRONICS... SOME KIND OF SIGNAL...
AUDIO, VISUAL... MAYBE BOTH.
IN THIS DAY AND AGE, THERE'S NO ESCAPING THAT.

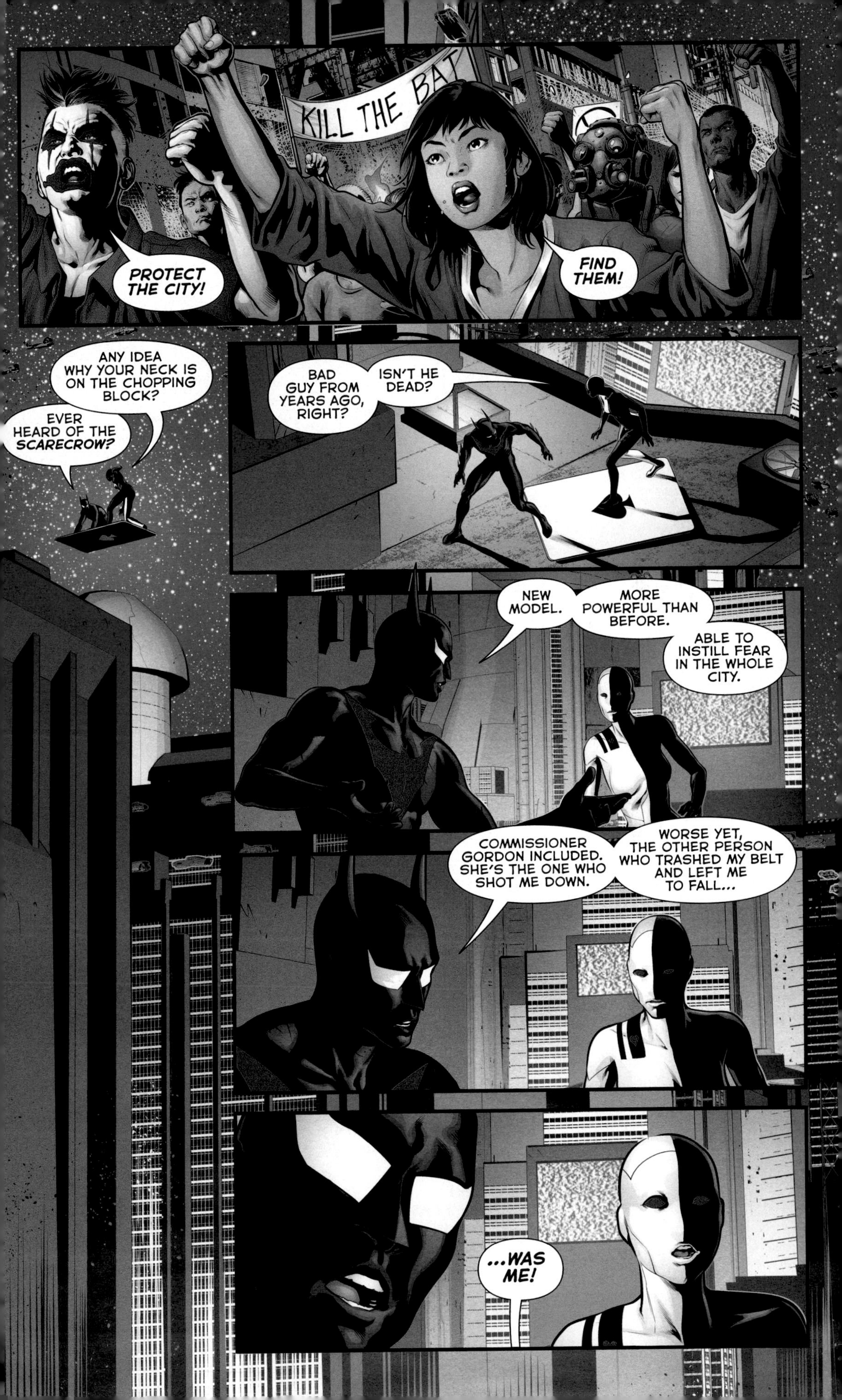
KILL THE BAT
PROTECT THE CITY!
FIND THEM!
ANY IDEA WHY YOUR NECK IS ON THE CHOPPING BLOCK?
EVER HEARD OF THE SCARECROW?
BAD GUY FROM YEARS AGO, RIGHT?
ISN'T HE DEAD?
NEW MODEL.
MORE POWERFUL THAN BEFORE.
ABLE TO INSTILL FEAR IN THE WHOLE CITY.
COMMISSIONER GORDON INCLUDED. SHE'S THE ONE WHO SHOT ME DOWN.
WORSE YET, THE OTHER PERSON WHO TRASHED MY BELT AND LEFT ME TO FALL...
...WAS ME!

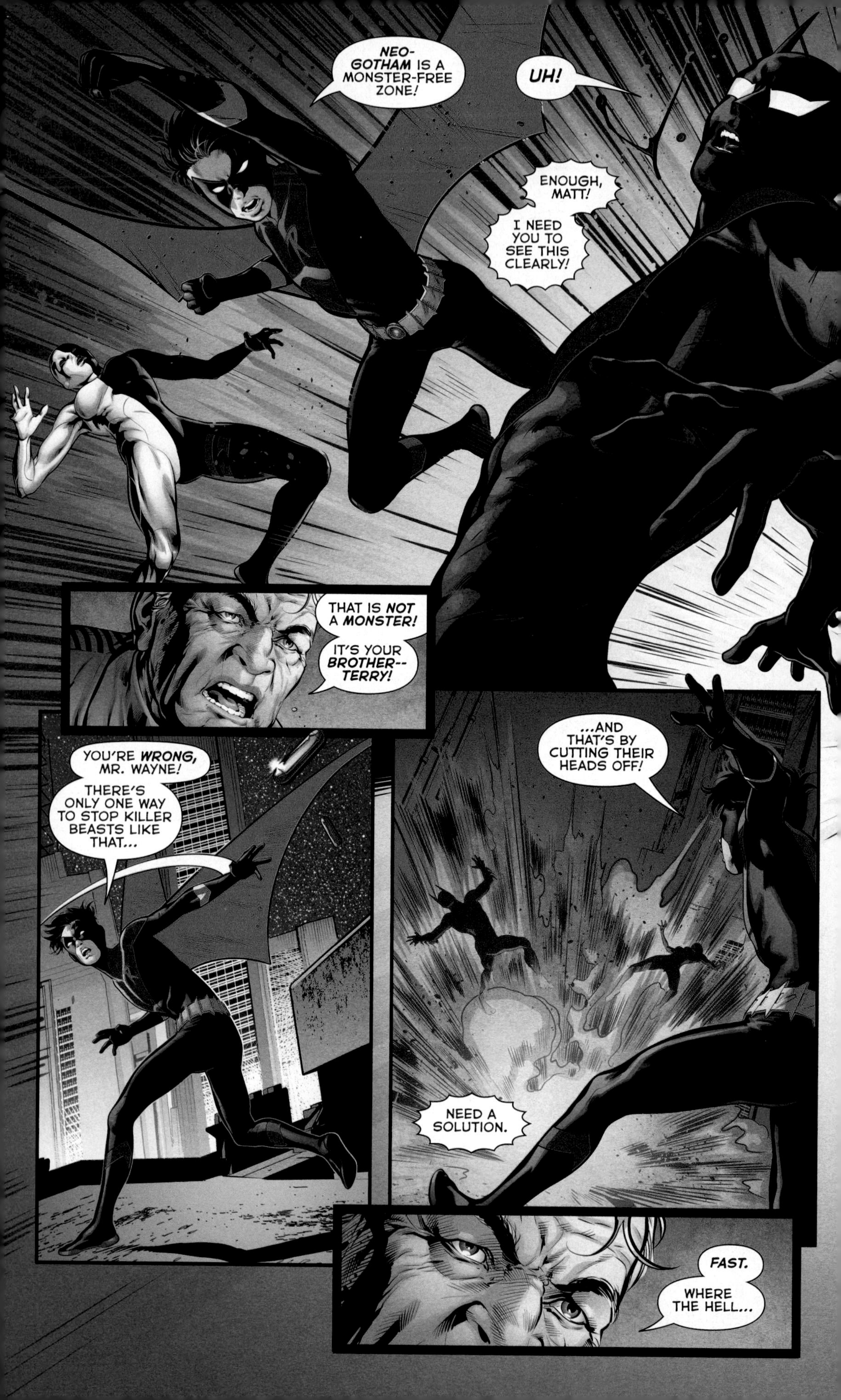

NEO-GOTHAM IS A MONSTER-FREE ZONE!
UH!
ENOUGH, MATT!
I NEED YOU TO SEE THIS CLEARLY!
THAT IS NOT A MONSTER!
IT'S YOUR BROTHER-- TERRY!
YOU'RE WRONG, MR. WAYNE!
THERE'S ONLY ONE WAY TO STOP KILLER BEASTS LIKE THAT...
...AND THAT'S BY CUTTING THEIR HEADS OFF!
NEED A SOLUTION.
FAST.
WHERE THE HELL...

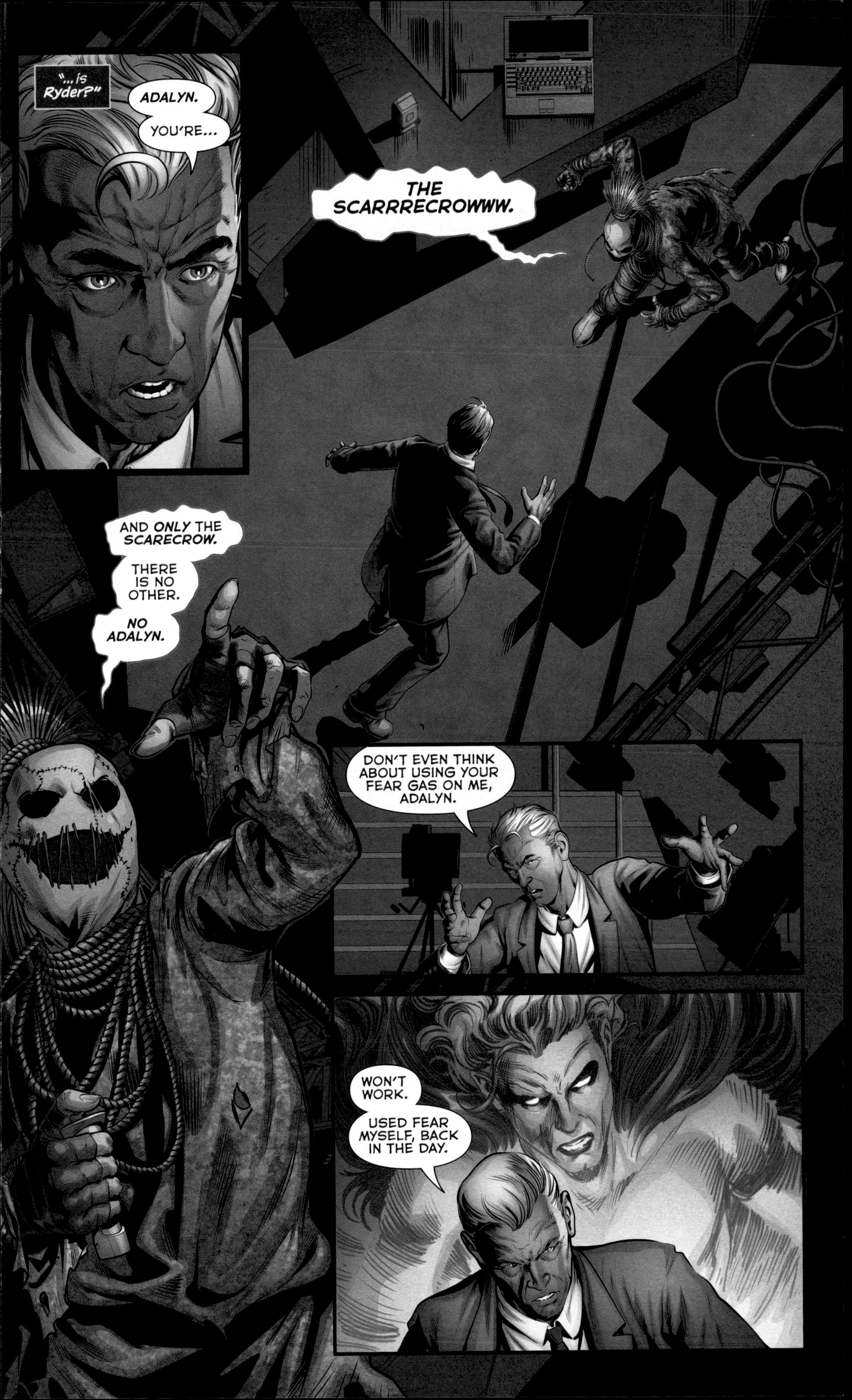
"...is Ryder?"
ADALYN.
YOU'RE...
THE SCARRRECROWWW.
AND ONLY THE SCARECROW.
THERE IS NO OTHER.
NO ADALYN.
DON'T EVEN THINK ABOUT USING YOUR FEAR GAS ON ME, ADALYN.
WON'T WORK.
USED FEAR MYSELF, BACK IN THE DAY.

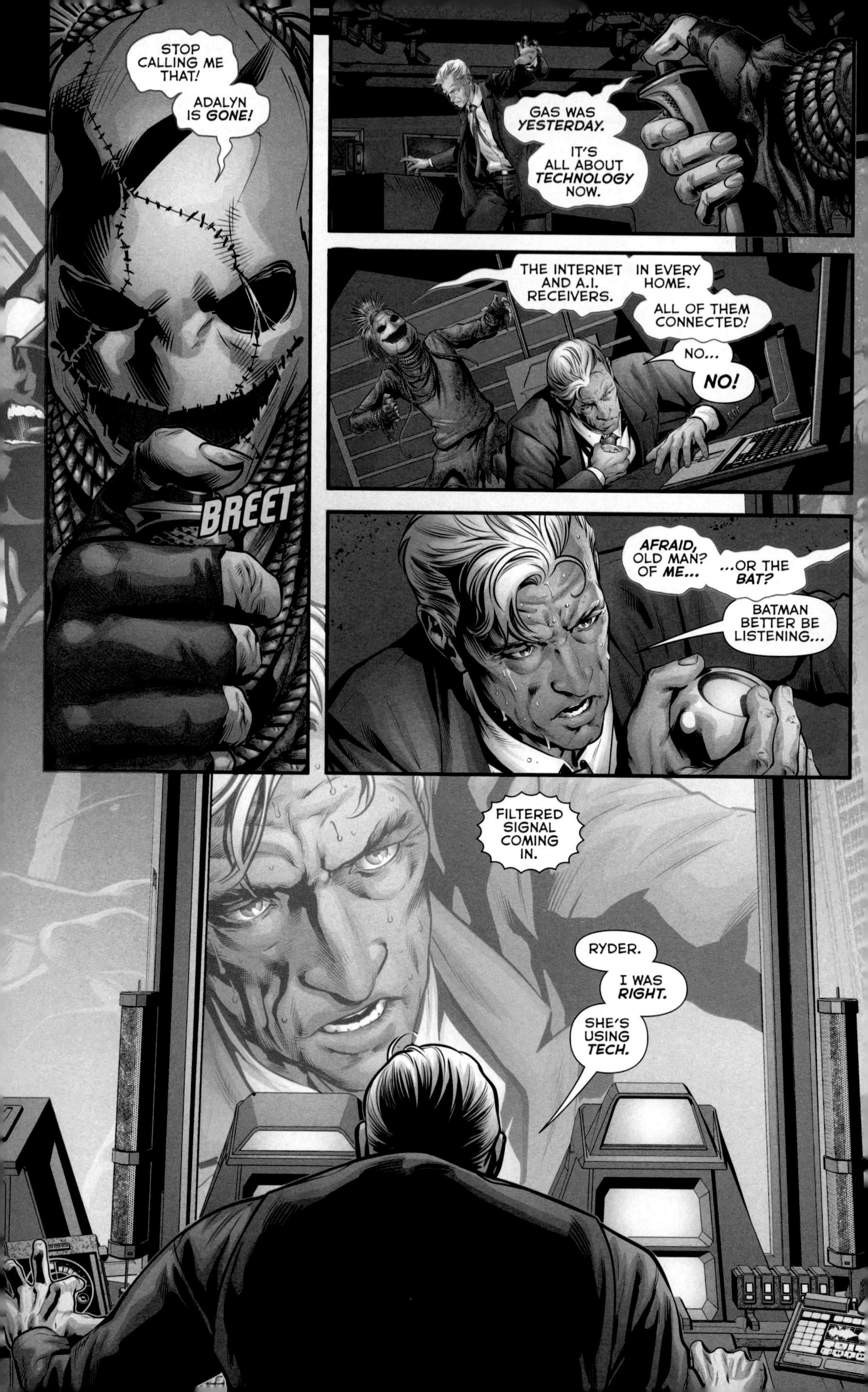
STOP CALLING ME THAT!
ADALYN IS *GONE!*
BREET
GAS WAS *YESTERDAY.*
IT'S ALL ABOUT *TECHNOLOGY* NOW.
THE INTERNET AND A.I. RECEIVERS.
IN EVERY HOME.
ALL OF THEM CONNECTED!
NO...
NO!
AFRAID, OLD MAN? OF *ME...*
...OR THE *BAT?*
BATMAN BETTER BE LISTENING...
FILTERED SIGNAL COMING IN.
RYDER.
I WAS *RIGHT.*
SHE'S USING *TECH.*

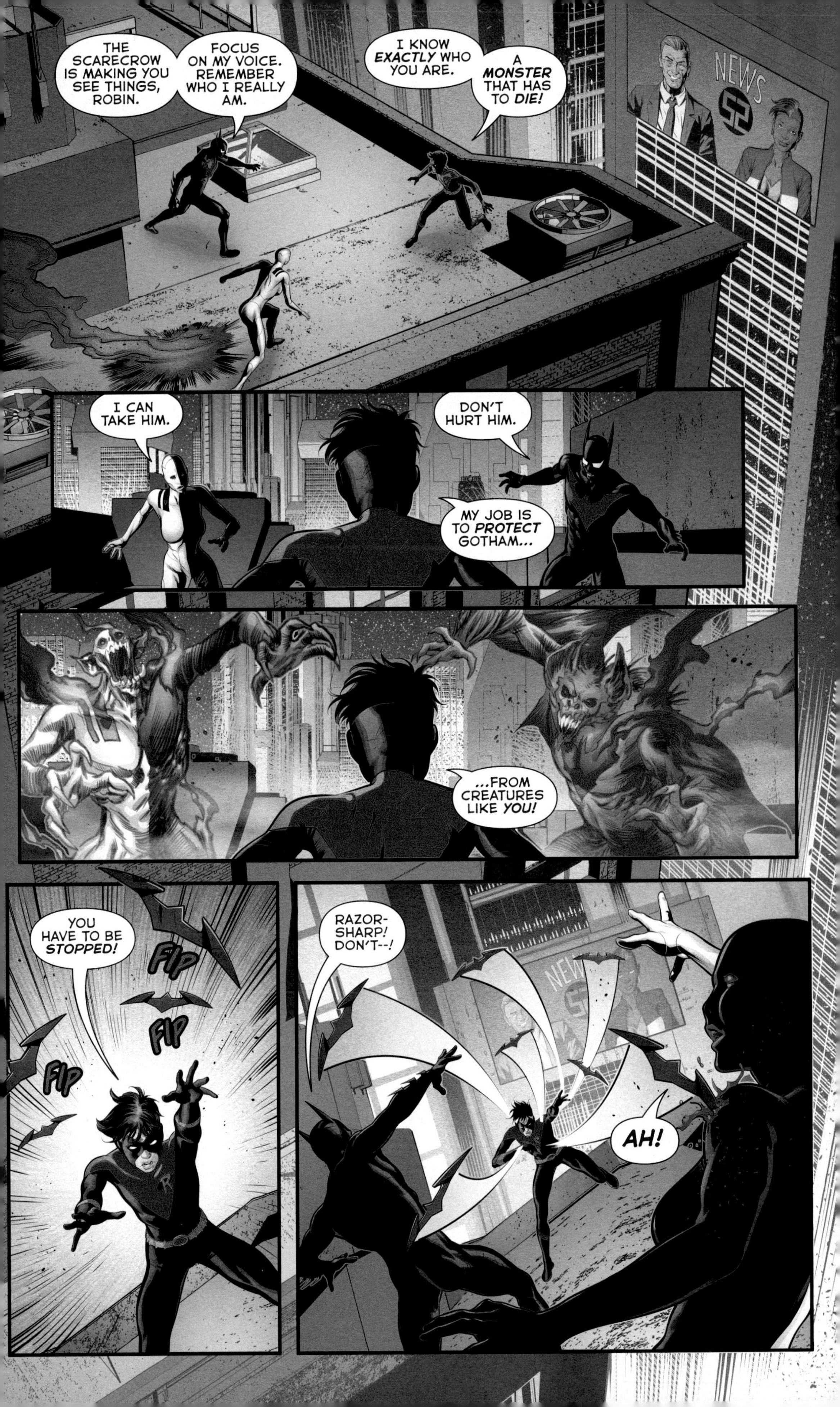
THE SCARECROW IS MAKING YOU SEE THINGS, ROBIN.
FOCUS ON MY VOICE. REMEMBER WHO I REALLY AM.
I KNOW *EXACTLY* WHO YOU ARE.
A *MONSTER* THAT HAS TO *DIE!*
NEWS 52
I CAN TAKE HIM.
DON'T HURT HIM.
MY JOB IS TO *PROTECT* GOTHAM...
...FROM CREATURES LIKE *YOU!*
YOU HAVE TO BE *STOPPED!*
FIP
FIP
FIP
RAZOR-SHARP! DON'T--!
AH!

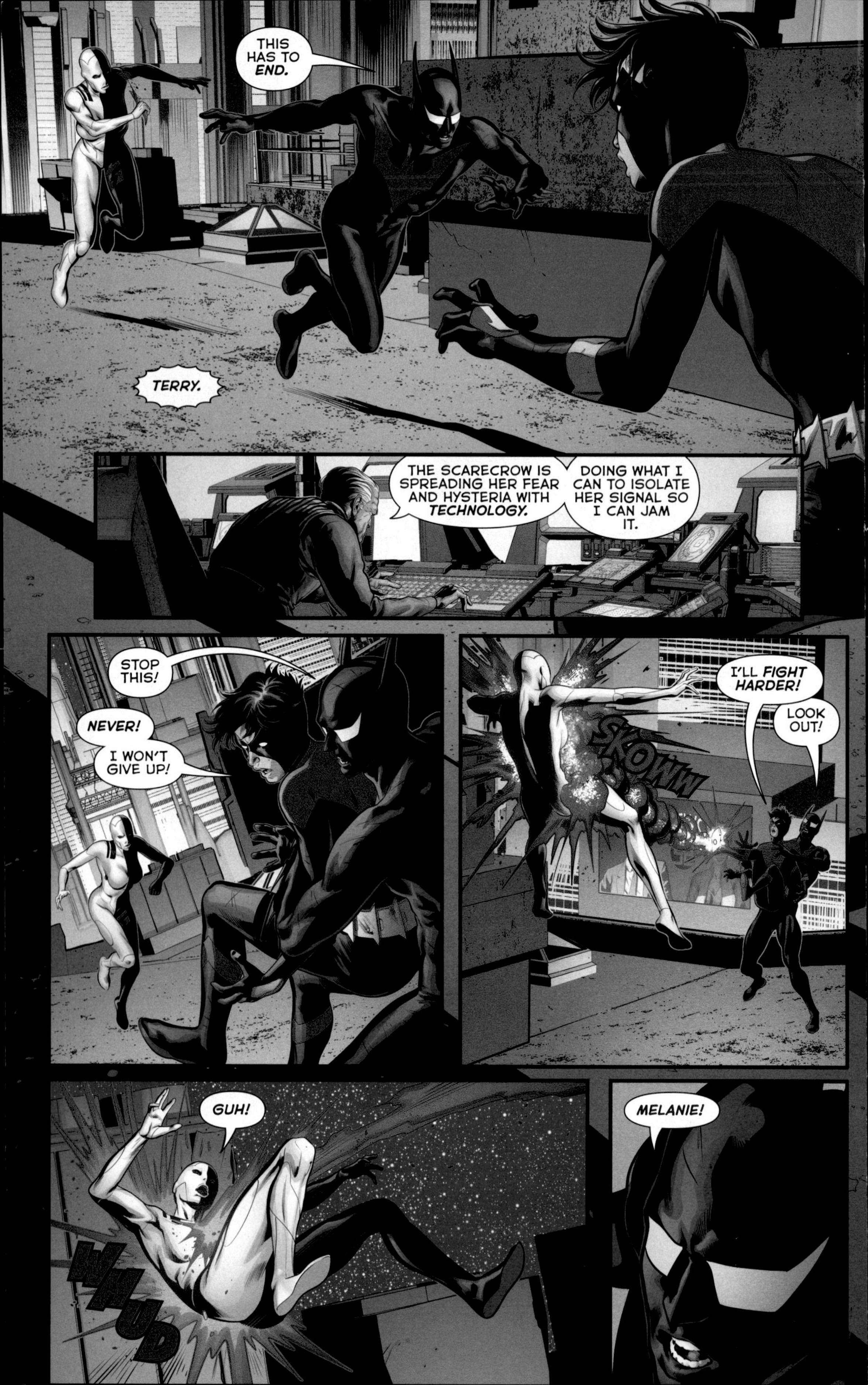
THIS HAS TO END.
TERRY.
THE SCARECROW IS SPREADING HER FEAR AND HYSTERIA WITH TECHNOLOGY.
DOING WHAT I CAN TO ISOLATE HER SIGNAL SO I CAN JAM IT.
STOP THIS!
NEVER!
I WON'T GIVE UP!
SKOWW
I'LL FIGHT HARDER!
LOOK OUT!
GUH!
WHUD
MELANIE!

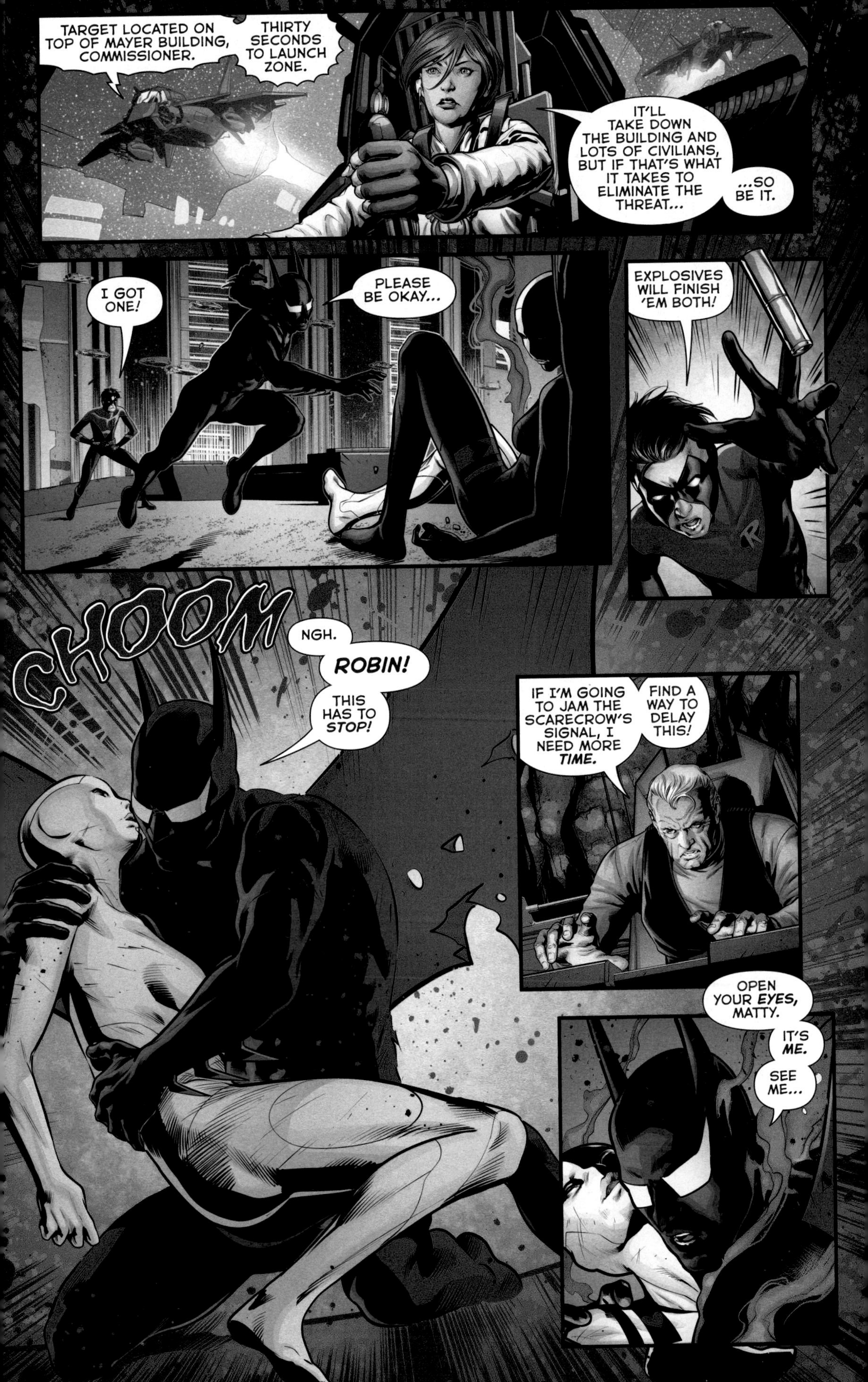

TARGET LOCATED ON TOP OF MAYER BUILDING, COMMISSIONER.
THIRTY SECONDS TO LAUNCH ZONE.
IT'LL TAKE DOWN THE BUILDING AND LOTS OF CIVILIANS, BUT IF THAT'S WHAT IT TAKES TO ELIMINATE THE THREAT...
...SO BE IT.
I GOT ONE!
PLEASE BE OKAY...
EXPLOSIVES WILL FINISH 'EM BOTH!
CHOOM
NGH.
ROBIN!
THIS HAS TO STOP!
IF I'M GOING TO JAM THE SCARECROW'S SIGNAL, I NEED MORE TIME.
FIND A WAY TO DELAY THIS!
OPEN YOUR EYES, MATTY.
IT'S ME.
SEE ME...

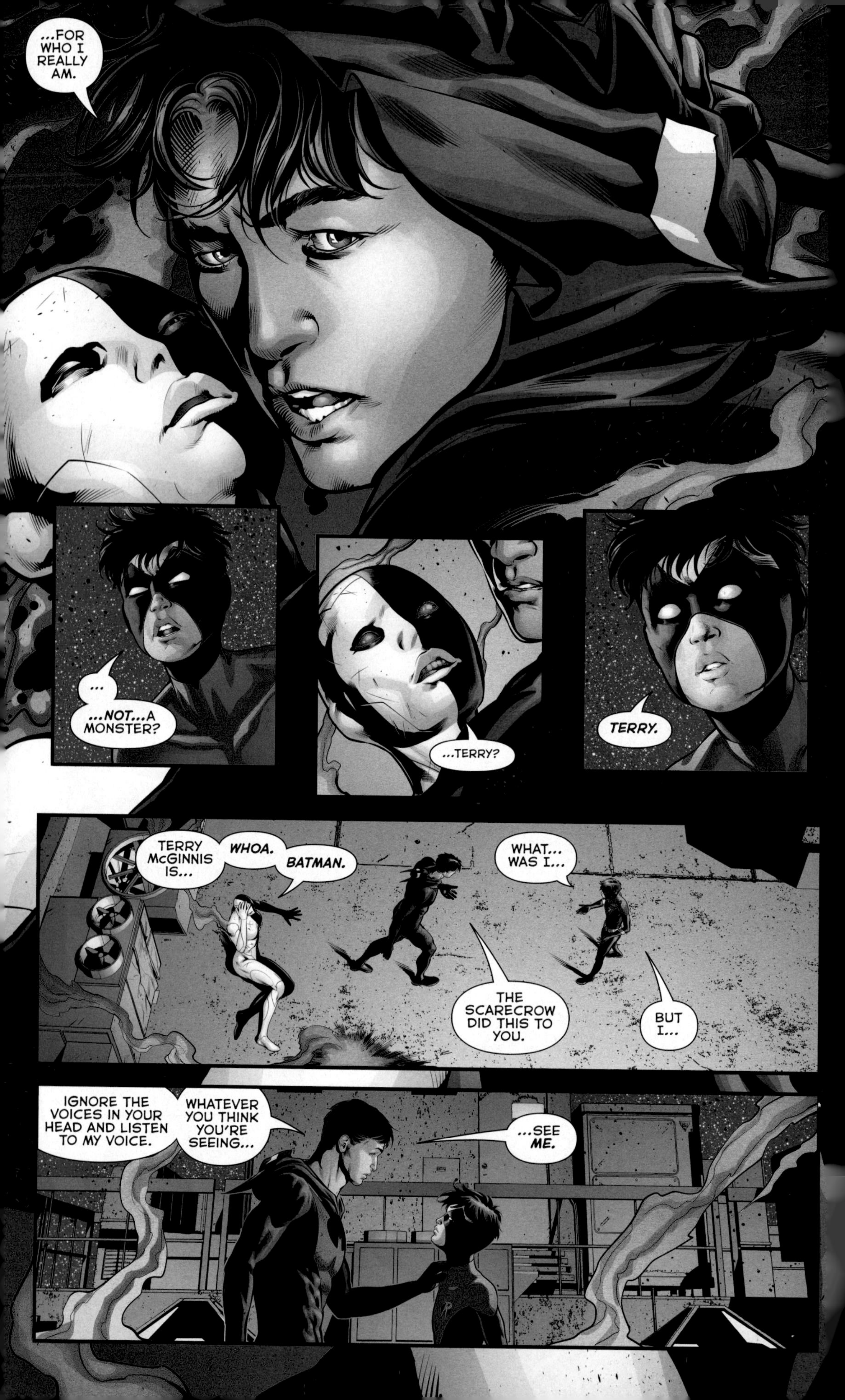
...FOR WHO I REALLY AM.
...
...NOT...A MONSTER?
...TERRY?
TERRY.
TERRY McGINNIS IS...
WHOA.
BATMAN.
WHAT... WAS I...
THE SCARECROW DID THIS TO YOU.
BUT I...
IGNORE THE VOICES IN YOUR HEAD AND LISTEN TO MY VOICE.
WHATEVER YOU THINK YOU'RE SEEING...
...SEE ME.

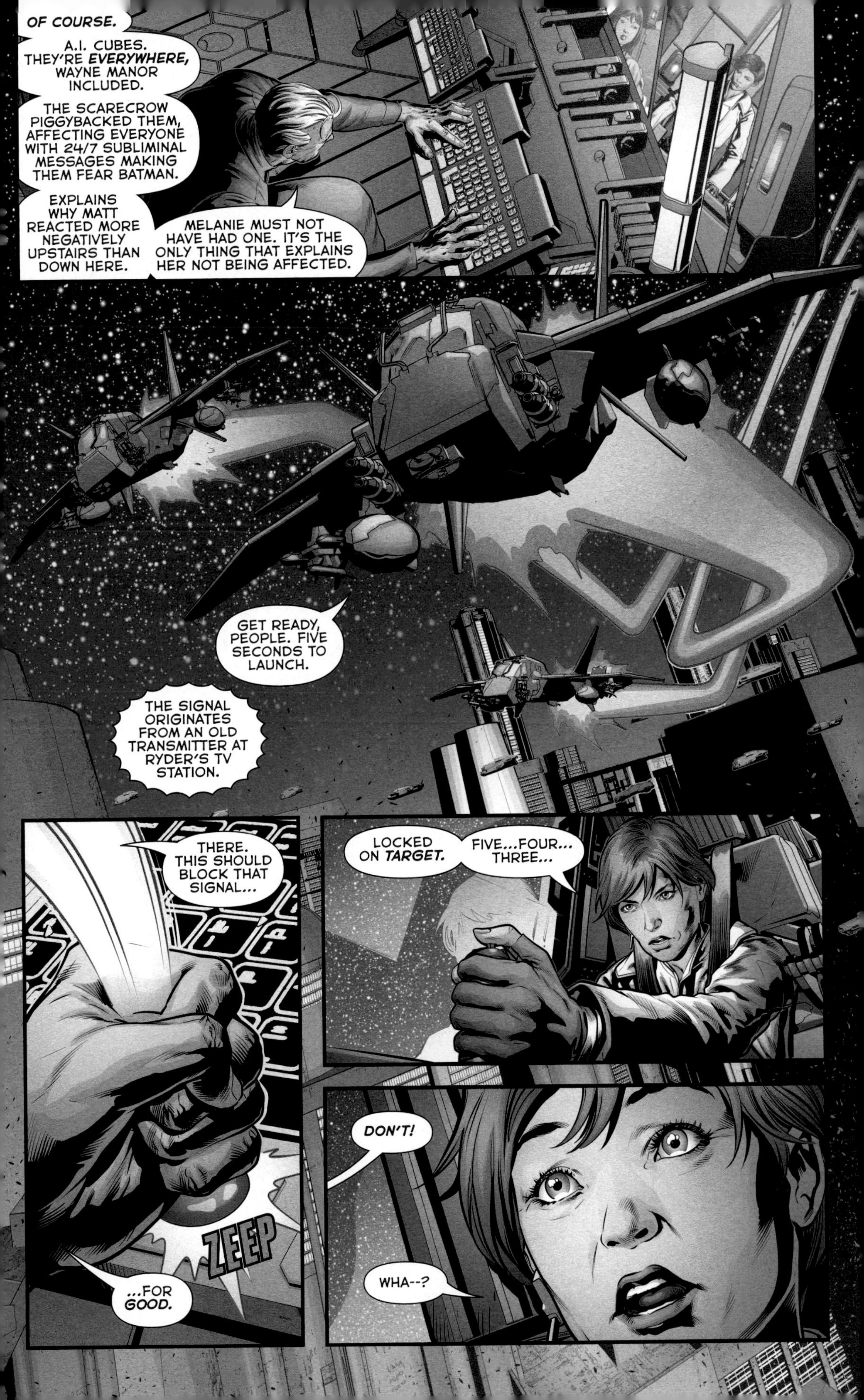

OF COURSE.
A.I. CUBES. THEY'RE *EVERYWHERE,* WAYNE MANOR INCLUDED.
THE SCARECROW PIGGYBACKED THEM, AFFECTING EVERYONE WITH 24/7 SUBLIMINAL MESSAGES MAKING THEM FEAR BATMAN.
EXPLAINS WHY MATT REACTED MORE NEGATIVELY UPSTAIRS THAN DOWN HERE.
MELANIE MUST NOT HAVE HAD ONE. IT'S THE ONLY THING THAT EXPLAINS HER NOT BEING AFFECTED.
GET READY, PEOPLE. FIVE SECONDS TO LAUNCH.
THE SIGNAL ORIGINATES FROM AN OLD TRANSMITTER AT RYDER'S TV STATION.
THERE. THIS SHOULD BLOCK THAT SIGNAL...
ZEEP
...FOR *GOOD.*
LOCKED ON *TARGET.*
FIVE...FOUR... THREE...
DON'T!
WHA--?

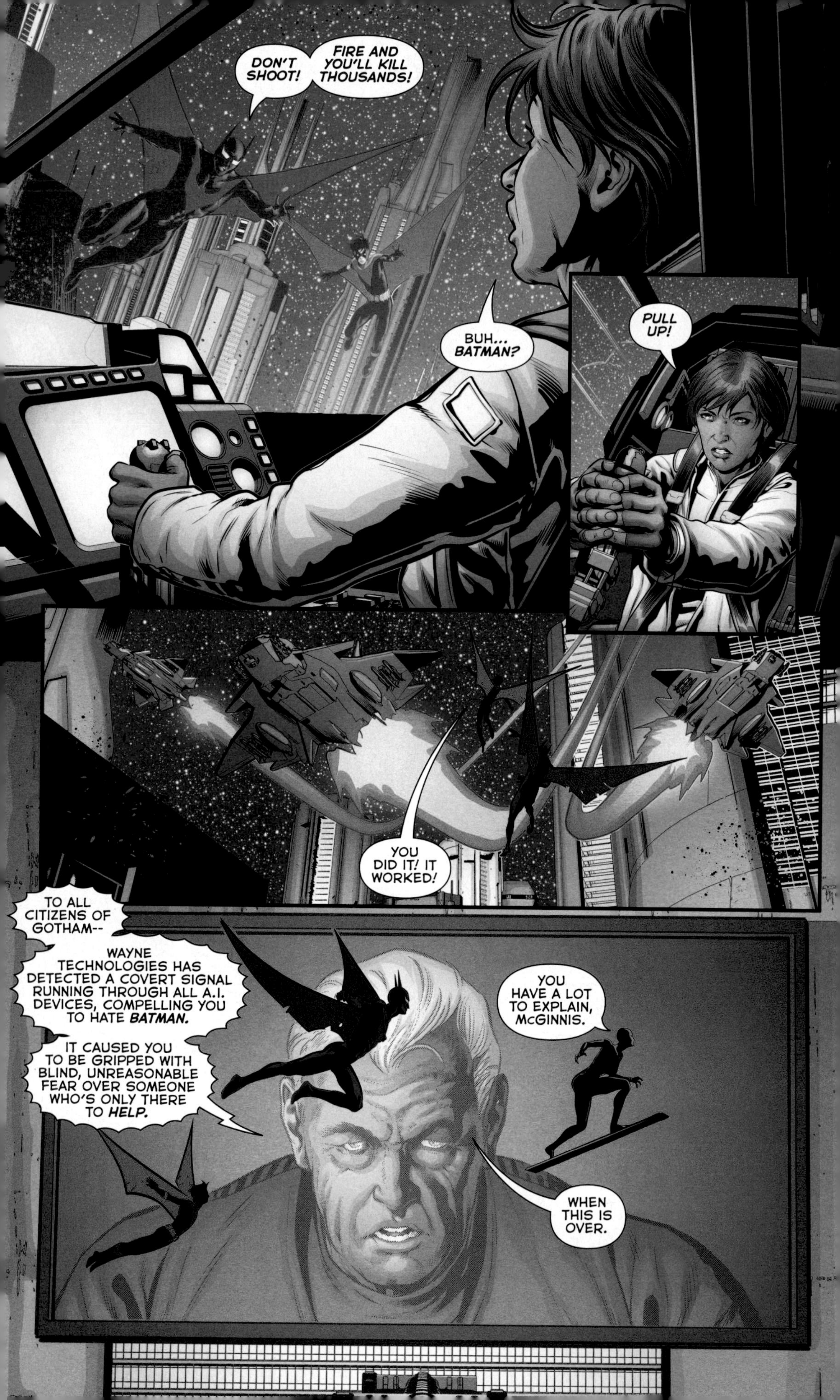
DON'T SHOOT!
FIRE AND YOU'LL KILL THOUSANDS!
BUH... BATMAN?
PULL UP!
YOU DID IT! IT WORKED!
TO ALL CITIZENS OF GOTHAM--
WAYNE TECHNOLOGIES HAS DETECTED A COVERT SIGNAL RUNNING THROUGH ALL A.I. DEVICES, COMPELLING YOU TO HATE BATMAN.
IT CAUSED YOU TO BE GRIPPED WITH BLIND, UNREASONABLE FEAR OVER SOMEONE WHO'S ONLY THERE TO HELP.
YOU HAVE A LOT TO EXPLAIN, McGINNIS.
WHEN THIS IS OVER.

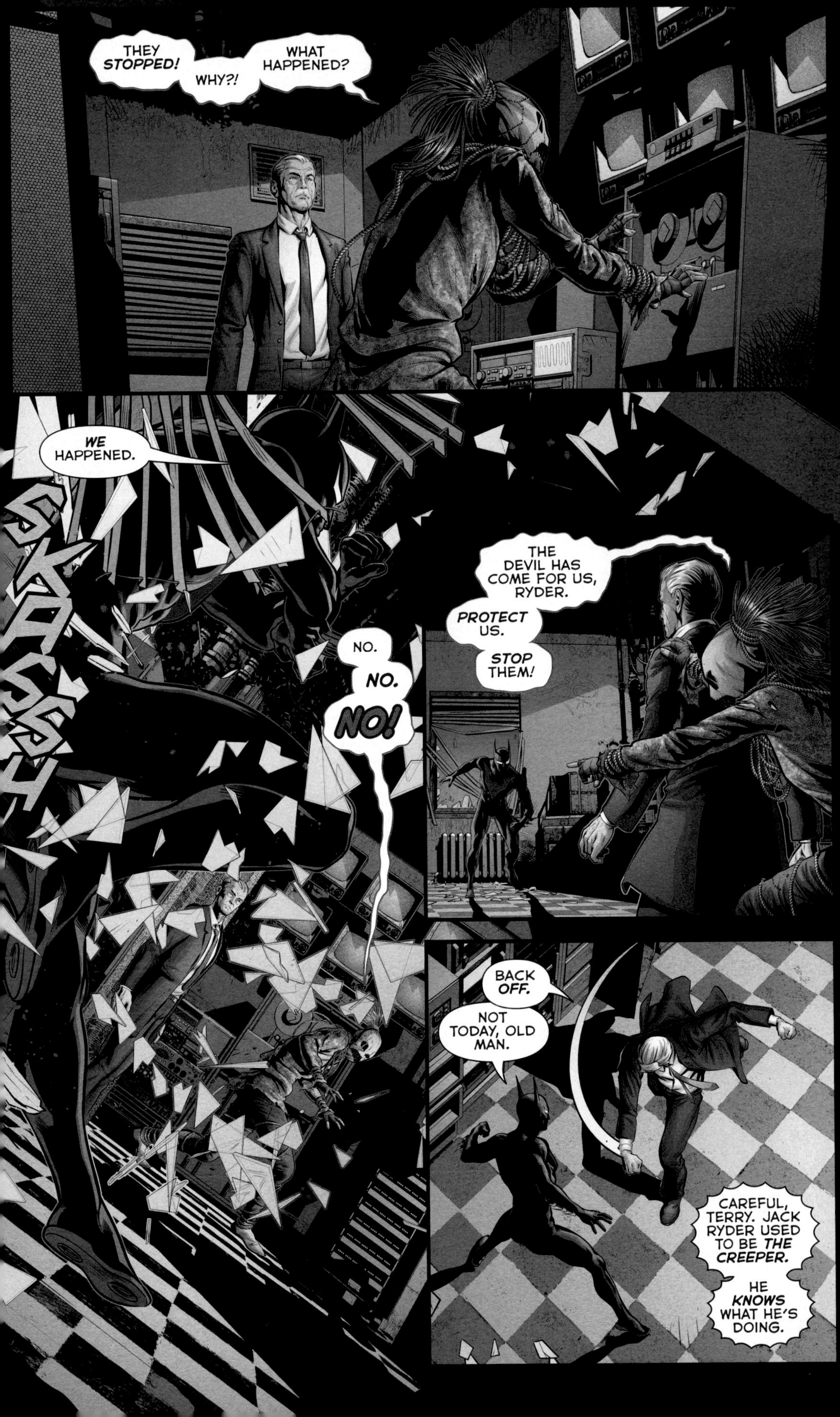

THEY STOPPED!
WHY?!
WHAT HAPPENED?
WE HAPPENED.
SKASSH
NO.
NO.
NO!
THE DEVIL HAS COME FOR US, RYDER.
PROTECT US.
STOP THEM!
BACK OFF.
NOT TODAY, OLD MAN.
CAREFUL, TERRY. JACK RYDER USED TO BE THE CREEPER.
HE KNOWS WHAT HE'S DOING.

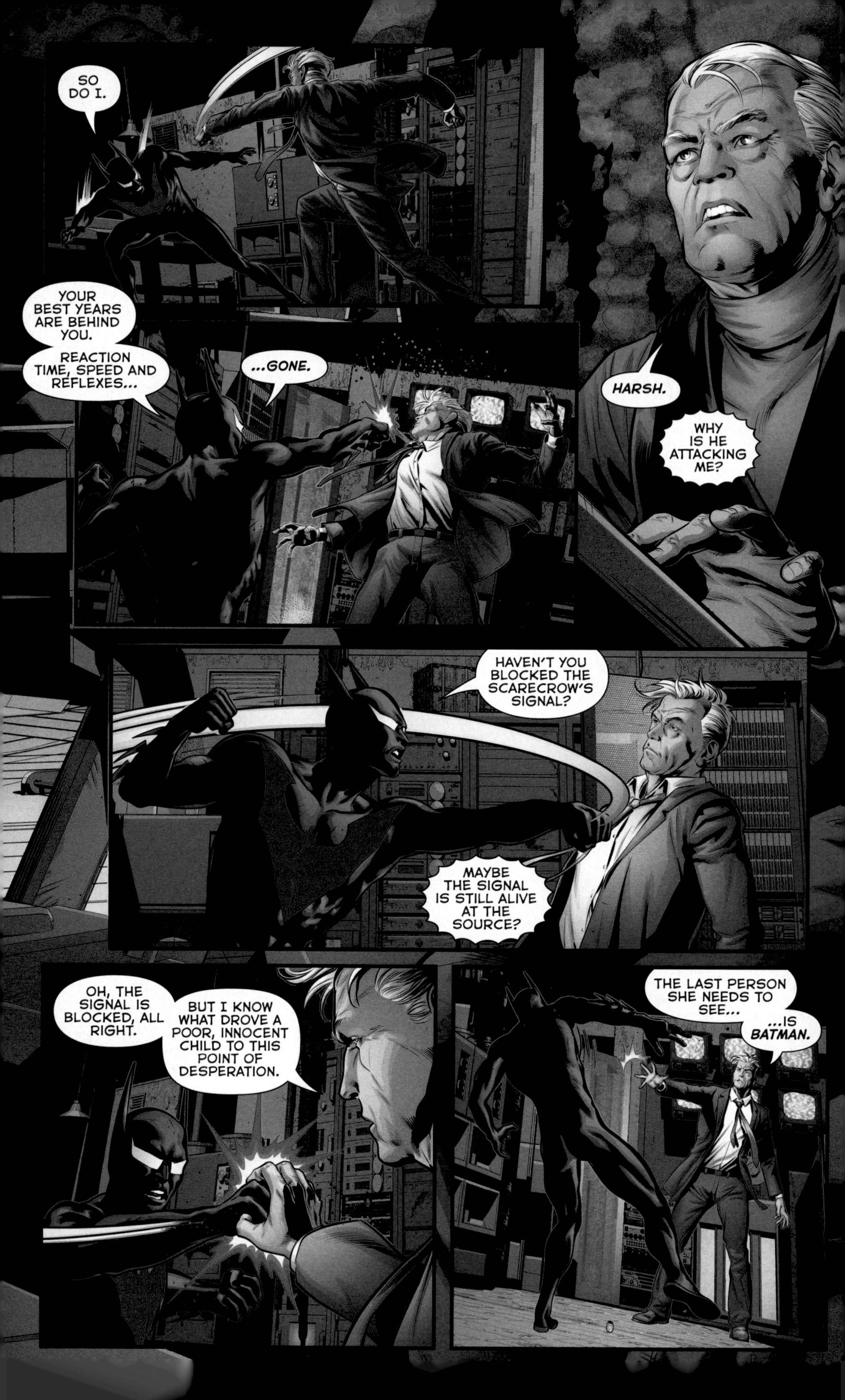
SO DO I.
YOUR BEST YEARS ARE BEHIND YOU.
REACTION TIME, SPEED AND REFLEXES...
...GONE.
HARSH.
WHY IS HE ATTACKING ME?
HAVEN'T YOU BLOCKED THE SCARECROW'S SIGNAL?
MAYBE THE SIGNAL IS STILL ALIVE AT THE SOURCE?
OH, THE SIGNAL IS BLOCKED, ALL RIGHT.
BUT I KNOW WHAT DROVE A POOR, INNOCENT CHILD TO THIS POINT OF DESPERATION.
THE LAST PERSON SHE NEEDS TO SEE...
...IS BATMAN.

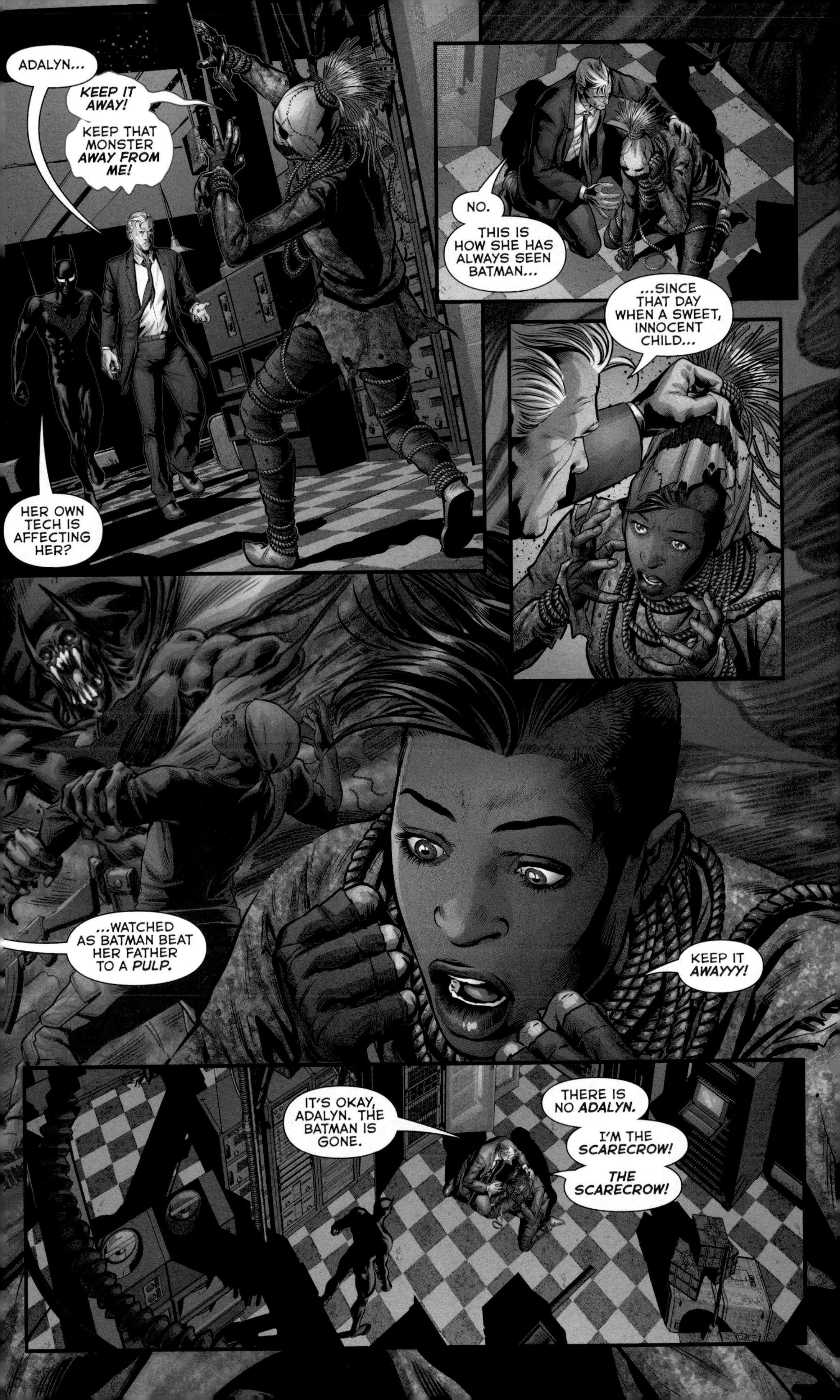

ADALYN...
KEEP IT AWAY!
KEEP THAT MONSTER AWAY FROM ME!
HER OWN TECH IS AFFECTING HER?
NO.
THIS IS HOW SHE HAS ALWAYS SEEN BATMAN...
...SINCE THAT DAY WHEN A SWEET, INNOCENT CHILD...
...WATCHED AS BATMAN BEAT HER FATHER TO A PULP.
KEEP IT AWAYYY!
IT'S OKAY, ADALYN. THE BATMAN IS GONE.
THERE IS NO ADALYN.
I'M THE SCARECROW!
THE SCARECROW!

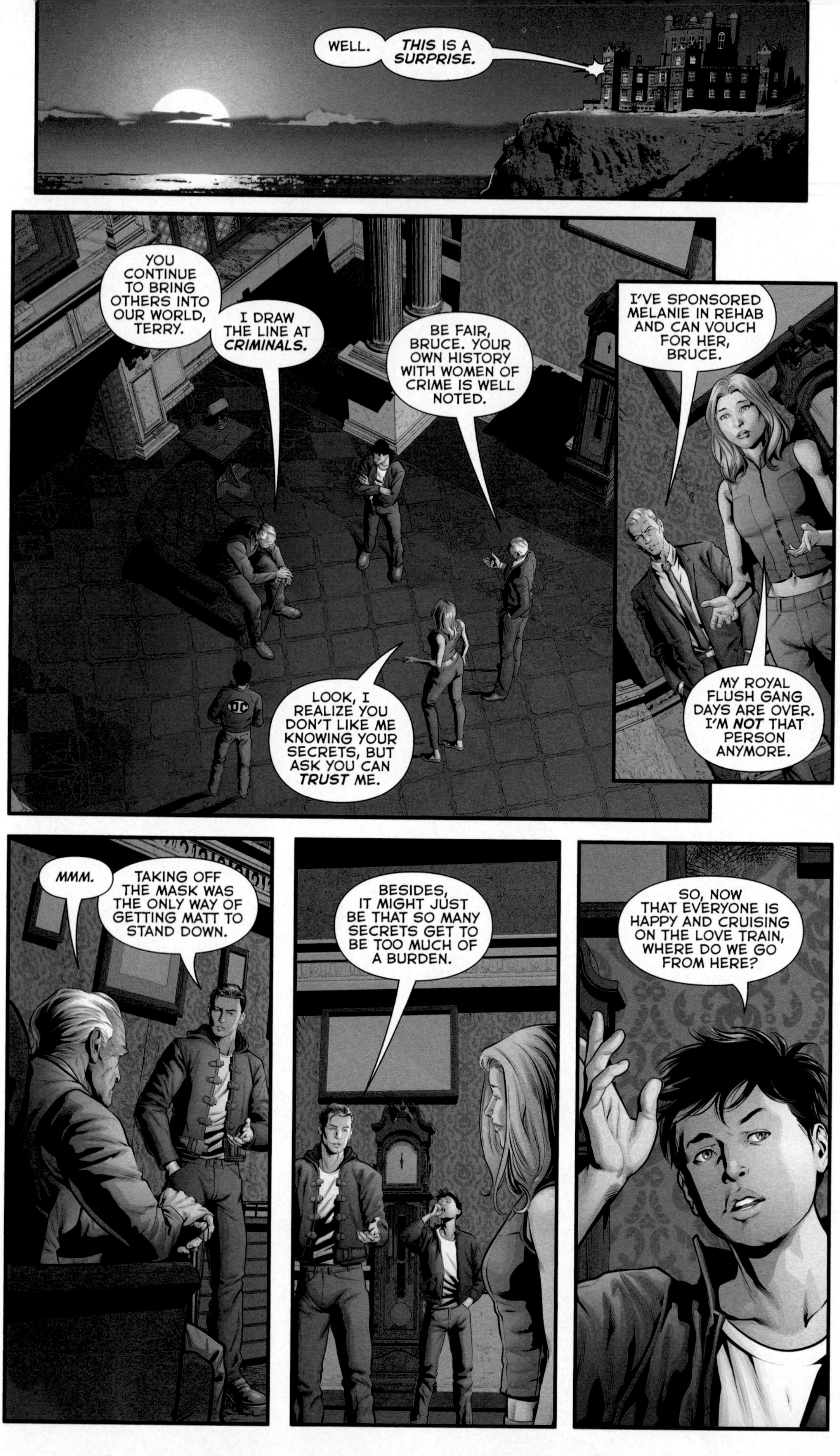
WELL.
THIS IS A SURPRISE.
YOU CONTINUE TO BRING OTHERS INTO OUR WORLD, TERRY.
I DRAW THE LINE AT CRIMINALS.
BE FAIR, BRUCE. YOUR OWN HISTORY WITH WOMEN OF CRIME IS WELL NOTED.
LOOK, I REALIZE YOU DON'T LIKE ME KNOWING YOUR SECRETS, BUT ASK YOU CAN TRUST ME.
I'VE SPONSORED MELANIE IN REHAB AND CAN VOUCH FOR HER, BRUCE.
MY ROYAL FLUSH GANG DAYS ARE OVER. I'M NOT THAT PERSON ANYMORE.
MMM.
TAKING OFF THE MASK WAS THE ONLY WAY OF GETTING MATT TO STAND DOWN.
BESIDES, IT MIGHT JUST BE THAT SO MANY SECRETS GET TO BE TOO MUCH OF A BURDEN.
SO, NOW THAT EVERYONE IS HAPPY AND CRUISING ON THE LOVE TRAIN, WHERE DO WE GO FROM HERE?

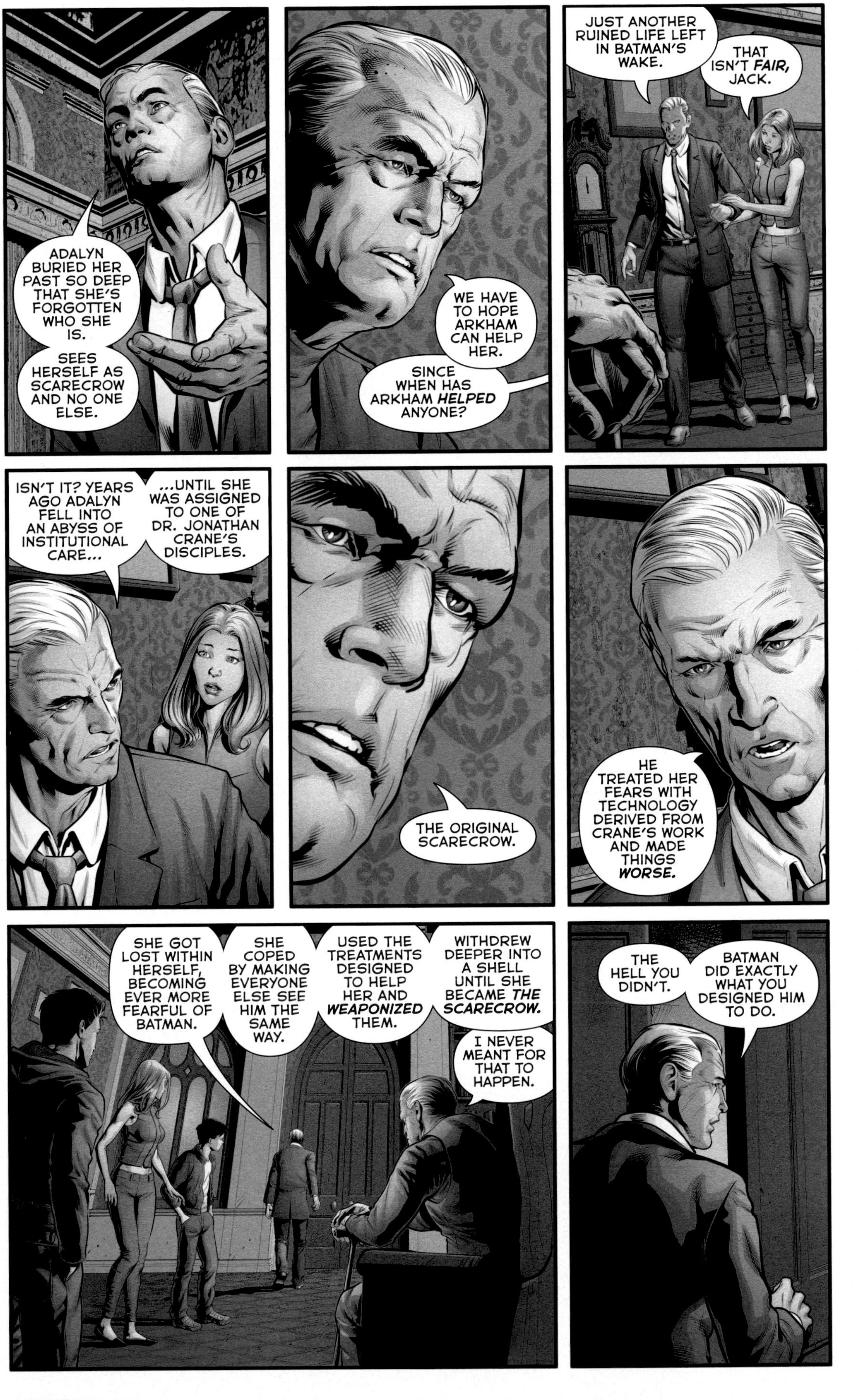
ADALYN BURIED HER PAST SO DEEP THAT SHE'S FORGOTTEN WHO SHE IS.
SEES HERSELF AS SCARECROW AND NO ONE ELSE.
WE HAVE TO HOPE ARKHAM CAN HELP HER.
SINCE WHEN HAS ARKHAM *HELPED* ANYONE?
JUST ANOTHER RUINED LIFE LEFT IN BATMAN'S WAKE.
THAT ISN'T *FAIR,* JACK.
ISN'T IT? YEARS AGO ADALYN FELL INTO AN ABYSS OF INSTITUTIONAL CARE...
...UNTIL SHE WAS ASSIGNED TO ONE OF DR. JONATHAN CRANE'S DISCIPLES.
THE ORIGINAL SCARECROW.
HE TREATED HER FEARS WITH TECHNOLOGY DERIVED FROM CRANE'S WORK AND MADE THINGS *WORSE.*
SHE GOT LOST WITHIN HERSELF, BECOMING EVER MORE FEARFUL OF BATMAN.
SHE COPED BY MAKING EVERYONE ELSE SEE HIM THE SAME WAY.
USED THE TREATMENTS DESIGNED TO HELP HER AND *WEAPONIZED* THEM.
WITHDREW DEEPER INTO A SHELL UNTIL SHE BECAME *THE SCARECROW.*
I NEVER MEANT FOR THAT TO HAPPEN.
THE HELL YOU DIDN'T.
BATMAN DID EXACTLY WHAT YOU DESIGNED HIM TO DO.

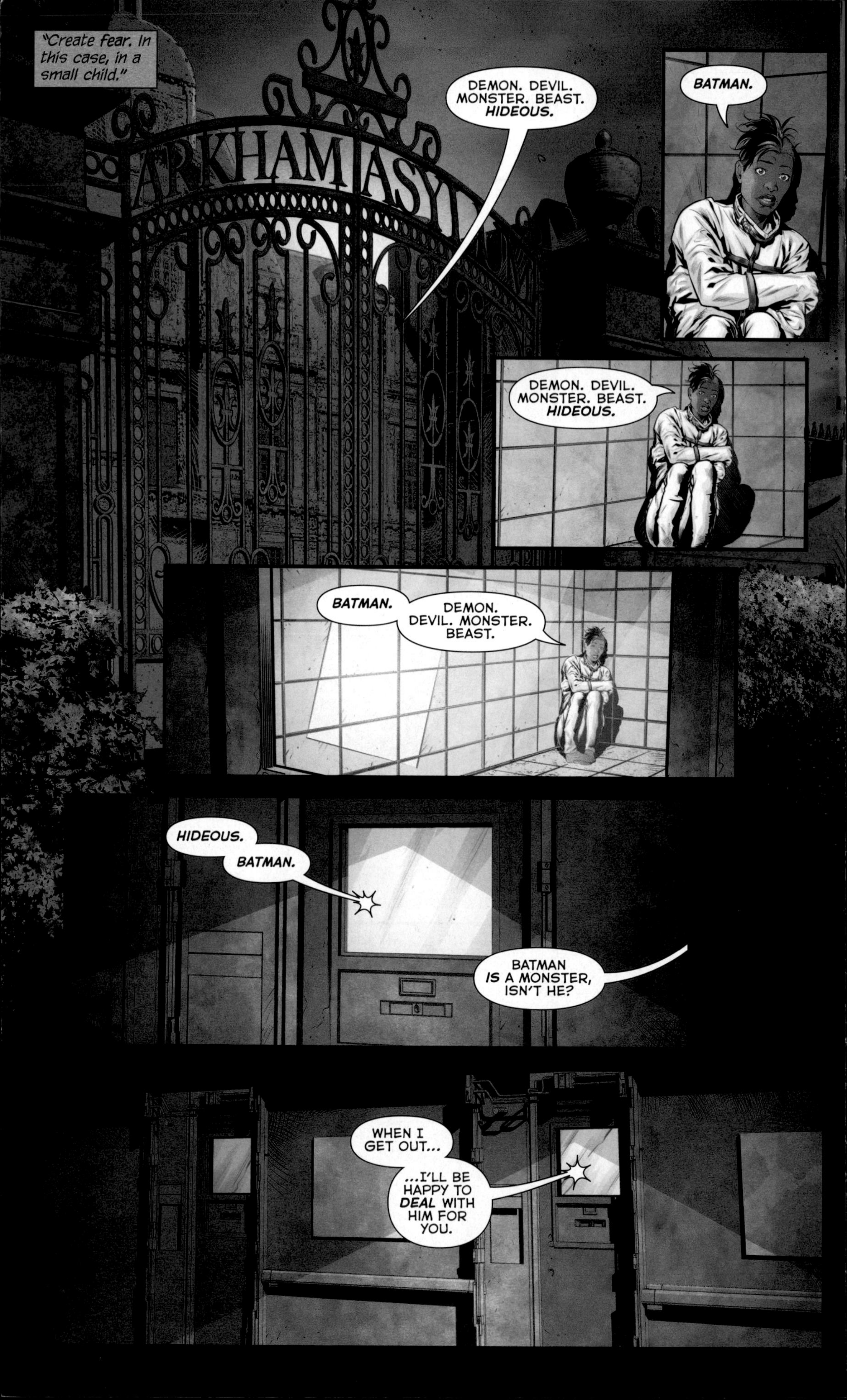
"Create fear. In this case, in a small child."
ARKHAM ASYLUM
DEMON. DEVIL. MONSTER. BEAST. HIDEOUS.
BATMAN.
DEMON. DEVIL. MONSTER. BEAST. HIDEOUS.
BATMAN.
DEMON. DEVIL. MONSTER. BEAST.
HIDEOUS.
BATMAN.
BATMAN IS A MONSTER, ISN'T HE?
WHEN I GET OUT...
...I'LL BE HAPPY TO DEAL WITH HIM FOR YOU.

BATMAN
BEYOND

VARIANT COVER GALLERY

BATMAN BEYOND #20 variant cover by SHANE DAVIS and WIL QUINTANA

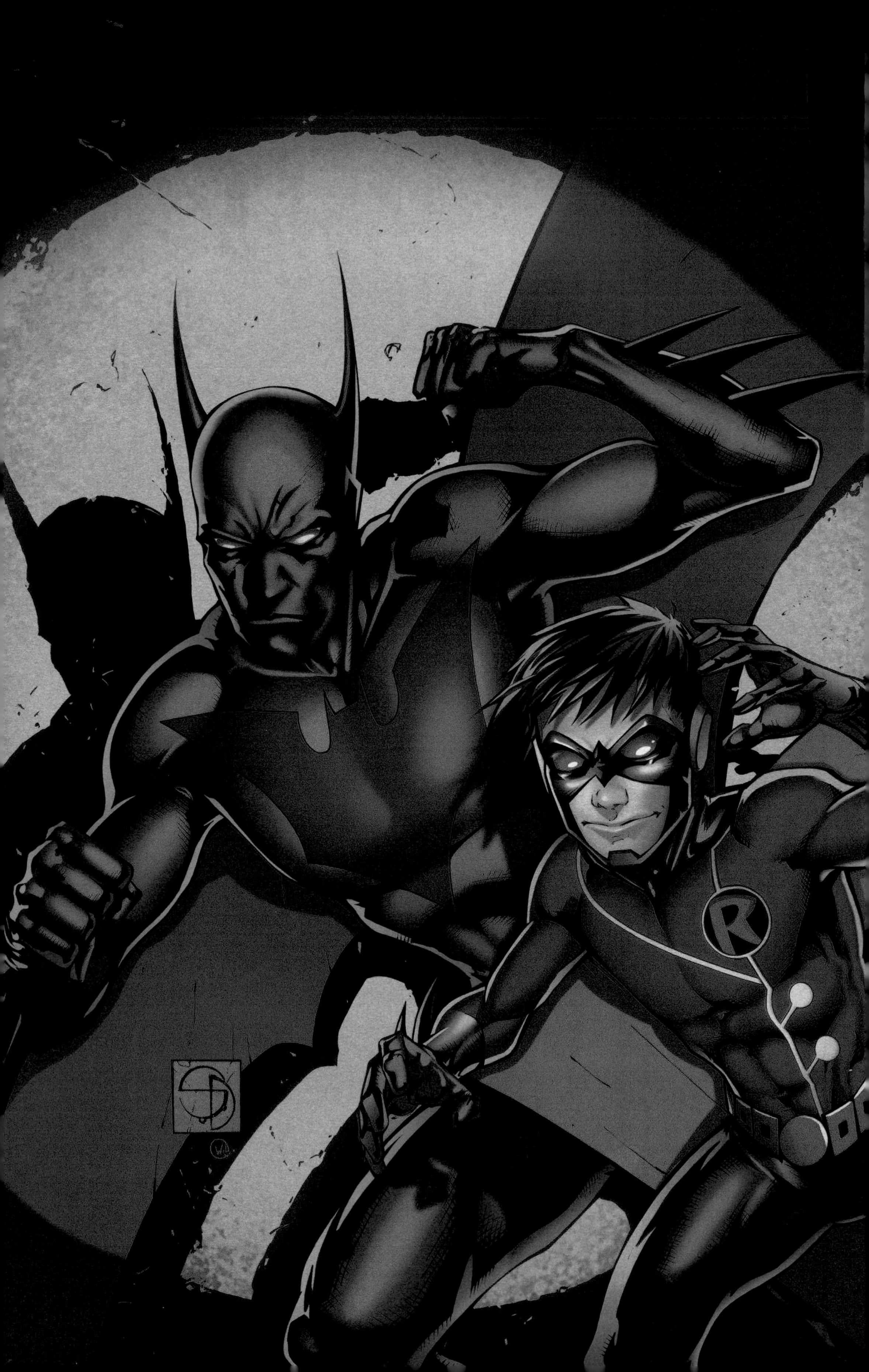

BATMAN BEYOND #21 variant cover by DAVE JOHNSON

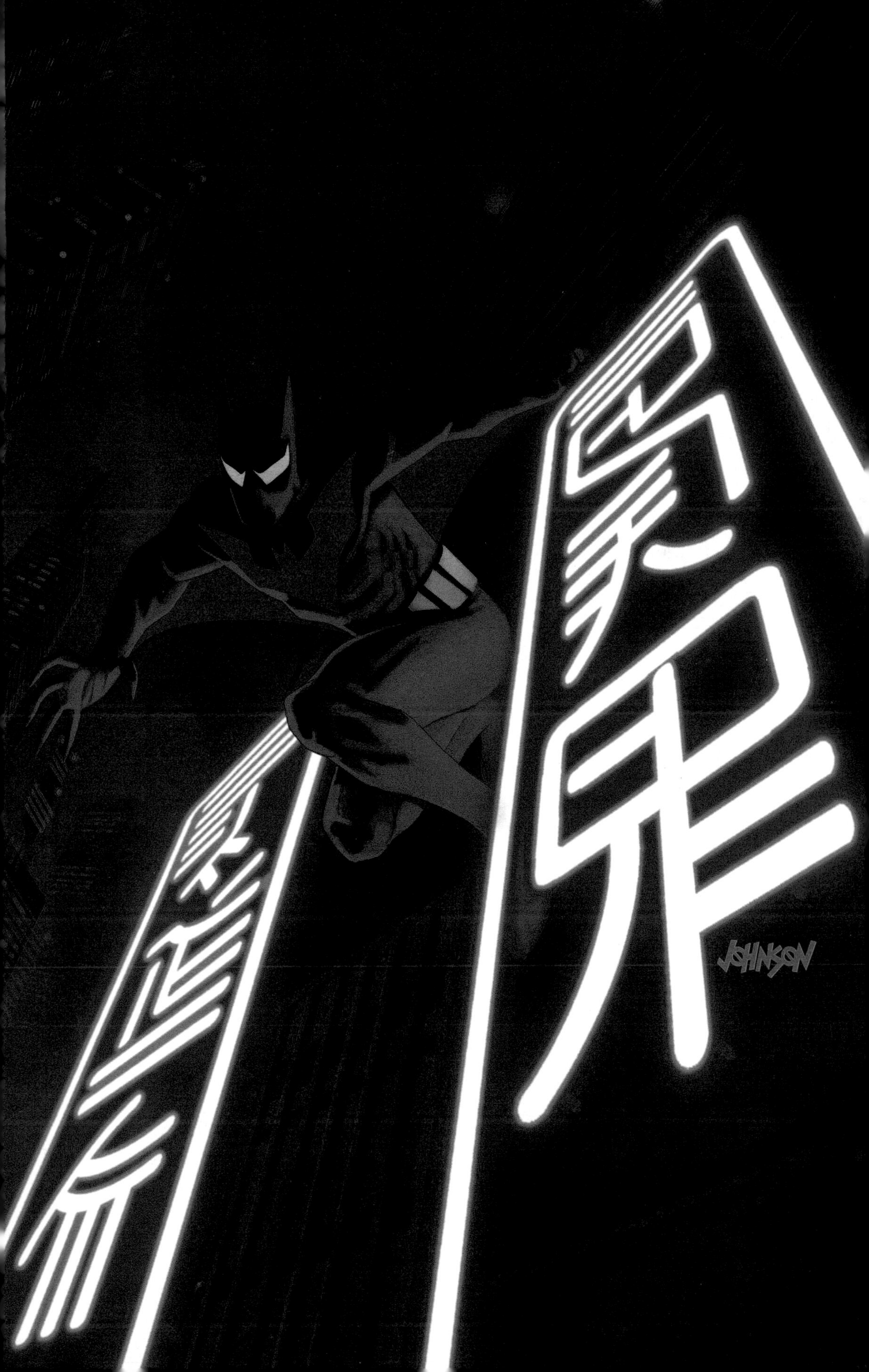
JOHNSON

BATMAN BEYOND #22 variant cover by DAVE JOHNSON

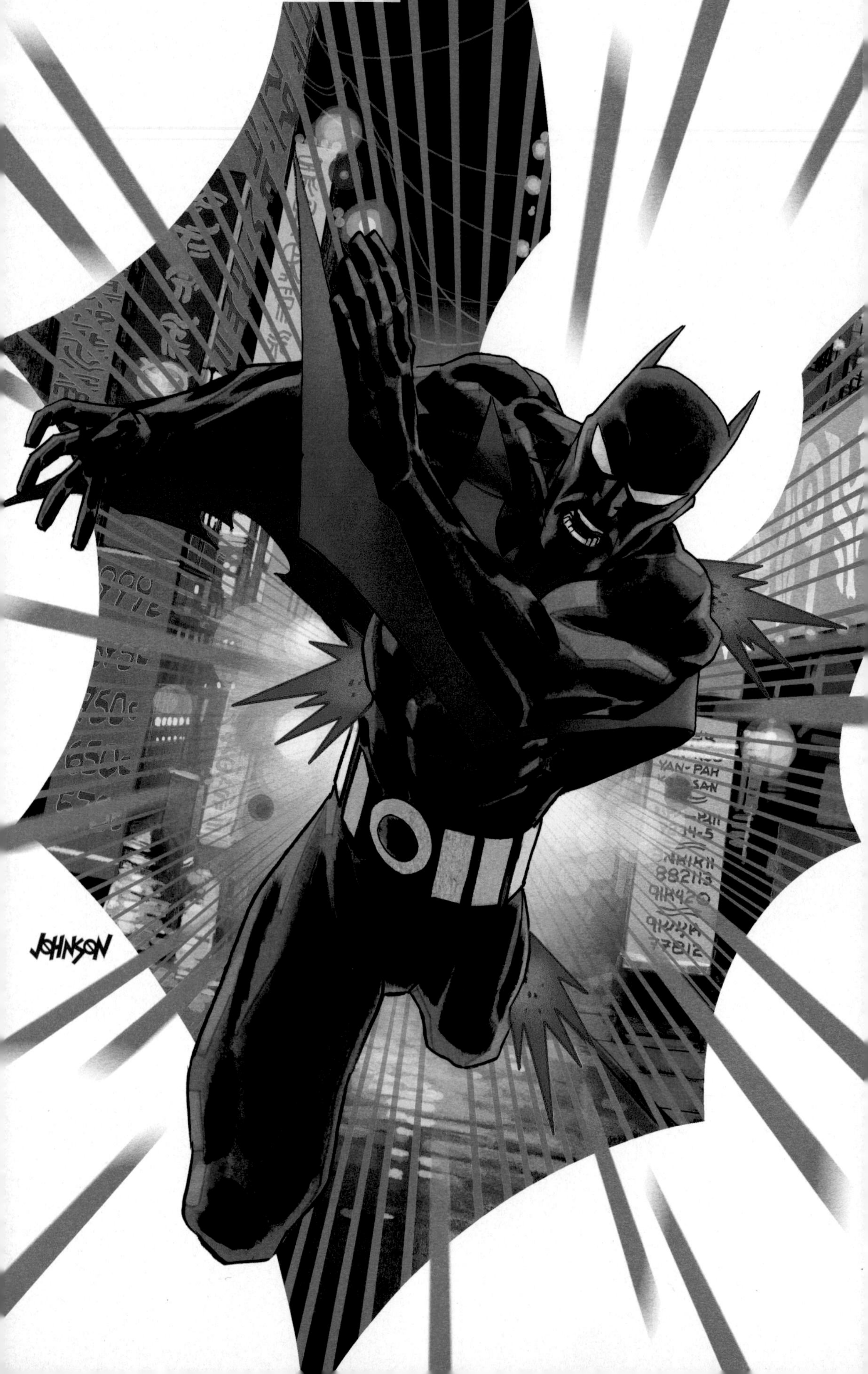
YAN-PAH
SAN
14-5
JOHNSON

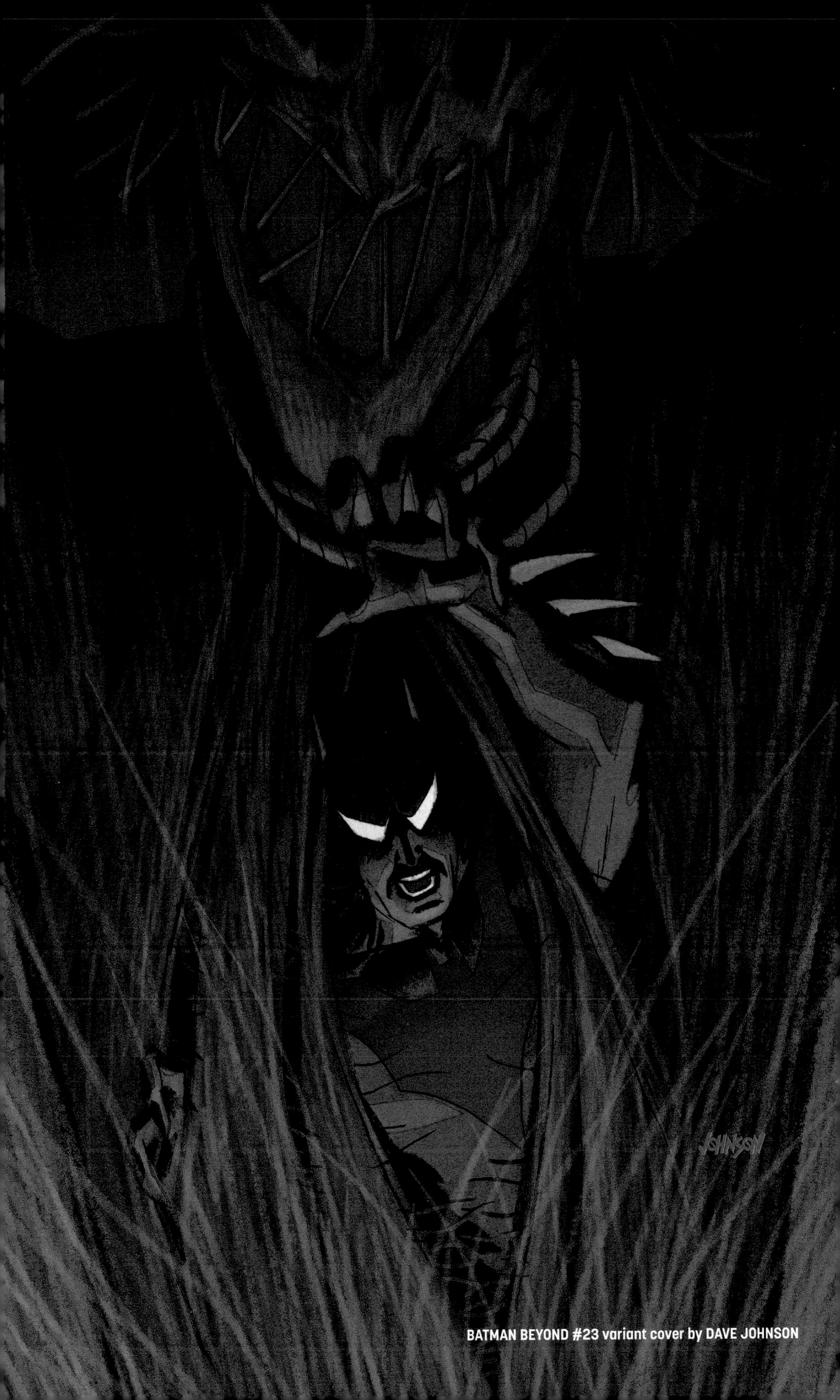
JOHNSON

BATMAN BEYOND #23 variant cover by DAVE JOHNSON

BATMAN BEYOND #24 variant cover by DAVE JOHNSON

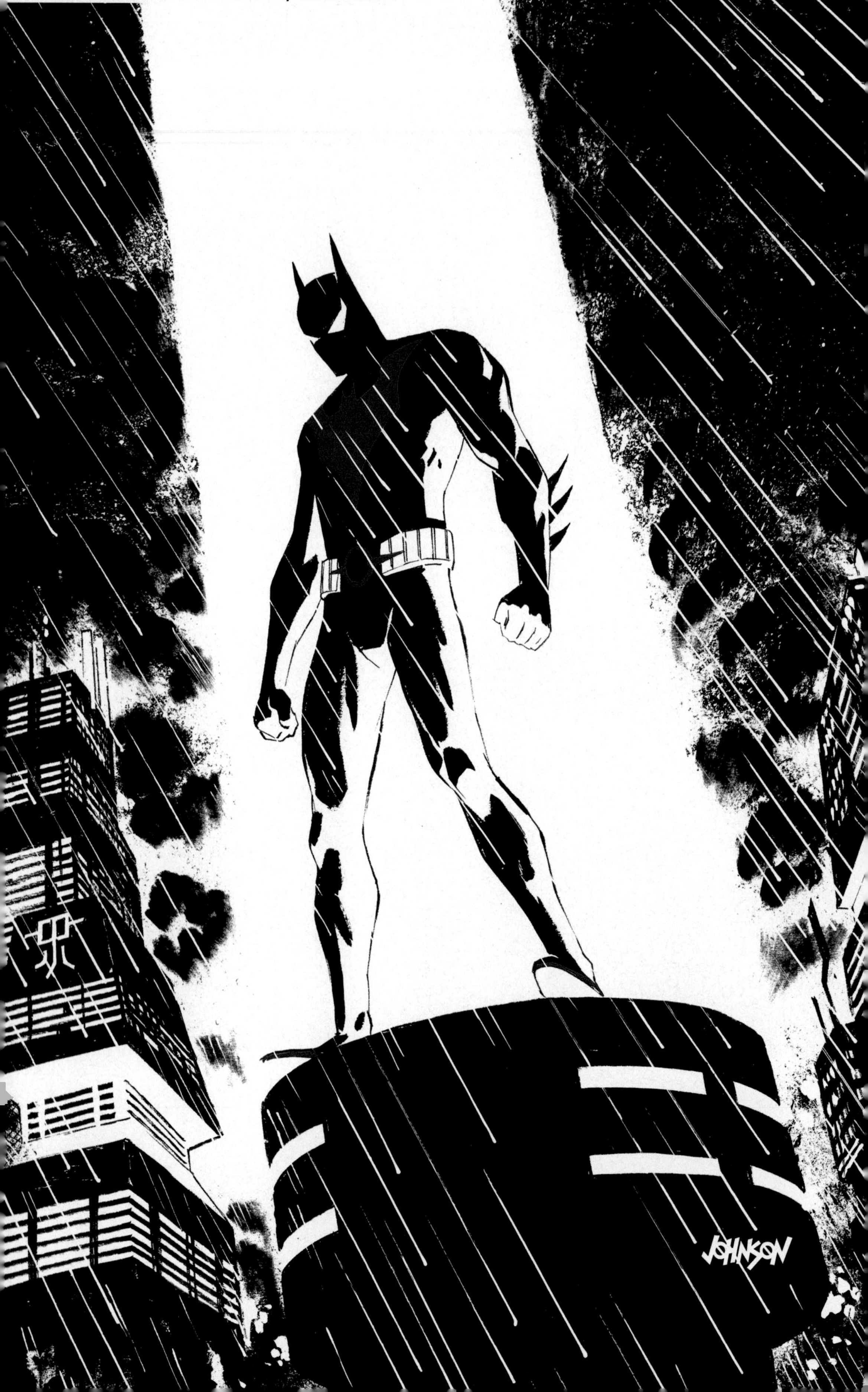
JOHNSON

BATMAN BEYOND #20-22 cover sketches by VIKTOR KALVACHEV

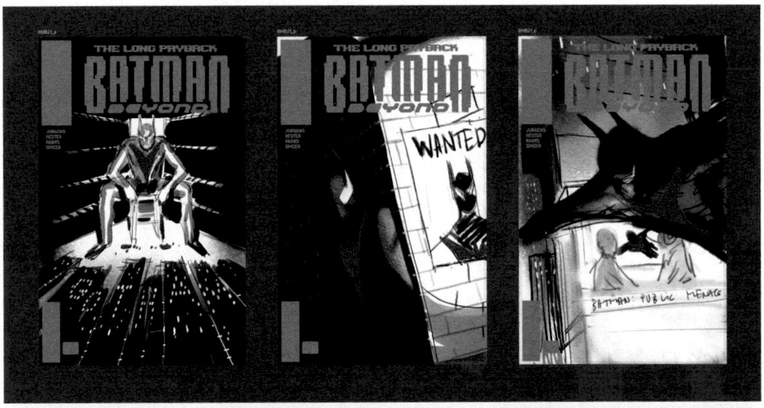
THE LONG PAYBACK
BATMAN
BEYOND
JURGENS
NESTER
PAINS
SPICER
WANTED
BATMAN: PUBLIC MENACE

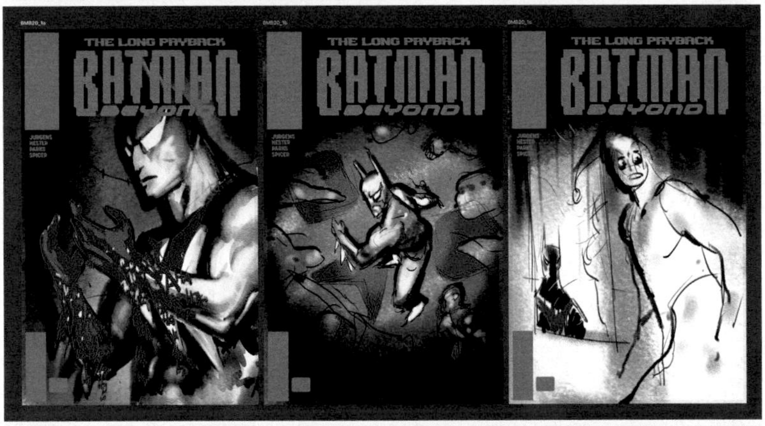
THE LONG PAYBACK
BATMAN
BEYOND
JURGENS
NESTER
PAINS
SPICER

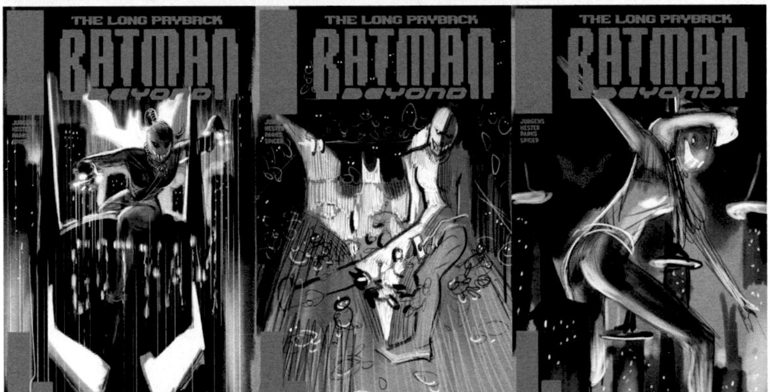
THE LONG PAYBACK
BATMAN
BEYOND
JURGENS
NESTER
PAINS
SPICER

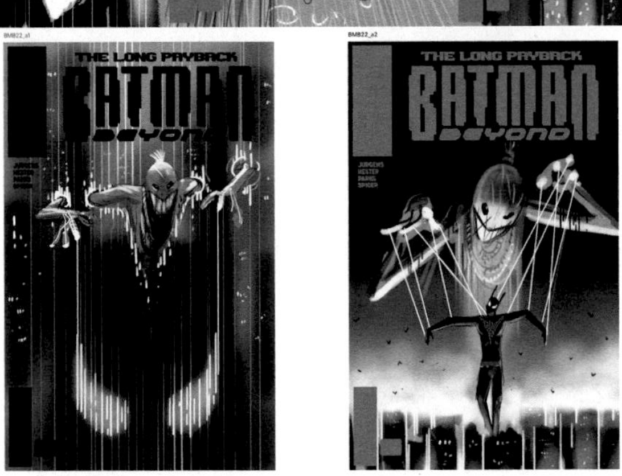
THE LONG PAYBACK
BATMAN
BEYOND
JURGENS
NESTER
PAINS
SPICER

BATMAN BEYOND #23 cover sketches by VIKTOR KALVACHEV
ROBIN BEYOND character study by DAN JURGENS

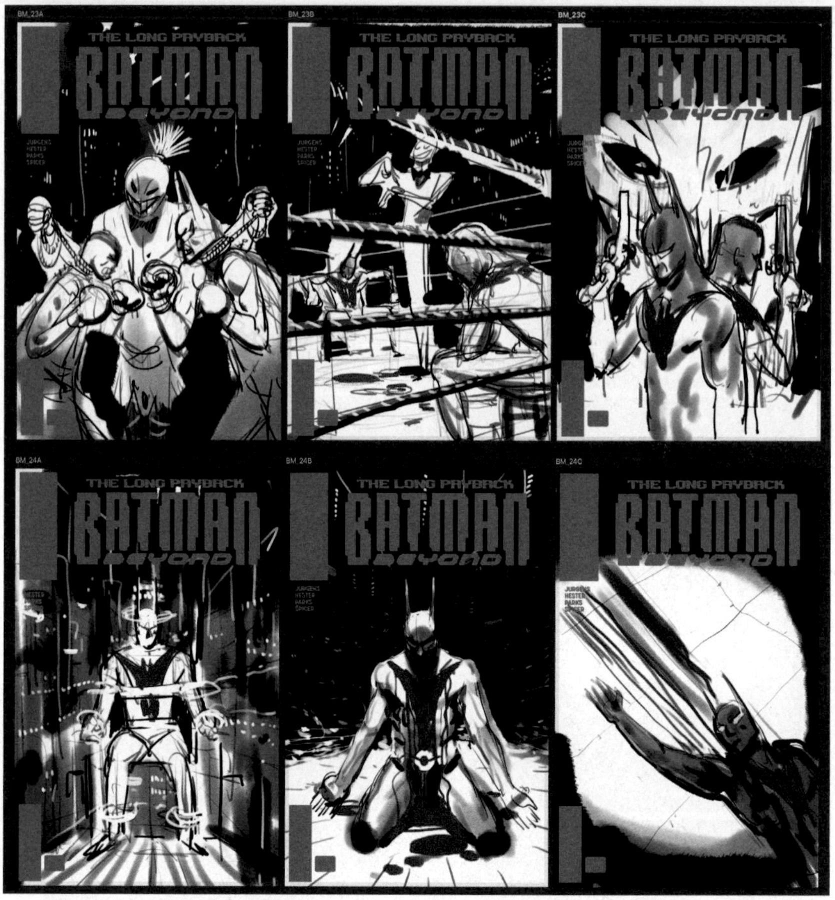

BM_23A
THE LONG PAYBACK
BATMAN BEYOND
JURGENS HESTER PARKS SPICER
BM_23B
THE LONG PAYBACK
BATMAN BEYOND
JURGENS HESTER PARKS SPICER
BM_23C
THE LONG PAYBACK
BATMAN BEYOND
BM_24A
THE LONG PAYBACK
BATMAN BEYOND
BM_24B
THE LONG PAYBACK
BATMAN BEYOND
JURGENS HESTER PARKS SPICER
BM_24C
THE LONG PAYBACK
BATMAN BEYOND
JURGENS HESTER PARKS SPICER

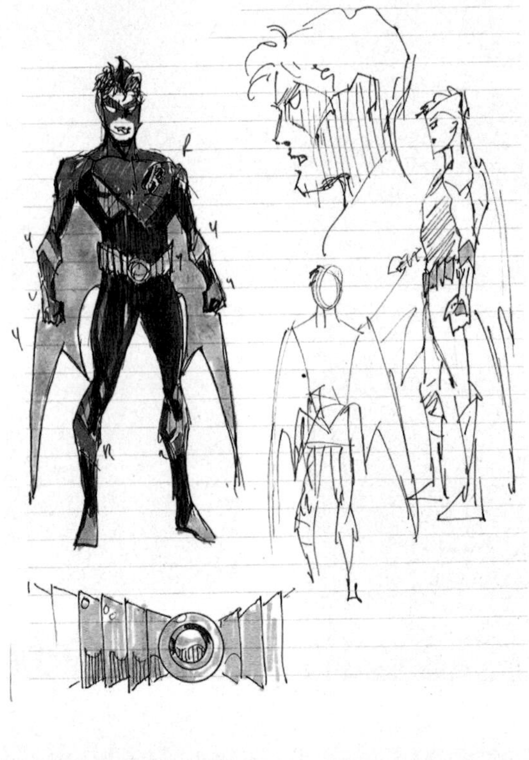

ROBIN BEYOND character studies by SHANE DAVIS

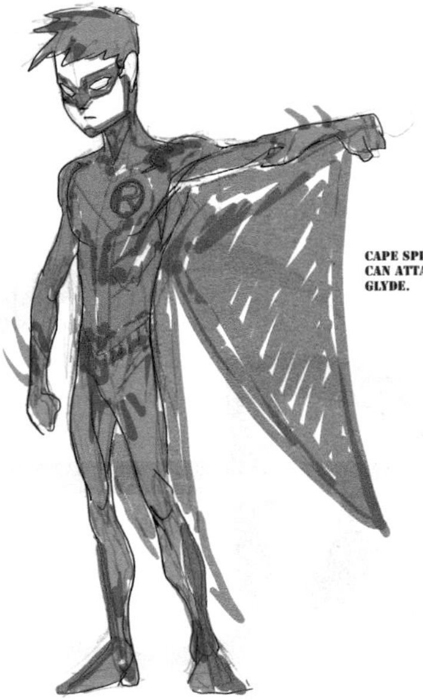
CAPE SPLITS IN BACK,
CAN ATTACH TO ARMS TO
GLYDE.

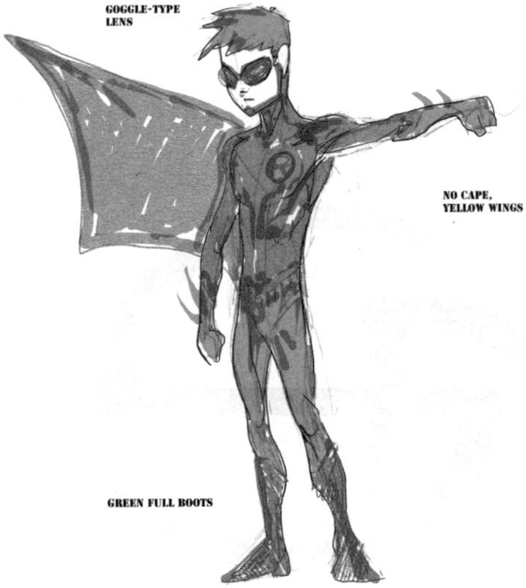
GOGGLE-TYPE
LENS
NO CAPE,
YELLOW WINGS LIKE BB
GREEN FULL BOOTS

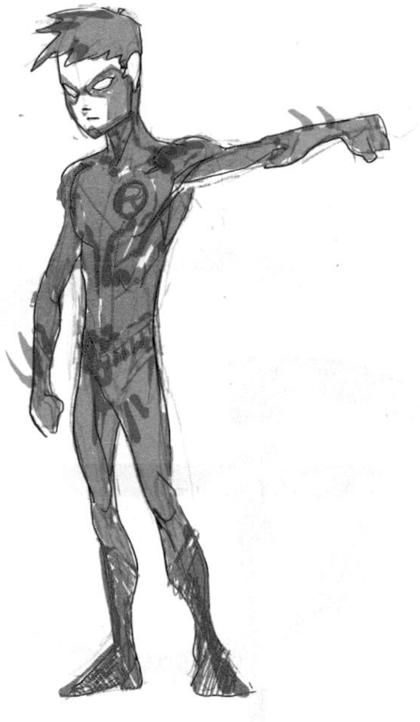

BATMAN BEYOND #20 page 13 pencils by MARCO CASTIELLO and inks by MARK MORALES

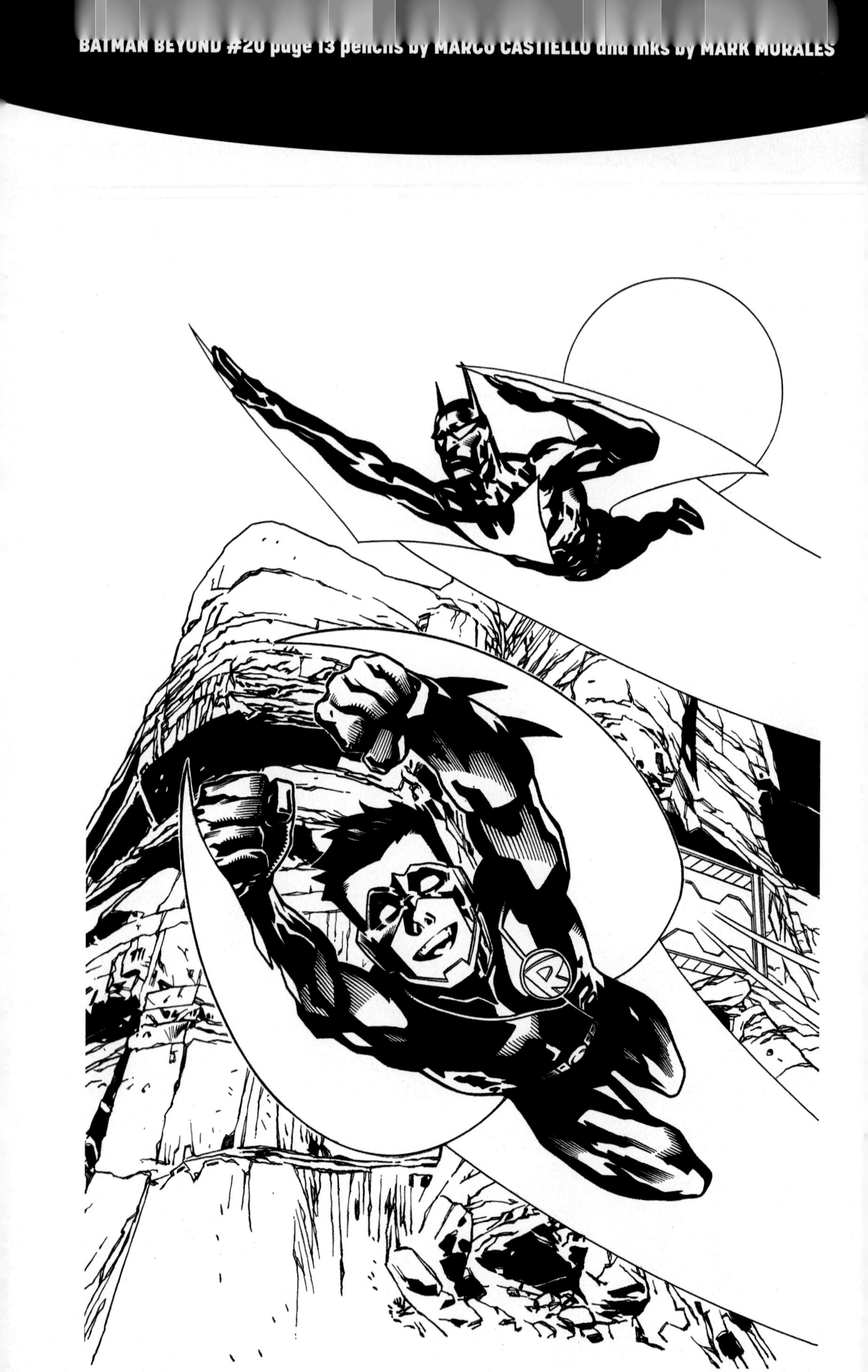

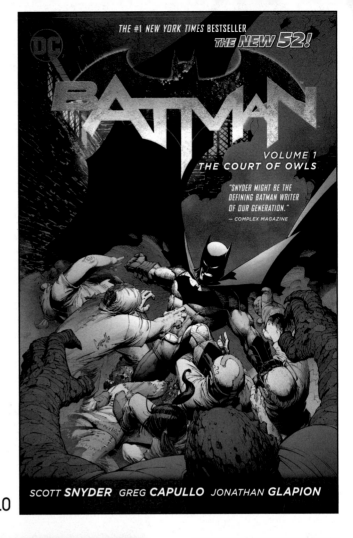

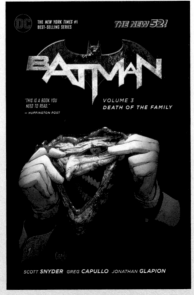

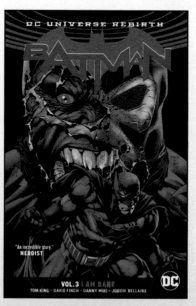

"The rare comic-book 'event' that lives up to its own hype."
–WASHINGTON POST

"Recapturing much of the original's unique visual flavor."
–IGN

BATMAN: THE DARK KNIGHT: MASTER RACE

FRANK MILLER with
BRIAN AZZARELLO,
ANDY KUBERT and KLAUS JANSON

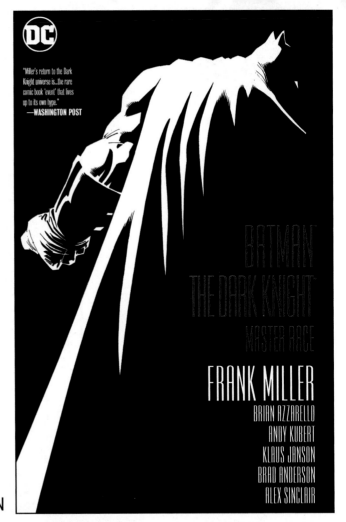

BATMAN: THE DARK KNIGHT RETURNS

BATMAN: THE DARK KNIGHT STRIKES AGAIN

BATMAN: THE DARK KNIGHT: MASTER RACE : THE COVERS

Get more DC graphic novels wherever comics and books are sold!

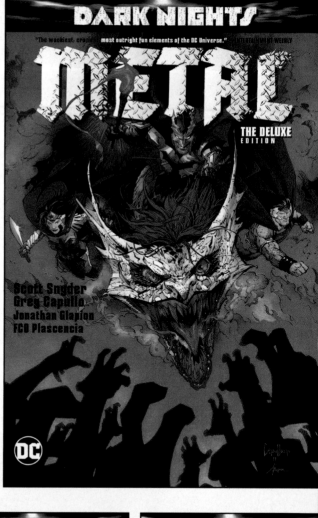

"This is the work of two men at the top of their games."
–THE NEW YORK TIMES

"Where nightmares and reality collide."
–THE WASHINGTON POST

"The Batman of your wildest nightmares."
–POLYGON

DARK NIGHTS:
METAL
SCOTT SNYDER
GREG CAPULLO

**DARK DAYS:
THE ROAD TO METAL**

**DARK NIGHTS: METAL:
DARK KNIGHTS RISING**

**DARK NIGHTS: METAL:
THE RESISTANCE**